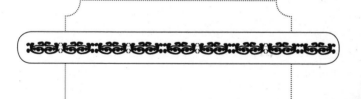

Tea Time with Terrorists

A Motorcycle Journey
Into the Heart of Sri Lanka's Civil War

Mark Stephen Meadows

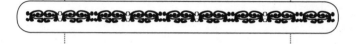

Soft Skull Press • New York

Library of Congress Cataloging-in-Publication Data

Meadows, Mark Stephen.
  Tea time with terrorists : a motorcycle journey into the heart of Sri Lanka's civil war / Mark Stephen Meadows.
      p. cm.
  Includes bibliographical references and index.
  ISBN 978-1-59376-275-9 (alk. paper)
    1. Motorcycling–Sri Lanka. 2. Meadows, Mark Stephen–Travel–Sri Lanka. 3. Sri Lanka–Description and travel. 4. Sri Lanka–History–Civil War, 1983-
I. Title.
  GV1059.54.S72M43 2010
  796.7095493–dc22

Cover and interior design by Mark Stephen Meadows
Printed in the United States of America

Soft Skull Press
An Imprint of Counterpoint LLC
2117 Fourth Street
Suite D
Berkeley, CA 94710

www.softskull.com
www.counterpointpress.com

Distributed by Publishers Group West

10 9 8 7 6 5 4 3 2 1

Thanks & Acknowledgments

This book was about seven years in the making, and during that time I interviewed many of the major actors in the Tamil–Sinhalese conflict in Sri Lanka, India, Canada, and the United States. But many people who are not visible in the manuscript also made the book possible and guided me through some dangerous waters. There are some people I can no longer thank, as many of them, including Shankar Rajee, are now dead. I would, however, like to send undying thanks to both the living and the dead, including Bandula Jayasekara, David W. Lewis, Anita Pratap, Y.K. and Pushpa DeSilva, Dayan Master (whose lessons echo from cover to cover), the Goviyapana Boyz (especially Prabath, Krishan, and their families), Enno, Mercedes, Naranj Wijeera, Lucas Path, Mr. W. Edwin of the Aluvihara Buddhist Library, and many, many others.

Anne Horowitz, supereditor, put in big energies and tiny attentions to make this thing legible and real. Input and realism were also added with the help of Andrea Matson-DeKay (and the rest of the 4-PACK crew), E.W. (don Eduardo) Kutner, Angela Klaassen, Heather Noone, Brian (Kogen) Lesage, and my wife, Amélie, who not only fielded the idea in the first place but saw it all the way through until the final draft of the manuscript.

Thanks most of all to each of the patient individuals who were interviewed. Here's hoping I've relayed your stories with the same precision and at least a portion of the passion with which you generously offered them.

Contents

This book is dedicated to anyone who
has reasoned along enemy lines.

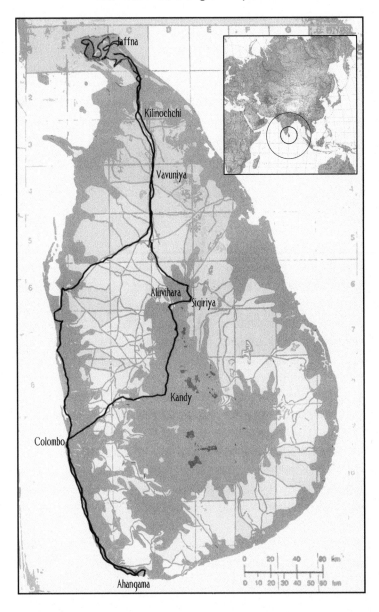

Tea Time with Terrorists

A Motorcycle Journey
Into the Heart of Sri Lanka's Civil War

Chapter One:
COMPROMISES

"We took some tea as a symbol, as a gesture,
to the Palestinian people, picked by the Tamil
people, as if to say, 'This is our sweat and blood,
this is the only thing we have to give.'"
—Shankar Rajee

The Day That Started with a Bang

The hand that set the 1984 bombs, Colombo, Sri Lanka

It was 5:01 AM, October 22, 1984. It could have been a morning two thousand years ago. Sri Lanka's capital city, Colombo, slept under the pink clouds of dawn, palm fronds nodded in the tropical breeze, large-billed birds summoned up the sun, and the 5:00 AM train blew its whistle. In the street below, a couple of three-wheeled tuk-tuks sat, their engines puttering: taxi drivers waiting to take children to school or businessmen to their desks. One of these drivers leaned forward to turn on his radio, and his tuk-tuk was thrown backward in a spray of dust and debris, as if by a silent hurricane. The corner of the church across the street rose several meters from the ground. It sagged back down, crushing a Tamil man underneath, and then it rained cement shards and pieces of glass for a full minute afterward as people scrambled awake.

The explosion was heard over ten kilometers away. Since the country was in the teeth of a civil war, this wasn't as much of a surprise as if it had happened in, say, Oklahoma City, but, just to be safe, security forces, medical personnel, and a bomb squad were deployed, quickly scurrying to the address that was broadcast on the radios. They expected that the mop-up would be quick and minimal. Multiple ambulances were called—again, just to be safe. The Sri Lankan army was put on alert. More than a few people assumed that the explosion was caused by a gas line that had caught fire, or that maybe the church had collapsed just because it was so old.

These teams pulled up to the front of the smoldering church at the moment that another bomb, at the south end of town, ripped open a bus station. Phone lines started to jam up, police and security forces were told to station themselves at the edges of town, and the Sri Lankan army picked up its weapons and headed over to the bus station, since these events were turning the dawn quite dark.

Five minutes passed. As this second emergency team arrived at the second scene, a third bomb, this one at the west end of town, detonated at a television transmission station owned by the state-run Sri Lanka Broadcasting Corporation, dropping the tower into a smoking mess of steel shavings. Five minutes later, an office building downtown erupted in a spray of concrete, spitting pebbles, rebar, plaster, carpet, and a few twirling chairs into the sky. Then, as if inhaled back into the building, the material returned to earth, floor after floor collapsing under its weight, instantly burying four people.

In a suburb, two people, clueless as to what was happening in the city at that minute, opened a box they found on the sidewalk. An enormous smoking mouth opened in the middle of the road, and their limbs were launched more than ten meters away. About two minutes later, at Fort Railway Station, an unexploded bomb was found by the police. While the Sri Lankan army was busy defusing that one, a second detonated nearby, flicking a train car that had just blown its whistle onto its side like a matchbox.

Six minutes of peace followed. Just as the police dispatch began to breathe a sigh of relief, someone called in to report a blast near the foreign ministry office.

There were no more emergency workers available, and the Sri Lanka Broadcast Corporation, from what remained of the broadcast tower, pleaded that people stay indoors, remain calm, and wait for authorities to unwire a city that had been turned into a distributed detonation device.

But it wasn't over. Five more explosions were yet to come in the next ninety minutes. And since that morning in 1984, more than a hundred thousand people have died early deaths in Sri Lanka as a result of "civil war," "terrorism," and "political unrest."

The attack was organized by a man named Shankar Rajee, who, over afternoon tea, told me why he had done this. He said his intent was to cause terror. He said,

> We realized that we needed to make the ruling class and the bureaucrats feel the pressure and tension of the war. We needed to make them listen to our grievances. With this in mind, we drew up an action plan . . . These would be symbolic explosions that would be designed to create enough panic, and, well, terror . . . to make the government realize that they were not as powerful as they thought.

Rajee brewed many dangerous ideas in the course of his life, and he spread the danger generously. An exporter of the concept of suicide bombing to the Middle East and one of the founders of the Sri Lankan Tamil militant movement, he fueled enough terror on that October morning to draw the attention that the Tamil cause needed. He felt justified. He had grown up under the heavy weight of riots, lynchings, arson, refugee camps, and an intimate education on the finer points of segregation. Raised in the war zones of Sri Lanka, and finding himself muzzled because of his ethnicity, he'd had enough. So in his early twenties he moved to London. While there he met Palestinian militants, traveled with them to Beirut for training, pulled a trigger on the front lines, and explained the basics of suicide terrorism to the Fatah party. He left with a souvenir given to him by the PLO: enough ammunition to start a small war. Which he did promptly, as soon as he arrived back home.

The decade leading up to this bombing had been a politically charged competition of physical force between the Tamil minority and the Sinhalese majority (both of whom have been living on the island of Sri Lanka, formerly Ceylon, for as long as either group can remember). Up until Rajee bombed Colombo, the civil war had grown gradually from attacks by petty criminals to deadly discharges launched by organized groups. Murders committed out in the farms triggered riots in the towns, which in turn provoked multiple murders in temples, which then set off massive riots in the cities. With each blow, the government grew more hardened and conservative—and this in turn led to more hardened and conservative militant groups.

One of the militant groups born in these hotbeds was the Liberation Tigers of Tamil Eelam (LTTE)—or the Tamil Tigers. Founded in 1976 in the extreme north of the island, the LTTE waged a violent campaign against the Sri Lankan government and, like most Tamil groups, sought to create an independent Tamil state in the north of the island, which would be named Eelam.[1] The LTTE became notorious for civilian massacres, child conscriptions, drug smuggling, weapons stockpiling, and high-profile assassinations. They came up with the wearable detonation device known as the suicide belt, invented suicide bombing, pioneered the use of women in suicide attacks, and were proscribed as a terrorist organization by more than thirty countries by 2002. And they had their dark side too.

The Tamil Tigers waged war with the Sri Lankan state for three decades. Nearly a hundred thousand people died in the longest-running civil war in South-

---

1. There is great irony in the fact that the name itself is neither purely Tamil nor purely Sinhalese but a cognate of the two cultures' languages.

east Asia. The Tamil Tigers attacked not only shrines and monuments of symbolic importance, they also carried out the assassinations of public figures such as Sri Lankan president Ranasinghe Premadasa and former Indian prime minister Rajiv Gandhi. Then, on May 17, 2009, the Sri Lankan government announced the death of the elusive and dictatorial Vellupillai Prabhakaran, the founder and leader of the LTTE, claiming victory in the war and an end to this chapter of a three-thousand-year-old story.

The war the LTTE waged was cultural, ethnic, social, and economic. What I saw was a cultural dialogue: Sinhalese chauvinism fueling Tamil chauvinism, and vice versa. The LTTE argued that the ruling Sinhalese (primarily Buddhist) majority was suppressing the Tamil (mainly Hindu) minority. The LTTE's justification for its felonious acts was simple: Ethnic suppression demanded military response. Indeed, over the years the vision and mission of the LTTE managed to earn some support among the diaspora of seventy-four million Tamils currently living in Europe, North America, and India.

Rajee's goal, like the goal of many Tamils, was to make the government realize that it was not as powerful as it thought. A former colleague of Rajee's and one of the cofounders of the Tamil Tigers, Dharmalingam Siddharthan reiterated Rajee's message when he told me, "The only way to move the elephant is to prick it with something small. You can't move it. You have to make it feel something."

Sama

Sama the Elephant, Pinnawala Elephant Orphanage, Sri Lanka

In Sri Lanka, the elephant is a symbol of governance. The effigy of the elephant (and the deity Ganesh, in particular) keeps an easy eye on restaurants, in bedrooms, over cash registers, next to telephones, and, down by the ocean, at the beach where the tourists turn red. Local craftsmen hawk tiny elephant sculptures for a few pennies apiece. They sit on dashboards and on roadside advertisements. There are huge temples dedicated to the elephant.

The power of Ganesh is based on the esteem that Hindus have for elephants. The elephant represents kingliness, kindness, power, wisdom, wealth, authority, and the removal of obstacles. The elephant is governance itself and the model that government workers attempt to emulate.

It has been correctly said that, aside from being as stubborn as a grandpa hogs, elephants have a fine memory. For thousands of generations, Sri Lankan elephants have traveled the length of the isle on paths they've worn smooth over the years, ambling slowly in lines of families hundreds of elephants long, each touching the one it follows, slowly polishing their route, heavy footstep by slow tread, along the shining eastern seaboard of the island. Woe unto construction workers foolishly building on these ancient trails. Since the pachyderms are large enough to push over a house with a shove of a shoulder, smart enough to consider the process before beginning it, and passionate enough to intentionally trample the little humans who get in their way as easily as you or I might step on one of those little purse dogs, it's not hard to understand a Sri Lankan's childlike awe of elephants. They are four-legged gods.

A few years ago there were several farmers who were growing sugarcane on one of these elephant paths in eastern Sri Lanka, along the outskirts of a national forest. Naturally, after months of careful plowing, weeding, and watering, they didn't want a multi-ton animal stomping up their field. So the farmers erected a fence. That year the elephants knocked it down and walked through. The farmers then erected a bigger fence, and the next year the elephants knocked that down too. By the third year, determined to solve the problem, the farmers put up a very big electrical fence. Thinking they had the problem licked, they returned home to their families, ate dinner, and went to sleep, peaceful in the knowledge that not even a four-legged god could get through that.

The next morning, when they returned to their fields, they found a strange raft-like structure on top of their fence. It was made of several dozen palm trunks, each one laid carefully next to the others, forming a bridge over the very big electric fence that was now pressed very deep into the mud. They soon discovered that their fields had received an abusive stomping that had nothing to do with the path the elephants had walked in the past. This sort of behavior, it hardly needs pointing out, needs be interpreted as a reprimand.

Elephants will do as they deem appropriate. An elephant is far too large to be forced, too smart to be herded, too strong to be threatened, and too confident to be cowed; but it can be trained with a curious process that looks a bit like negotiation.

The first step in training an elephant is to catch one. In order to do that, you need to find one of the elephant paths. You should bring along some good strong rope, about a hundred candies, and a few boxes of crackers. It is recommended that you also bring along several brave friends. To catch your elephant, you must first tie nine or ten very strong deer-hide ropes to large trees (deer hide is almost as strong as hemp but is more pliable and lighter). Tie one end to a tree, and tie the other into a noose. Set the noose on the path, being careful not to disturb the bushes, then go hide with your friends and wait until the elephants come. You'll hear them. It may take a few days. When an elephant steps in one of the nooses, pull it tight. This is where things get difficult, because the elephant will make lots of noise. He will stomp around and try to free himself. As he does, make sure one of your friends is keeping an eye on where the elephant's other feet land. When he steps in the second noose, have your friend pull that noose tight too (but don't let the elephant catch him doing it or the elephant might pick him up like a doll and throw him down to the ground, and that would be the end of your friend). Now you have two of the elephant's legs tied to two trees. If you can get all four you'll be in good condition, but three will definitely do the job. With his legs spread out like this the elephant will be unable to walk. He will also be mad as a wet cat, and so this process is dangerous, but if you can manage to get that far, you have the hardest part of the job complete.

Wait two to five hours until the elephant calms down. Talk to him; say nice things to him. Tell him he'll be okay. Talk to him just like you would talk to a person. This is very important. Fortunately for you, elephants have a sweet tooth of legendary proportions, so give him candies as another way to calm him down. Just toss them in front of him, and he'll pick them up. Crackers also work. It's important that you stay calm and let him relax. Don't hit him. You won't accomplish anything that way other than getting yourself killed. Elephants have been used as execution machines, wrecking crews, and lumber lifters for good reason. Even a small elephant could pluck you from the ground with less risk and less effort than it would take you to pick up a drugged dog.

Now that you've caught your elephant and have given it all of your candies and crackers, bring in another elephant that you or your friends have already domesticated. If you're lucky enough to have a tame female on your side, everything will go smoothly. Some reports say that males don't even need to be caught, as they will just naturally follow a female back to the stables, but I'm recommending a safe and tested approach.[1] The elephant that you have tied up will greet the strange tame elephant. Keep the tame elephant around for four to five days. If you need to move your captive to a better grazing area (they eat about 250 kilograms, or 550 pounds, of foliage a day), release a couple legs, let the elephant walk a bit,

---

1. Elephants have a matriarchal society. The alpha female generally keeps approximately fifteen to twenty males. If one of them is making some sort of trouble, she throws him out of the herd. No one seems to know exactly how.

then tie him to a new tree. By the end of the week, with the other elephant nearby, all should be fine. If you aren't lucky enough to have a tame elephant on hand, then patience, kind behavior, and more candies can also do the trick.

The elephant will soon see (since behavior is more learned than taught) that life isn't so bad as a captive: He gets cookies and new friends. Generally, things will go fine, and he will come along to work with you more out of the cooperation of friendship than the shackles of necessity.

Mahouts are an Asian kind of cowboy. They capture, train, raise, and work with elephants for a living in both India and Sri Lanka. Over the millennia, mahouts have developed a vocabulary they use when they talk to their elephants. Remember, talking is very important; any mahout will tell you that it is key to his relationship with his elephant. The words are derived from Hindi. *Daha* means "go forward," *ho* is "stop," and *deri* means "pick that up." Some of them are more complicated, like *meheidan*, which means "move to this side." The "sic 'em!" command, *pour-duh*, tells an elephant to drub a poor sap with his trunk, but only once. The words can be strung together to form short sentences such as *daha deri meheidan*, which means "go forward, pick up that object, then step sideways toward me." This means that you can lead an elephant to water, and you can tell him to drink, too.

Mahouts carry long sticks with a hook and a pointed tip—something sharp that makes an elephant move. They might, for example, say mehe-idan and hook the elephant behind the ear with this tool to reinforce the verbal message. Occasionally they poke the elephant with this stick. But the elephant will be pricked only gently, and only if he has already been trained. Unwise or aggressive mahouts simply don't die old.

Elephants do what elephants must: They drink over one hundred liters of water each day, eat trees for breakfast, and need a river for their daily bath. Since humans do similar things with similar resources, competition for space and water has grown increasingly acute. Humans erect a fence, the elephants push it over, and the humans retaliate. The elephants then retaliate for the retaliation. This ancient war, which is called in a perfectly serious tone, "The Human-Elephant Conflict," is going very poorly for the elephants, great symbols of governance and power though they may be. The 2002 census set the score at twenty-five million people and twenty-five hundred elephants.

I have personally seen about a hundred elephant veterans of this conflict. Most of them are at the Pinnawala Elephant Orphanage, a conservation breeding center run by the National Zoological Garden of Sri Lanka. The orphanage, established in 1978, is a government-sponsored institution aimed at preserving elephants. If a wounded elephant is found, the animal is brought to the orphanage, given the best medical care in the world, and offered residence with the others that live in the refuge. Some of these elephants are found separated from their herds, some are sick or wounded, and some of them simply get caught in the crossfire of Sri Lanka's civil war.

In 1984, only a few weeks before the morning bombs went off in Colombo, the elephant orphanage received news from up north that a small female elephant had been found lying in a ditch outside of some rice fields. Dr. Rajapaksa and another veterinary surgeon from Pinnawala drove their jeep up to investigate. When villagers led them to where the elephant was lying, they saw that the calf's front leg had been blown off after she had stepped on a land mine. Unable to walk, she had lain herself down and prepared to die in that ditch, one more casualty of the war. But Dr. Rajapaksa would have none of that. He and his colleague bundled her up, hoisted her onto a trailer, and carted her back up to the orphanage. There they wrapped her stump in a very large white bandage and gave her a massive dose of medication, a dozen buckets of fresh water, and a fresh pile of palm fronds. They named the young elephant Sama, which means "peace."

Dr. Rajapaksa worked steadily with Sama for five months. He gave her vitamins, talked with her, fed her freshly cut foliage, and kept her stump clean and in fresh bandages. There were four daily baths, medication, and cleaning. Eventually her health returned. But problems of a lost a leg don't go away, especially if you need to have three feet on the ground at all times, as elephants, massive as they are, do. Sama started having difficulties since she simply wasn't able to keep her weight well-enough distributed for her other limbs to bear.

As soon as the problem came to light, Pinnawala contacted an engineering firm in Germany to manufacture a prosthetic leg. The limb, a flexible cylinder made of steel girders and cotton fabric, fit Sama perfectly, but she took it off and threw it against the wall. The following day, the good doctor fastened a couple of loose screws back into their sockets, bent the frame back into shape, and gently reattached it to Sama's leg with Velcro and a cotton wrap to keep her comfortable. That afternoon it was found at the base of a different wall, again bent.

After three tries, Dr. Rajapaksa decided that Sama had executive power on this topic and that there was no room for negotiation.

These days, more than two decades after her accident, Sama and the other elephants of the Pinnawala orphanage continue their daily routines. When the mahouts bring the elephants to the river to bathe, Sama can be found at the back of the group, slowly swinging her mass under a misshapen spine, making what pace she can manage. The mahouts follow her patiently, and the tourists gather at the railing. All of the onlookers have the same pitying expression written on their faces as they watch this symbol of government, this little veteran god, find her way to the river below for her afternoon bath.

Original Coat of Arms, British Colony of Ceylon

Chapter Two: Ahangama

"They hate our freedom."
—George W. Bush, March 18, 2002

The Island

Yakkinidua Island, Ahangama, Sri Lanka

The brooding blue of the Indian Ocean stretches for thousands of miles, slowly echoing waves between continents until, finally, the waters break upon the island's yellow and green flanks. For as long as the record books go back, Sri Lanka has always been a densely populated island brimming with rich vegetation. Just south of the Indian subcontinent, Sri Lanka stubbornly guards her spot near the middle of the ocean, where there are no neighbors, except India to her north. There is no land for over a thousand miles in any other direction.

People live in Sri Lanka today in much the same way as they have for about eighteen hundred years. Water is pulled from the wells, coconuts are knocked from the trees, fish are dragged from the sea, and the big tropical sun swings overhead, tying the days into each other in a steaming, sweaty rhythm of ancient customs. People eat more or less the same food they've eaten for the last several millennia (curries), and the language hasn't changed much either (unlike India, Sri Lanka never adopted English as an official language). Most Sri Lankans live in little houses that are built of coconut fronds, and the roofs are replaced seasonally. The monsoons roll through the skies, usually arriving in May or June, and the dust of the previous year is rinsed down into the sea so that the year can begin anew.

Some things have changed. Schooners and brigs of the sixteenth century used to stop here often to take on water, food, and wood before moving on. It was common for shipping lines from Singapore, for example, to stop over in old Ceylon before taking a southwesterly bearing toward Madagascar. As a result of this traffic, the island attracted the notice of the Chinese, Dutch, and Portuguese, who each took turns chasing out their predecessors. For most of the rice farmers, mahouts, and monks, these conquests were no more than skirmishes localized within the capital city and hardly had any effect on their lives, if they were heard about at all. But then the British arrived, bringing to the island not only a new and harsher definition of imperialism but the industrial revolution as well.

Just before 1900, some metal railroad tracks came slithering out of the jungle. A few years later a big black strip of asphalt road snaked its way down the coast, and soon cars and motorcycles were chugging through the towns. The mob of cars carried an increasing number of tourists, many of whom brought enormously fat wallets. Televisions appeared in some people's living rooms. Bizarre advertisements followed, and in the heartbeat of a generation, Sri Lankans saw the arrival of industrialization and its children: pollution, automation, overcrowding, malnutrition, and factory mass production.

During the monsoon season, however, the island becomes ancient again, and silent. Both the trains and the tourists make fewer appearances, going back to whatever time they came from. If you allow yourself to pay attention to the details of the island, the jungles brim with strange voices, hoary-toothed phantoms, and the old gods that step quietly through the jungle just before a storm arrives. The ocean whispers some dreadful secret again and again, the winds argue a more complicated rebuttal, and the fronds listen to both sides, one, then the other, then back again. Then the falling rain starts simply enough with a few sprinkles. These build to an applause and then a roar as the streets fill with water and run brown with the jungle silt on its way to the sea. And each drop in this huge falling crowd is saying the same word they all have said, over and over again, in precisely the same way since Vishnu came down from India and lifted the island of Sri Lanka up out of the sea.

The monsoon rains become sheets, and the sheets

become descending walls of water, magic walls full of falling lenses, and through it, if you look closely today, you can see things just as they were, thousands of years ago, before all the wars and empires and spice traders. Sri Lanka remains Ceylon and all of her old lessons roam, like ghosts, among the modern wars of today.

It wasn't the spice trade or imperial conquest that brought me to Sri Lanka, or even tourism, but media. My interest grew when I began to encounter the word "terrorist" so often on television, radio, the Internet, and in print that it seemed terrorists must be very important, and very frightening, people.

Terrorists had already had a big impact on my life. In September 2001, I'd been in Europe. I'd been clowning around at an event in Linz, Austria, and after the festival I motored back to Paris, planning to spend a few days there before flying home to California on the twelfth. While I was taking a nap on the afternoon of the eleventh, the phone rang, and a friend told me to turn on the television. So I stood there, staring at the screen, with millions of others around the world, as planes sliced first into one World Trade Center tower and then the other, launching the twenty-first century with the most fantastic media event in history.

The next morning, news outlets were scrambling to find an explanation for what had happened, but I finished my coffee and planned on going to the airport anyway, only to find out my flight home had been canceled. As a result, I was stranded in Europe, which led to my getting rid of most everything I owned, staying in Paris for over a year, and being separated from friends and family for far longer than I had imagined possible. September 11 had an immediate and profound impact on my life.

"Terrorists," they told me, were the reason.

Then, after George W. Bush got back from wherever he was in the week following September 11, he was all over the airwaves with the same word. "Terrorists" was on the front page, headlines, splash screens, television banners, and everyone's lips. And it didn't let up in the months and even years that followed September of 2001: Terrorists were responsible for everything bad.

But was this fear caused by terrorism, or by the media that was spreading terrorism? If no one had filmed September 11, 2001, what impact would it have had? What was the link between terrorism and media? And what was a terrorist, anyway?

I'd never seen a terrorist with my own eyes, nor had I ever talked to anyone who had. If it weren't for my faith in the integrity of editors at my news sources, I'm not sure I could even have said that terrorists were real. It was a bit like everyone in the neighborhood telling me to watch out for Sasquatch: I'd seen videos of him, and he seemed strange and different, but I was just not getting the entire picture as to why I should be so, well, terrified.

The media had left me with more questions than answers. I wanted to know how, for example, someone could justify to themselves the killing of thousands of people for a political cause. What ethical complaint or grievance could be so sharp you'd decide to become a suicide bomber? I had read of terrorism schools, so I guessed you got, what, an MA in terrorism? I was also confused about the way terrorists lived: in caves, in the wilderness, and hating me for my freedoms? Maybe a terrorist is more like a golem than a Sasquatch, I thought, but it was too simple to believe and I was suspicious; right and wrong were too clearly demarcated for this portrayal of terrorists to be true. I finally hypothesized that the myth of the monster was not the thing to be feared; it was, rather, the media that was to be feared, because the media was causing terror by reporting on terrorists. I decided that if I couldn't solve this equation, then I would at least muck it up further.

For me, believing is seeing. If terrorists were dangerous enough to provoke sweeping changes in our federal laws, I felt, then they were dangerous enough for me to try to understand them. If the government was passing laws to protect me—laws that determined what I could and could not do, laws that changed what I could and could not say, laws that affected habeas corpus, even—then I figured I should go find out what it was I needed to be protected from.

The laws seemed potentially more dangerous than the terrorists themselves. Several months before I left on my monster-hunting expedition, I found out I could be jailed simply for talking with terrorists. A recently issued presidential decree, the "Detention, Treatment, and Trial of Certain Non-Citizens in the War Against Terrorism" military order, stated that what I was setting out to do could potentially get me tossed into a secret jail far away from home. Since Germany had a similar policy during the Second World War (they called it, far more poetically, *Nacht und Nebel*[1]), I became more afraid of my own government in nearby Washington than of terrorists in faraway caves. More important, however, was the fact that I didn't want to be afraid. I wasn't interested in buying into what I saw as a nation of people reduced to a slobbering insane asylum of terrorized lobotomy victims watching television. The fears were not, nor would be, mine. And making sure of that required some action on my part.

Enjoying a career well scarred from a lifelong

---

1. *Nacht und Nebel*, or "night and fog," was the Nazi directive essentially legitimizing the kidnapping of anyone distributing anti-Nazi propaganda.

habit of touching stoves, I bought a ticket despite my fears, packed a bag with a small laptop, camera, and voice recorder, and got on a plane. The instruments I brought were my terrorist-trapping tools. I also brought my favorite boots, some clothes, a couple of books, a lighter, and my sunglasses (my pocketknife and shampoo didn't make the journey, however, as they were confiscated at the airport).

I decided to take the job because I fit the role. As a boy I lived for nearly eight years in rural areas without electricity, I had worked in high-risk environments as a forest fire fighter, I had been trained to provide emergency medical care, and I was able to document what's happening from a first-person point of view. I fit the qualifications. It wasn't about adrenaline addiction. Calling me an adrenaline addict is a bit like calling me a curry addict; neither have anything to do with why I went. Surely both curries and adrenaline were on the road ahead, but it wasn't necessary to buy an airline ticket to get them. No, I took the job because nobody else was stupid enough — or was possessed of the (rapidly evaporating) sense of immortality I still doggedly maintained — to visit a war zone, act as a witness, and collect and document alien points of view, all without the backing of a major media outlet.

Corporate news is unclean, untrustworthy, and made to satisfy the agendas of those who can afford to buy the truth. Believing that there is no such thing as objective news, anyway, even if it's statistical information (stories we have to tell are always more true, even if less accurate), I set out to find and report the most subjective and inaccurate news I could. If a terrorist existed, I would talk with him. I would see for myself and write about what I found.

I would go because knowledge is terror's strongest antidote.

So I decided to do a little terrorist ethology. It was not terrorism that interested me, mind you, because that is just the act; rather, I was interested in the psychology of the people who undertook the acts—specifically the people who were involved in suicide terrorism, which seems to be the most feared (and therefore the most effective) form of terrorism. At first I considered going to Afghanistan, then decided I should study a purer specimen, as it were. Afghanistan was too anti-American, and I wanted to talk with terrorists who had little to do with the United States or with American or anti-American causes; I wanted, instead, to find a group of terrorists who had evolved their own local gripes yet had also influenced other terrorist groups with their own unique solutions. I was interested in seeking patterns and models that could be generalized, then compared with the behavior patterns of those who did have a gripe with my country. I wanted to find a way the United States (and other countries) could learn something from that petri dish. I wanted to find something like a Galapagos, a place where the evolution was contained enough to be unique, so that it might offer general information applicable elsewhere.

Looking at terrorist watch lists, I finally came across what I had been looking for: a small island; an ancient conflict; racial, religious, and political boundaries that were all in a tangled contention. By 2003, India, the United States, England, Canada, and the European Union had all designated the Tamil Tigers a terrorist organization. I decided to go because, just as a bird thrives in the sky and a fish comes from the sea, it would be necessary to go there to learn about their country, customs, and culture, to understand their context, the conditions that created them. Plus they invented suicide bombing.

I told my wife about it. We weren't married at the time, but we were in Paris (she's French) and it was springtime in 2002, and we were walking through Place St. Michel and I said that I was going to go interview terrorists.

She stopped, turned to me, and said, "That's so American of you."

Now, I found the village where I'm staying, Goviyapana, after a good deal of research about the island. I knew that I wanted to be on the beach, I knew I wanted to start my investigation in a small town, and I knew I wanted to start in the south, where there is a considerable tourism industry. It was legally easier as well as logistically simpler to start here, since finding a hotel in the demilitarized zone, much less the active war zones up north, would have proven impossible before arriving. So I decided to wade into the shallow end first, and the southern end of the island was just that. This small village of Goviyapana happened to be located between the tourist resort, the deep jungle, the coast, and the museums and libraries I wanted to research, and meanwhile at the extreme opposite end of the island to where I'm ultimately headed.

Goviyapana has electricity, but I haven't seen a working phone; the village has water, but I haven't seen a running faucet.

I'm staying in a tiny hotel that is quiet and clean and very inexpensive. It is full of disturbing dreams and harmless nightmares. There is a bed that is made each morning by a bent old man who comes in and arranges the sheets in a fancy way and puts a flower on the pillow. This is lovelier than chocolate, and he organizes whatever I happen to have knocked over during the previous day and brings in milk tea and hoppers (a kind of griddle cake made of rice) before he makes the bed. He's generally nearby, as there aren't many guests other than the stray dog that he throws rocks at, an occasional gecko, and the silent bald man from Austria who mostly hides in the room upstairs. This man comes to the hotel at this time each year (the cook has told me) and talks with no one but simply rotates himself and his lawn chair with the sun each day, eats his curry in the evening, and hides again at night. He reminds me of Kurtz. Sometimes I see a young woman dressed in a sari walk up the stairs to his bedroom, usually around sunset. I don't know who she is, but the man seems lonely nonetheless.

My bedroom, which costs about U.S. $12 a night and overlooks the ocean, has a small and prissy Victorian-style writing desk and a patio where my food is brought in the evenings. My bedroom is large, and I spend time here peacefully. The other room here is the bathroom. It is a large and square concrete room with a shower spigot shoved into the wall at about chest level, and a short garden hose on the floor (the green kind, about as long as my forearm), and no shower curtain—but in a land as wet as Sri Lanka no one really cares if a little water falls on the floor. Next to the shower are two foot impressions with a hole behind them. This area, if I happen to miss my mark, is easily rinsed off with the rest of the floor. Just for practice I turn around and put my feet in the impressions like they're stirrups, then step out again for fear I'll be catapulted or receive an enema. I'm not used to this.

Okay, I tell myself, this is not a bad idea. This is a simple toilet that doesn't waste water, doesn't use nasty cleaning products, and doesn't have any moving parts, and so it doesn't require replacement plastics to be manufactured. It is simple and easy to maintain. It is so simple it seems superior to the toilets I grew up with. It's connected to the city's plumbing, or seems to be, I think, as I look down the hole. So I suppose it is hygienic. But, wait. There is no toilet paper here. Is it not customary to use toilet paper, or did the old man that changes my sheets just forget? There is no roller on the wall. It would be nice if there were toilet paper. Perhaps that, also, is what the hose is for.

A hole in the floor I can deal with. But not having toilet paper is leaving me feeling abandoned. This seems primitive, especially since the right hand, rather than the fork or spoon, is the national eating utensil of Sri Lanka. In such an otherwise nice hotel this shortfall seems so uncivil.

But the truth is, civilization and industrialization have nothing to do with each other. A country can be ancient and civilized and not have any of the manufactured appliances that we Westerners might consider essential. Perhaps civilizations should be measured by their toilets. A rudimentary toilet can be a sign that the civilization in question is not concerned with unimportant matters. I have seen in both Los Angeles and Tokyo heated toilets that measure the pH level of shit, its consistency, and its quantity. I've seen entertainment toilets in Sydney with video games mounted on them. I've seen luxury toilets in Paris that squirt mint-blue water into the bowls when you turn the gold-plated flush handles. And I've seen little antisplash shelves in the bowls of toilets in Berlin that would make any scatologist or coprophiliac smile. These toilets, however, are harder to maintain, are more expensive to buy, use more resources (plastic, metal, glue, and, most of all, water), and are, ultimately, complex sales efforts. They have nothing to do with being civilized, or even civilization. Maybe industrialization, the cause of so much pollution, is itself uncivil.

The notion of "First World" is absurd.

Maybe the societies with the simplest toilets are

the most civilized. Maybe what makes a civilization such is not the things we buy but how we treat one another— how we, if you will, avoid getting ourselves and others dirty. That a country's toilet uses a nearby shower as a flushing system says nothing about how its people greet one another, about what guides their moralities and thoughts, about their history, what their dress codes represent, or how their families interact. What this hose next to my shower, next to my toilet, says is what any toilet in any country says: Don't shit on the floor. But this is hard for me to understand, and so I spend a good twenty minutes in the bathroom pondering over such things, then I go downstairs to ask if I can have a roll of toilet paper.

I'm walking along the beach. It is warm, and the wind is lifting ribbons of coconut smoke out of the jungle (presumably from a farmer's campfire?) into the air and tracing strange designs out over the sea. The beach is a beautiful slab of paradise with all the trimmings: the bent fronds hanging over opaline blue, waves sliding up and over the white sand, one or two people bathing, gentle clouds hanging on the horizon, and all of it slowly turning cardamom yellow as the sun exhales into the sea. A skinny man with a turban sits on a single stilt that holds him some two or three meters out of the water. One leg up, one net down, patiently fishing.

About a quarter mile off the coast a perfect equilateral triangle of an island holds its place in the swell of the Indian Ocean. A footpath on the island spirals up past a cluster of boulders, through some patches of grass, and— above the steep face of the cliff—into a thatch of trees, which stand on the top of the island like a clod of hair on a triangular head submerged up to the eyebrows. Faces can be seen among the reeds and thorns—the faces of ghouls and devils that still guard the island and work its machinery. But you can see them only with your peripheral vision. If you concentrate on them, they quickly change into rocks, or trees, or shadows of the two. The island is perfect, pristine, and suspicious.

For the last five or ten minutes, two young men have been walking behind me, not saying a word. With skeletal high cheekbones, long noses, and dark eyes, these two look like they've lived on a diet of amphetamines for the last twenty years.

I stop and turn around to find out what's happening here.

They smile at me.

"What is your name?" asks one.

The other asks, "Where are you going?"

I ignore the questions and ask the name of the little island.

The shorter one, his skin a bluish black, smiles at me with huge teeth as sharp as coral and white as ocean spray, and this surprises me, this contrast, because he looks so beautiful.

"Yes, it has name!" he shouts. "It is name Lace Rock!" He has a disarmingly large smile, and his eyes shine with a pride that I'll probably never know.

"Yakkinidua," the other one quietly adds.

"What does that mean?"

"Yakkinidua?" the less-tall one steps in again. "Ghost Island." Then he smiles again, and I'm shocked again so I smile back.

The taller one looks at his friend, and they say something in words of spice and flame—nearly Spanish lifts in the tongue combined with Chinese and the sound water makes as it runs over rocks.

Then they look at me and are silent for a second.

"Witch's Rock," they both say.

Once upon a time Hanuman, the monkey god, stole some potent juju from Kali. Hanuman, medicine in hand, scampered down the coast, and Kali, vowing to retrieve her magic, sent a black storm of vengeance and death after him as a plague. Hanuman hid among the rocks here at Yakkinidua, and Kali thundered past because the island is so good for hiding and has, as the young men tell me, "many secrets."

Once upon a different time, much later, a woman lived on the island, and she knew how to knit. She lived on the island with her husband and sold under dainties to the ladies on the weekdays—nicely woven petals to surprise the unsuspecting husbands. She picked berries and pounded leaves into a paste that could close a cut in a day, and everyone knew, even without asking her or visiting her on that triangle of an island, that she was also a witch.

Of course, "yakkini" means "devil" or "ghost," as well as "witch"—I can't quite get it straight from these guys, they don't know—and so this is why it's got so many names: Lace Rock, Yakkinidua, Witch's Rock, Ghost Island, and, most simply, the Island. My two new associates find nothing strange about the legend, and so it doesn't cross my mind that it might be a fiction. We all seem to agree that these stories are fact. Believing is the most important part of any reality.

The two young men I have met, Prabath and Krishan, are both in their early twenties. They're out of school and not in need of jobs because they have food and friends and all that they require except entertainment, since the cricket match isn't until tomorrow and there are no car accidents, fishing trips, or freshly dead people to investigate. They're just looking for something to do, and it doesn't matter what. This explains their interest when I walked by, since being white, I'm also a novelty. They've seen tourists walking down the road from time to time, or behind the fences and on the private beaches, pink, puffy, reclining, and sipping, but Prabath and Krishan haven't talked with many of us. For them, we tourists are a sort of different species that's interacted with only for business reasons, or if there's an emergency that breaks a hole in the thick social barriers of race, ethnicity, and money. Thus I'm their solution to boredom, as they are a solution to mine, and so we discuss the island.

Prabath, the shorter of the two, with the big white teeth and eyes like those of a rabbit that's come back from a long journey, takes my hand and startles me at first until his sincerity stops me from moving. He even has long eyelashes, which make him look as guiltless as Grünewald's little lamb. Prabath seems alien, with thin forearms that taper down to meet a block of a wrist, leading into his large knuckles and twig fingers. With his hands pulling at my own, he asks me to sit down on a tree to talk, and so I learn that a couple of years ago he passed his advanced-level exams. Now he lives next to the railroad tracks under a cluster of trees with his mother, father, sister, and two brothers named Lalith and Shamesh. They live in a small concrete house with the standard outfitting of an entry parlor, a living room, three bedrooms, a kitchen with a woodstove, and a backyard. In the backyard is a palm tree. In the living room they have the customary arrangement of two chairs that face a sofa with a coffee table in between. He doesn't have a dog or any pet. Dogs aren't kept here in Sri Lanka, because they, as a species, misbehave and carry fleas. A Sinhalese will tell you dogs are filthy, just as any New Yorker will tell you pigeons are disgusting.

Prabath and Krishan are cousins. Krishan, probably twenty-three or twenty-four, lives next door. He's taller, not at all like a lamb, a little smarter than his cousin, and behind his eyes is not a pleading interest, but storms of comprehension and patience. Krishan is angular and smiles too but his eyes register deep knowledge, like a Buddha. His fingers are more serpents than sticks. As Prabath and I talk, Krishan rolls a cigarette, wipes his lip, glues the cigarette together, blows softly once to dry it, and pulls out his lighter.

Prabath, still holding my hand, carefully explains that their family has owned the land for a long time, though the two of them cannot agree upon the details. They break into a good five-minute conversation over this point, neither one of them being able to go back much more than three or four hundred years. Maybe more, but they decide they don't care. At least three hundred years, it is agreed.

Their English is crummy, but a helluva lot better than my Sinhalese, since I can say only "thank you," "please," "friend," "we go," and "do you speak English?" They call me Marx since that's the closest thing they've heard to a name that unhinges an underbite as badly the word "Mark."

The days pass, and I've found that my mind is slowing down and my heart is speeding up. My life has been blown fresh, I have no responsibilities, and my third eye is squinting its way open. I didn't know I had one until a bald monk in a saffron robe poked me in the forehead and told me so. Now I do. Sri Lanka shifts you. I have stopped eating lunches since there's so much else to be done in the middle of the day. One of these activities is fishing with Prabath and Krishan. We catch crabs, also known as *cacadua*. We just pick them up, fast before they run, then we take a stick we've sharpened with a rock and push it through the crab's soft torso, baiting the hook for the fishing line. We sling them back into the sea, their fingerlike legs desperately clutching at the air as they slowly fall over the deep water. Then we catch a fish and bury him in the sand for safekeeping (he is still trying to breathe as I cover him with dirt, but this is the way of life, and the crabs had it no better, worse even, and this is how it ends for everyone, anyway).

Other activities of the afternoon include learning about the people in the village. An old woman who lived just up the beach in a cinder block house has killed herself. Prabath explains that she just walked into the ocean. The water was up to her waist, then her breasts, then her neck and her jaw, then she disappeared, only to reappear, salty, still, and scratched (and only a little nibbled upon) on the beach the very next day. The ocean just spit her back out at the same place she went in. It didn't care for her and nobody else in the village seemed to have either. "She was crazy woman," Prabath tells me matter-of-factly, and so the village people took her body from the beach and into the house, and they'll bury her too.

To Yakkinidua. We swim, splash hard, our heads out of the water, race. It is a twenty-minute swim, then a scramble over some rocks, a view down a two-hundred-foot chasm where an British imperialist killed himself in the 1920s, an ascent up some warm boulders into the sun, an elbows-and-knees military-style crawl through a thorn tunnel (I have the little red designs down my back to prove it), a walk over some more boulders, a climb up into some other trees, up another cliff, and then into a clearing. Two hours later we are finally breathing hard and looking off of the pointed forehead of the island where the witch lived. We are far out and high up, and they tell me that there's a good view up in the tree.

Gabriel is one of two friends of Krishan's who are with us today. He shows me which tree to climb for the 360-degree grand view. On his cue, they all lift me into the lower branches, and I climb far up into an aquamarine heaven that hangs high above a miniature landscape of millions of palm hands reaching into the curry winds. The ocean is glittering like an enormous jewel, a great spread-out goddess that is making love to the sky, and I can tell them apart, but not where they join, because it is far away, tucked under a coming storm, and great activity is brewing. I laugh for the longsighted joy of being able to get high enough that you can see where you are, and my friends on the ground below are laughing at me laughing because they all know this beauty, too. I can see mountains far off in the distance. There is a tiny bus on the road down the coast. Little people are getting off now, and those who were waiting get on. They are only specks next to the yellow bus. Other people are swimming in the river. They are naked because their mothers are washing their clothes on the shore nearby. I can smell tea and the salt from the ocean. A black-and-white bird, some refugee from prehistory, swings by with a question in his eye. My hand aches and my feet are cut from the rocks, and the wind kisses my hair, gentle and cool.

"Be careful, Marx!" Prabath advises.

He sounds like a panicked mother.

I have no clue what he's worried about so I look down, half expecting to see a leopard climbing the tree. But it is just Prabath, with that shiny blue face of his and those crazy teeth, and he is smiling at me, and he laughs.

Gabriel is picking up berries nearby. Ripe, they've fallen from a small bush. Gabriel speaks the best English of the group and has appointed himself the Guide. Gabriel has a serious face, as if he's been bred for fighting, but his hair hangs loose, and it has its own sense of humor. He is a lighter shade than Prabath and Krishan. Gabriel's father was, as I understand it, Weligama's medicine man—Weligama is the town just up the road—for several decades until he moved down here to Goviyapana. I climb down from the tree and help Gabriel pick small red berries out of the dirt for thirty minutes while Krishan and Prabath take their turns in the tree or wander out to the edge to see the blue line of the Indian Ocean, past the Tropic of Capricorn, where the next piece of land is Antarctica. We're at the very edge of the world, standing on the pointy corner.

Krishan rolls a joint.

Ten minutes later, it's time to go, and those of us who are not observant Buddhists are stoned and running down the hill like young boys. The afternoon, as all afternoons, asks that more things be done, and none of us care at all about anything in particular.

"Come, Marx!" Prabath yells.

"What is it?" But I'm asking the back of Prabath's head, because he's already running down the hill, jumping from stone to stone. We are all barefoot, only they are used to it. I ask, "Where?"

"The tunnel with the breath sea," Gabriel kind of explains.

I look at Krishan, hoping he can help out.

"Very good," he says and smiles the smile of a great secret, with the edges of his mouth curled.

The other boy, to whom I haven't spoken, as I just met him today, runs ahead of Prabath. Krishan is polite enough to wait for me. Then he decides that he should lead.

So I follow.

We scurry down the back face of the island, the southern part that faces Antarctica, and I see Prabath and the other boy crawl into a dark cave. Gabriel slides in, then Krishan. They're quick like spiders, and they know, from lifetimes of practice, where to put their hands and feet. Mine are now bloody; the soles of my feet are shredded. I'll have to stay off of them for a bit, here in the tropics. This is my last day out for a while.

Squatting down to look in, I hold my chin to my chest and peer out from under my eyebrows. It's a long, creepy, dark damn cave. The tunnel is deep and narrow. I can hear the ocean thunder-bumping inside the rocks, and I can't see the light at the exit end. The boys' voices ricochet and reverberate. The surf, hitting the island face, makes a crack, then a boom, and that energy ripples across the island and here, at the mouth of this cursed hole, the energy even touches my intestines with a dull and deadly voltage. I take a deep breath and put my hand on my knee. This tunnel is serious as birth. I swallow my claustrophobia and follow them, figuring that if they've already gone in and they're still laughing, it can't be that bad. There is a forty-five-degree angle in the rock, and I lean back into it, putting most of the weight on my feet, using my arms to support myself from behind. Holding my neck stiff, I have to turn my head to get through the narrow opening. It's barely large enough to crawl through. My chest is getting stuck between some sharp rocks since I'm both taller and thicker than most Sri Lankans. I exhale, slide forward, and can breathe again. It smells like earth, womb, and tomb garnished with sea salt.

Many unnerving minutes pass, and I'm concentrating on foot, hand, putting foot down (ouch, more blood) then hand again until suddenly I'm again borne into the sun, but my feet are right at sea level, and we're all standing in a shadow, watching a wave roll toward the cave that is our little porch. We are standing in a blow-hole cavern that looks out at the ocean. The entire Indian Ocean is in front of us, framed by black and wet rock.

I look at my feet. Yes, I am standing at the same level as the ocean. I look out. Yes, that wave, beautiful as it is, clad in mint blue and shining sun, is rolling toward us, its face more than six feet high. It's going to crush us into the back of our little cave, smash us against these rocks, and then drag us back out for the sister wave that follows to mash us against the rocks again. This is going to be a week at the hospital. I look at Krishan and Prabath. No, they are not panicking; they are looking at me, smiling. I take a step back toward the tunnel (as if it would be any kind of escape route) and watch.

"Marx!" Prabath echoes.

"Come!" Krishan waves at me to step closer to him, and to the ocean too.

The wave gathers, inhales, buckles over the churning boulders on the sea floor, lurches higher, crests, and slams into the tunnel opening, like a big palm clapping over an open mouth. The spray explodes out over this opening, and on the other side we can see the wave, stopped dead in its tracks, a huge gelatinous screen, the sun shimmering on the other side, fish silhouettes pulsing and wiggling in a neon wall of holy blue sapphire, as big as a cinema screen, but far, far livelier.

It is at this moment, as we stand in awe before a magic wall of seawater, that I feel like a Tom Sawyer turned Johnny Quest who is exploring the haunted island with my cadre of Sinhalese compadres. Aside from my bleeding feet, thorn claw marks down my back, my sunburned head, cut fingers, scraped chest, receding fear, and dirty hide, I am really clean for, perhaps, the first time in years. There is no problem anywhere in the world. I look at the smiling faces around me. They are proud of their Yakkinidua Island. These black faces, with sharp white teeth, thin Indian features, and skinny, muscular bodies, are proud of their heaven-high tree, their cannon-firing ocean, their sun and berries and magic ghosts that swirl about, singing spice songs in the warm, windy airs of ancient Ceylon, as it has been for thousands of years.

And, that same day, at that same hour, about ninety miles north of us, a politician is pulled out of his car, shot once in the back of the head, once in the back of the neck, shoved face first onto the sidewalk, and left to be picked up by the police force of Colombo.

Honorary Dinner

Curry lunch, South Sri Lankan style, Ahangama, Sri Lanka

The two families, if they are even separate families, live close together and share a well. Prabath's backyard is linked to Krishan's backyard by a small trail that curls through the coconut trees, twists around a couple of papaya stalks, hops the creek, and exits near the railroad

45

tracks, where the well sits inside of a small square piece of concrete.

Only 2 percent of Sri Lanka's population has septic systems similar to what you might find in North America or Europe. Most of the country is just a few feet above sea level, so the island's main water table is a cocktail of what goes in and what comes out of a population as dense as New Jersey's. People drink what's there, and their immune systems adapt. For the most part, across most of Sri Lanka, if you step into a river, you're stepping into a whole new world that is probably best kept on the outside of your skin. If not, and if you're from the West, your immune system will have one hell of a time handling this particularly rich soup. Dysentery leakage for this Westerner notwithstanding, it's important to note that to the average Sinhalese or Tamil, there is nothing wrong with any of this water. If Prabath were to come visit me in California, he'd have a hard time too but for very different reasons. But the fact of the matter is that there is a standing water table of sewage next to the railroad tracks and between the houses. It's not that you notice this, not visually, or olfactorily, because the vegetation of the area filters and the rains dilute and the sun bleaches and things don't really get too bad. But it is the tropics, and this is fecund, and you can smell it in any well if you have a sharp nose.

Lalith pulls the bucket from the hole, and the smell doesn't make me want to pour it over my head, as if I were in a 7-Up commercial, but as he smiles his satisfied grin I'm reminded that we like what we're familiar with, and to him this is the water from his home. He hands me two buckets, fills his two, and we take the path back to the house, he in the lead and I following with a very simple satisfaction, as if I were a stupid golden retriever, carrying a stick for my master. I want to participate as I can in Sri Lankan living, make myself useful, and learn something in the process. The thought that I could ever blend in, or make any impression subtler than a huge, pink, strangely dressed, and illiterate Westerner such as I am, is an absurd notion. But I offer entertainment. Children can pluck my skin, adults can examine my palms, dogs can bark, babies can cry, women can stroke my hair, and everyone is provided with the uncommon diversion of a living freak show, while I, happy from the attention, am also saddened that I can never really be a part of this world.

Despite this gap, Prabath's family welcomes me as his good friend, and I help with the chores around the house during the days. I've found that work is the best way to get to know people, and I like to help out when I visit someone whenever I can. It's a sign of appreciation, it's a way to temporarily join their family, and I learn the details of their lives that way. Plus, I was born in Mississippi, so it's somehow bred into me to try to be polite, even at the risk of getting in the way.

So we carry water back from the well and help his mother spin string with coconut husks. They show me how to climb a coconut tree. It's done by making a loop out of cloth, or rope, a little longer than the trunk is round. That loop is then thrown around the trunk and leaned into while facing the tree. Testing the loop, it can now be used as a counterbalance to the feet, toes pointed out, that hold the climber just long enough to again flip the loop up, then again hop up with his feet, ready to flip the loop again. The more vertical a coconut tree is the more difficult it is to climb, but Prabath and Krishan don't have any such inconveniences on the property. Only the big yellow coconuts are knocked down to the waiting crowd below. They teach me how to tie my sarong (both Sinhalese and Muslim style). After work we roll cigarettes with leaves from a local shrub and smoke fumes that taste like singed cow dung cured in gasoline.

Knowledge is traded on both sides, though my set of skills is neither as interesting nor as important to living in Sri Lanka as how to weave a rope or knock down a coconut. There are a few things I know how to do, like plumbing and electric work, and I offer to show them what I know, but they don't use what I think of as infrastructure and so they do not care about such unimportant things; instead, I show Prabath and Krishan how to repair a boat and patch a surfboard, and I advise Prabath against going to work in the factory in Colombo, the city which for him is the epicenter of success and a guaranteed path to wealth.

If he could be rich, he could get a blonde wife. He informs me of this simple equation one afternoon while we are standing in the dusty town of Galle watching a television in a shop window, staring at the dancing figure of Britney Spears.

Today is the eighteenth of March and there's a full moon. This is Poya Day, and Prabath has told me that a full moon is good for at least three reasons:

First, the Buddha hit enlightenment on one, so a full moon is a bell that hangs bright in the sky, calling people to temple once every month. This is the sign for everyone to dress in white and to consider what the Buddha had to say. I like this. I like traveling in Buddhist countries for their sense of meditation, sincerity, and the cultural undercurrent of real tolerance. Difference runs against the grain of monotheistic cultures, but Buddhists tend to let people each do their own thing. Temple here is more of a party, fluffed up with flowers and tea, even for foreigners like me.

Second, during Poya Day, the village sparkles from house to house with small parties and post-temple dinners. The friends who gather, dressed in white, sit around the table talking about the children down the street, about work, about the chicken that was just bought, about the weather, and about health. Prabath, having cleared it with his mother and brothers, has invited me to his family's house for dinner tonight. The entire family spends only a few dollars each week, so it was impossible to refuse the offer. Generosity must be measured by intent, so the same afternoon he made the invitation I took a three-wheeled taxi, a tuk-tuk, up to the town of Galle and bought a white sarong and a nice new shirt. It was cut to my fit, perfect clean cotton, tightly sewn, neatly pressed, and cost U.S. $4. As I stepped out of the store, the smell of rotting trash, Clorox, and moldy pineapple slithered up my nose, and I wondered about the tact of going to dinner at someone's house dressed in a week's worth of pay. I hoped they would understand that I was honored by the invitation.

Third, Poya Day is good simply because Prabath has said so.

When he explained it to me, I asked him, "What is Poya Day?"

"It is good, Marx. You see!" is all he had to say.

And so we go.

Gussied up in my new white outfit for dinner, I walk up the moonlit railroad tracks toward Prabath's and Krishan's houses. The jungle is crackling with life, humming low with a rhythm of small insect songs. A huge snake buckles its way over the tracks. Monkeys argue in the trees, then make daredevil jumps, leaving large branches high in the canopy swinging. A small girl darts behind a bush, and I hear a boy yell, "Hellooo!" I wonder how many eyes are on me. There is always someone nearby. Privacy simply does not exist here.

I shout back, "Suboratria, machang!", a phrase Krishan gave me, an important one that means "Hello, friend!" The children's giggles bubble out of the leaves because I have such a thick accent and look so freakish to them—a white man dressed in white—walking down their railroad tracks on a Poya Day. Prabath's family lives immediately next to the railroad tracks, which double as a primary footpath, a pedestrian thoroughfare.

The boy practices his English and yells, "What is your name?"

"Poya!" I yell, and this gets me a scream of laughter from at least six hidden children because it means both "shut up" and "full moon." There is rustling everywhere in the bushes. Branches crack as the children run away. The air is rich and damp with oxygen from all the breathing plants, and my arms hang simply and easily from my shoulders. Overhead the man in the moon, ageless and vigilant, gives me his strange sideway grin.

Prabath is standing in the doorway. He has been waiting. He impatiently says hello; then, before I can answer, he rushes to tell me that his brother Lalith is busy cooking my dinner. "Your dinner" are the words he uses, which is my first sign of what's coming.

It's a small house and very simple, as I mentioned, with a concrete porch. Sandals are left at the door. I step inside, and my friends are only partly here because now formality has kicked in and I'm a guest of honor. I don't yet understand what this means, so I follow the cues and watch for more signs.

Asia is old, and therefore civilized, and therefore formal, and I tumble into an ancient system of practical kindness that I cannot understand.

"Sit, Marx," Prabath commands, and points at one of the two important chairs in the living room.

Again, by ingenuous good will on both of our parts, I am reduced to a dog, and I sit.

Everyone leaves. The chairs have green flower patterns on them. I think they were covered in plastic the last time I was here. I can't remember. Hands folded in my lap, I start staring at the painting on the wall. It is a print of an English clipper ship on a sea. The lower-right corner of the canvas got a little moldy, once upon a time. Before the painting got moldy, or was even painted, the English colonized Sri Lanka, and savagely, but this painting just hangs here. I hear noises in the kitchen. Something clinks, and Prabath scolds his older brother. The clipper ship is under full sail with a following sea, but you can see that the sailors are concerned. They are leaning off of the booms and over the gunwales and shouting, their hands to their mouths. The sea is a little intense for them. A fly lands on my knee, sniffing for dinner. I let it search. The table in front of me is covered in a thick sheet of clear plastic. It is yellowing and reminds me of my aunt's kitchen in Tennessee. Yes, the furniture was definitely covered with plastic when I was here before. Only the table is covered now.

I've heard it said that both the Sinhalese and the Tamils spray their furniture and wipe down their houses after a "pink" has visited. Some of them cover their noses because the white man is toxic. He has brought industry but no prosperity, money but no wealth, legislation but no order.

Prabath's mother startles me as she walks in with a cup of tea. She smiles and says hello in Sinhalese. I compliment her on her house, then think that it probably doesn't matter to her that much. She smiles, hands me the tea, and backs out of the room.

That was confusing, dizzying even, so I continue to sit.

The steam from the tea curls out of the cup and into the air and forms a face, smiling, welcoming me with a come-hither wink, smelling rich and abundant. I've been in the country formerly known as Ceylon long enough to have tea, but never in someone's house, served by his mother. This is my first taste of the real deal. Real milk tea. And I must add that I have never had tea smile at me. I push my nose into the steam and inhale an entire spice market in one breath. Cardamom and cinnamon and berries roll out with a sugary flavor that, despite being smelled, hits the sides of my tongue, making it water, and the smell also has a silver lining of something almost like a delicate soapy scent. The milk is strong, and smells condensed and sweet.

As I open my eyes, I notice that the light overhead is dancing on the surface of the magic liquid (because by now I can hardly consider this tea) like fire, and I realize that I haven't even touched my lips to the cup yet. This should suffice to say that the cost of a ticket to Sri Lanka is justified by a single cup of tea one may find in a friend's family home. This should also suffice to point out why the entire nation of England, that dour and gray land of people who eat beans and potatoes all the time, dwell on afternoon tea.

I look at the painting and want to stand up to look more closely, but don't.

The train comes roaring out of the jungle, threatening to shake the house to rubble, and I set the empty cup down. It feels like an hour has passed.

I dare not get up and ask for another cup. If they were wealthy, I wouldn't bother so much with manners and honor; but, ultimately, other than warmth and the exchanges and stories that a traveler can offer to people who have never traveled, these gestures are the only things I have to give.

I hear voices in the other room again and the snap-ping of a fire in the kitchen. I want to go look but will not be discourteous by leaving my assignment. A small *huna*, a little fellow of a gecko, clings to the wall and stares at me from where he hunts his bugs near the lightbulb. Do even the lizards stare at me?

Prabath comes running out of the kitchen looking panicked. His face is pale, his mouth open, and he's breathing as he stands in front of me for several seconds, confused and worried.

"What's the matter, Prabath?" (I now like using Prabath's name in every sentence, as he uses mine, because it makes it clear that I'm concerned and sincere and his friend. He's a good friend. We've been friends for about a month now, and we've seen each other almost every day, sometimes twice a day, usually with Krishan.)

"Marx! We have no *konko*!"

He turns and walks to the doorstep, slides into his sandals, out the door, toward the tracks. He's being a concerned host, and somehow I want to cry because it is too much for me to bear, that someone so poor would fret over a dinner for me, when I can just ask the cook at the hotel to make me a meal, and would cost less than a cup of tea in the place where I'm from. But Prabath is not to be bothered with complicated explanations; I have a service to provide him, as he is making such efforts with his family to serve me.

He stops, turns, looks at me, makes a scooping motion, and raises his eyebrows.

I stand up, jump over the threshold, and slip on my sandals, and we walk up the little trail through the night, crickets roaring, past the palms, under the bulb of the moon, up the little muddy hill, out onto the railroad track. He explains that this is all wrong and bad and no *konko* for dinner is like having no coconut, and he's upset with Lalith for not having already gotten the *konko* that afternoon. Prabath told him days ago and reminded him twice this morning, and Lalith is bad, bad, bad, and very bad.

I'm wondering to myself, No stores are open; it's 9 PM. Where could we get *konko* for dinner? I then pause and ask myself what, really, is going on. This dinner is too big of a deal. Prabath's display is almost suspicious. But, being trustworthy myself, I set these thoughts aside.

I have to jog to catch up with him, the width of each step made awkward as I thread the railroad trestles.

"Where are we going, Prabath?"

"Come, come, Marx," he says, and drops nimbly off the side of the railroad into a little ditch. Quickly he squats on his haunches and starts picking green hand-size leaves that are growing in dense clusters. They look like spinach.

I don't get this and ask, "Who owns the property? Your family?"

"The village."

"But then who's allowed to pick the *konko*?"

"The village."

"But doesn't it get eaten up?"

He stops his picking and looks at me, clearly irritated. "No, Marx." He looks at me sternly. "The village takes care." Then Prabath flips from stern to jubilant, flashing those teeth at me again through his brilliant smile, proclaims "There is enough for everyone!", and returns to the picking.

My suspicions about our foray evaporate and so I stoop down to help Prabath pick konko.

Sri Lanka is a piece of land covered with food. There is no need for laws that are based on models of scarcity. Sri Lanka is so rich in food, and so covered with it, that you could set down a healthy person, naked, on one side of the island, and that person could walk to the other side of the island, hundreds of miles across, without dying from starvation. The entire island is smeared thick, like a layer of butter on toast, with food. Starvation would never even remotely be a question. Not a day would pass without at least four different kinds of fruit to be picked from the trees. People here don't know what it feels like to come out of a five-month winter and see buds on trees. It's a perpetual growth season. Scarcity is scarce, so they don't know the need for greed since food is growing everywhere and always. They have no need of money for the same reason, and they don't know why we have shopping malls, overpasses, and models that are grinning and squirming on the covers of diet magazines.

But they want these things anyway.

Back at the house, I am sitting in the one chair at the dinner table. A beautiful curry is in front of me, along with a large plate of white rice and four small plates containing the *konko* we just picked, some fish that Prabath caught this afternoon, coconut that was pulled from the tree in the backyard (it has been ground into fine chips and roasted with chilies), and some jackfruit that came from the other tree in the back. The jackfruit has been fried. There is a large bowl of lentils mashed into a paste of *dal*. The plates are steaming, and Lalith is smiling proud. He stands to my right. To my left Prabath and his mother also stand, keeping watch. It is time for me to eat, and they will neither sit nor touch the meal until I'm finished.

It's mortifying, despite how good the food looks.

As noted earlier, the Sinhalese, like nearly half the world's population, eat with their hands — but the right hand only. The method is to hold four fingers close to each other, slightly cupped. You scoop up your food and take care to not sully above the third joints. Then, bringing your food to your mouth, you push it in with the back of your thumb. It's a simple system and it feels nice to touch the food. So, in deference to and respect for such a meal, and because I've grown fond of the process, I scoop my fingers, pile some warm rice, mix the *konko* into it, and take a mouthful. The *konko* was the most difficult to get, so I decide to start there.

Suddenly, I'm reminded of the well outside; the konko tastes like sewage. Raw sewage, the kind that rises in your nose and then drops into your chest. Images of rainbow-colored pork, rusted septic systems, and train tracks all blend together into a mental stew as I swallow.

But I smile, and I eat as much as I can, and I enjoy it all and deeply. Despite my tender stomach's yearning for customary, Western sewage-free fare, the way it was served and the love that went into it is a most delicious sauce.

Good and Bad

Prabath and Krishan, Ahangama, Sri Lanka

On the way home, after we have gone to temple and lit candles and visited the idols and placed flowers and paid all the respects and heard all the stories that have been told for thousands of years, our footsteps crunch the rocks down between the railroad ties. The canopy is a blindfold to that great Buddhist eye of the full moon. It is dark as only the jungle can be. But in the clear the railroad tracks are lit by the moon, so Krishan, Prabath, and I attend to weighty matters such as Enlightenment and Good and Bad. Prabath says that it is easy to tell good from bad. A man walks by us, and I ask Prabath, "Good man or Bad man?" Prabath smiles, then answers. He knows everyone in the village, of course, so he knows the answer. Despite Buddha's teachings.

A man on a bicycle passes us, and Prabath leans

over to me and says, "That is a Bad man."

"Why?" I ask.

"Because he drinks," Prabath hisses between his teeth, quite uncharacteristically.

Another man walks by, this one with sticks on his back, a sarong around his waist, and no shirt. He passes us, and we nod hello.

"Is that a Good man or a Bad man, Prabath?"

"That is a Good man."

"Why?"

"Because he is working."

"But how do you know he is Good, Prabath?"

"Buddha says."

So I ask Prabath whether Buddha was a Good man or a Bad man.

Naturally, Prabath says, "Good man."

"Why?"

"I don't know." Prabath laughs a little. "I don't know, Marx."

Krishan waits until Prabath is picking up a rock to throw, then leans and whispers, "Because he discovered."

On another evening, however, again walking home from temple (when we are all three primed for these sorts of heady discussions about morality, afterlife, and decision), I decide to throw a drifter, but easy, so I can be certain that Prabath understands.

Slowly, I ask Prabath, "What do . . . ? "

And Prabath immediately and implicitly agrees with my slow approach and replies, "'What do . . . ?'"

"What do you think . . . ?"

"'What do you think . . . ?'"

I wait.

Prabath says, "Marx wants to know what Prabath thinks . . . "

I continue, "What do you think about death?"

We walk in silence for some ten seconds.

Prabath says, "Marx asks, 'What does Prabath think about death?'"

"Yes, that's right."

We keep walking and chew on this.

Prabath says, "Death is Bad, Marx. Death is not Good."

"Yes, that is all." Prabath concludes, "Not Good. Bad."

It starts to sprinkle rain, and the stones on the path become translucent in a way that I have seen only in the tropics.

"Krishan?" I peer back over my shoulder and ask, "What do you think about death?"

Prabath interrupts him. "Krishan think same thing. The village people all think same thing."

I think I hear Krishan blow some air out through his nose in a soft snort.

This is not a linguistic barrier. When I've learned new languages, I sound like an idiot, sure, but I also know well enough to separate linguistic ability from experience and experience from intelligence. Prabath isn't stupid, and while his English isn't great, his exposure to the outside world has been limited living with his family in the jungle. The railroad tracks are, for him, the center of the world. If I believed in the myth of the noble savage, I might mantle this unfortunate burden on Prabath, but things aren't that simple, and people aren't that good. Prabath, though, is kind enough to be an exception to the rules.

Prabath stops. Through the grimy window of a local restaurant a stray television throws shifting blue light on the tamped-down mud under our sandals. It is warm and humid, and the three of us stand there and breathe quietly. A music video is playing. Someone who looks like Britney Spears or Christina Aguilera is oozing blonde goo all over the camera, slapping her hips, and wriggling like a fish on a hook. Horses are galloping around. A wind fan has been pointed at the girl's hair.

Prabath looks at me and says, "I want to marry an American girl. Do you know an American girl I can marry?"

Dancing Devils

Devil dance, Ahangama, Sri Lanka

A guy named Robert Knox was imprisoned on this island for twenty years back in the 1600s. From what I understand, he was just up the road, here on the southern side of the island. One of the Sinhalese kings kept him as a pet. Knox eventually escaped with a Dutch trading vessel and got back to London. Safe at home again in Mother England, he wrote a book about his life on the island, titled *An Historical Relation of the Island Ceylon*. It's a fine read, at least in part because Daniel Defoe's *Robinson Crusoe* was to some extent based on the story. I think Knox wrote this book as a kind of vengeance against the king of Ceylon and not at all for his reason listed in the book ("for my family"). I think he decided it would be a great way to help motivate the British to invade the place. Looking at the sequence of events, that book might have done just that.

> *THIS Booke was wrote by mee Robert Knox (the sonn of Robert Knox who died one the Iland of Zelone) when I was aboute 39 years of Age. I was taken prisoner one Zelone, 4th Aprill, 1660. I was borne one Tower hill in London, 8th Feb: 1641. My Age when taken was 19 years: 1 month & 27 dayes. Continewed prisoner thare 19 years 6 month 14 dayes. So that I was a prisoner thare 4 month & 17 dayes longer then I had lived in the world before, & one the 18 October 1679 God set mee free from the Captivity, being then with the Hollanders at Arepa fort to whome be all Glory & prayse. Robert Knox, 1696 in London.*

It's a sharp weave of colonial perspective. Since I'm cut from the same cloth, I thought the book might be a convenient and historical counterpoint to Prabath's black-and-white view of the world. I was reading about how Knox noticed three dances, one of which was a "devil dance." It was a means by which locals did everything from cure a cold to fix trade rates with foreign nationals.

One night, while I'm calmly reading Knox's narrative in my hotel room, Krishan, Prabath, and Gabriel knock on the door. They tell me that I need to get my camera and to hurry because this won't last long, and then they run away. I toss my book on the bed (thinking, What the hell is going on? It's almost ten in the evening, and usually the entire village is dead asleep by now!), grab my camera, poke my feet into my sandals, slam the door, and step out under the chirping night sky. The half moon is hanging overhead, and all the palm trees and the dirt road are lit gray and blue. It seems like a night to worship, die, or kill.

I have to jog to catch up with them. They say that it's just up ahead. I have no idea where we're going, but they're excited enough that I think it'll be good. And I hear drumming, fast. Someone screams.

As we cross the railroad tracks, one house stands out. The lights are on. No, not lights; I see the unmistakable shimmering red light of a large, open flame. It's not candles; it's torches, and it's moving fast inside the small house. Something inside is slowly exploding. It seems the house is on fire, and these three came to get me to watch a little human suffering tonight. But no, because there are people inside, and they are beating a drum, and through the window we can see that the fire is ceremonial.

Krishan's eyes are huge as he says, over the drumming, "The old lady died under the bridge. Two years. Daughter, and daughter's daughter, and daughter's daughter's daughter." He laughs at his English. "Now they all dream her! All night! Old dead woman needs to go away now!", and he starts laughing at his own joke, and I laugh back, giddy and confused but wanting to be friendly and wanting to appear as if I understand what the hell is going on.

A man dressed in a loincloth is dancing, and the beating of the drum is only barely muffled by the walls. The tiny living room is packed with people, maybe fifteen in all, and everyone is watching the man in the middle dancing with his two torches, whining his nasal ululation of divinity and death.

"Come, Marx!" Prabath says, and we go to the front door.

I'm not interested in walking in on someone's church service, so I ask to confirm that it will be okay. Prabath rolls his eyes at me and pulls hard on my wrist. He's excited to show me this, and he wants it seen, this fiery beauty that's inside the house. I'm pressed in with a crowd of boys, shoving me toward the living room. As we pass into the house, I can barely kick off my muddy sandals; it's hard to be polite in such a press.

We step into a flame-lit carnival of loud drumming and the man whining a song in something close to Sinhalese. The room is full of incense and palm fronds. There is a chicken running around. Seashells and dead white butterflies are scattered with the candles everywhere. Are they going to burn the entire house? There is a cow head with the eyes staring straight ahead, dry, and lots of bamboo or palm or something that's carefully woven into decorative spirals and swirls, and that part is on fire and all sliced up into tiny delicate braids around the ceremony, which is set up in front of these women — the one on the left, who is old; another in her early thirties; and the girl, her daughter, I guess, about three years old. They sit peacefully in front of the dancing and singing and drumming, their placid faces lit by the fire that is about to burn their house down.

Unsettled ghost dust has been floating over their beds, so they've hired a high-octane neighbor who knows how to deal with these duties to come over for some dancing, drinking, and dinner — someone who can send Great-Grandma to the other side.

Once I get used to the heat, I realize that this is

neither solemn nor scary; it's a party. I'm pushed to the front of the room, someone walks toward me waving a white plastic chair overhead, and I'm given the best seat in the house, while everyone else is sitting on the floor. Why the hell are they offering me a seat of honor? Because I came with Prabath? But before I can sit, another person hands me a chocolate cookie, and with the cookie a cup of that incredible tea also appears. Four people have handed these things to me, in concert, as it were. My hands are now full, and the drum is going faster than a pack of monkeys on methamphetamines, and I'm trying not to step on the chicken or get my head burned by the guy with the torch while they hand me another cookie.

Prabath still has hold of my wrist, and he pushes me to sit down near the front, next to the younger woman and her daughter. The woman looks at me and smiles. Feeling self-conscious and wanting to evaporate, I smile back. The little girl smiles. I smile. The man doing the dance screams, and we all look at him. Prabath releases my wrist, and I spill some of the tea on my foot.

Suddenly Lalith appears next to my head, and he tells me what the man dancing has to say: "Woman, woman, go home, you now need to go home, we love you, we love you, go, go, go, go, go."

Life and death must be balanced, and separated.

The tools that are used to placate (or vacate) ghosts are simple, and they can be found in a grocery store near you. The drummer and singer are most important (though these you cannot buy, as they are the neighbors from up the street, and they come from a caste that is specially designated to perform this magic ritual). The rooster has been through this a hundred times, and he keeps a beady eye on everyone but is calm as a back-road puddle. The cow's head, however (with its staring eyes and that dried tongue sticking out, just the tip, from the front of its mouth), isn't faring as well. The singer slaps it and puts his hand on the cow's forehead and says something to it. The rooster has it easy by comparison; he just walks around like a tough guy.

The people laugh, and there is no pomp here, only downright solid command. Nobody doubts this ceremony, which is the sole reason why it will work and part of why it is fun. Faith allows more than most people believe, and the more people believe, the more it allows. The Sinhalese believe humans are really that powerful, and so they are.

The gleaming white butterflies and flowers were caught and picked today. They're arranged next to a set of gold teeth that are on the table, whose origins are a complete mystery to Lalith as well. Perhaps they were the grandmother's? Everything is new, macabre, and peeled fresh from the belly of heaven. There is a can of kerosene, seven or eight small bags of spices (cumin and cinnamon on the list, naturally, since this is old school), reeds, and more flowers. Flowers, flowers everywhere. Someone spent the day plundering the backyard. It's a beautiful arrangement, especially with the waxen, staring eyes of the cow head.

The singer is a little king, a priest and a performer. He's a neighbor and a good friend. His faith is his reason. And it's easy to see why it works. If this guy came running at me with a can of gas in one hand and a big red rooster in the other, singing songs, beating a drum, and setting a fire in my living room, well, I'd leave this plane of existence too.

Of course it works. All cultures have strong reasons to keep death out of this world, since death, like water, is a part of everything. Maybe it's a bit like keeping the house clean: Keep the undead from loitering on the lawn. Phantoms, like animals, shouldn't be in the kitchen while we're cooking. It's just uncouth.

I look at Prabath, wondering if he will ever tell me why death is Bad. I see that his eye is trained on me, and he immediately smiles. I realize that his pleasure must lie in seeing his world through other eyes. I can't control any of this anyway, so I sit back, chew my cookie, and watch the show. But why, I wonder again as I look around the room, am I the only one sitting in a chair?

Another blast of flame warms the side of my face, and I watch the ceiling to see if it will catch fire. Somehow it doesn't. Lalith leans down and starts to talk in my ear. Between a few minutes' orientation and Lalith's staccato English, I'm getting a handle on what's going on, and it's making some sense. Dancer and Drummer know the magic combination, and they've spent the whole day preparing for this four-hour ceremony. It's a big deal, and they've been paid by the eldest of the women to do it. The woman and her daughter are the patients; Dancer and Drummer are the doctors. The women needed the help, so this is being done to them, and at them, and not with them, not at all. They are along for the ride, as are the rest of us. Drummer and Dancer are there to administer, and the Dancer is sweating even though he's shirtless and wearing only a white sarong. There is flame everywhere, and it smells like burned oats and chocolate and safety.

"Good, Marx?" Prabath has appeared next to my shoulder and has leaned down and asked simply. I look up at him and smile and nod. As the drumming and the singing and the burning go on, I can't help but wonder why I'm sitting in the middle of the room. But I have my camera, and I gently take some pictures, as if I were a burglar in a cathedral, collecting artifacts from the cloister. But then, this isn't a Western church, so why I'm behaving like this confuses me. I don't have any other ideas about what to do. Be still, smile, express appreciation, don't flaunt the massive wealth I possess, and don't distract whomever I might distract—the woman, the Dancer, the ghost—from doing this important work that needs to be done. This is witch-doctor hospitality.

Two hours pass, and it's break time; everyone is exhausted. I can't tell if this is just a momentary lapse or if things are over. But then another cow head is brought out, and fresh reeds and a second can of kerosene, and I have the sense that we're only getting warmed up. In the middle of the room, on the chair, with my fucking camera, I feel about as inconspicuous as a bullet hole in a forehead. So I tell Lalith that I'll be leaving and thanks, Prabath, thanks, Krishan.

But suddenly I'm being practically carried into the living room and told to sit in one of the two seats that, just like in Prabath's house, face the sofa with the painting above it: the seat of honor again. (What?) So I reluctantly sit on it, and I'm handed more tea, and an overflowing plate of cookies appears this time and some dates, or something wrapped in little sweet candy paper, and it's all just too much since I don't want to dent their dance by sitting in to see. This has to be the dead great-grandma ghost's fault, that I would be the exotic element in the middle of an exorcism. Then I see my own hand in front of my face, and I'm shocked at how white it is and how long my fingers are under strange translucent skin (it's been some number of weeks since I've looked in a mirror), and something makes some vague sense, as if I've just discovered that I'm a guest ghost at the village exorcism. I'm out of place, and welcome to it.

The two women come carrying the baby girl, and behind them is the Dancer. They all sit down to talk with me. They ask if I've seen ghosts before, and I have to be honest and tell them that yes, I've seen them and indeed I'm surrounded by them every day, and for the first time in my life people believe me. The Dancer laughs, and Prabath laughs, and everything unbelievable in the world seems as reasonable as the rooster standing near my chair, staring up at me with his black and comprehending marble eye.

It's noon. I'm restless.

An ocean breeze dances through my room. I'm sitting at my desk with my shirt off, pen in hand. Books and old newspapers and little scraps of paper, each held down by a rock paperweight I collected from the beach, blanket the bed and carpet the floor. Each document indicates someone who represents a political party, or a reporter who interviewed a terrorist, or someone who knows a friend of someone who worked with the LTTE or the PLOTE (People's Liberation Organisation of Tamil Eelam), or someone who works for the military, or someone who was shot, or someone whose uncl e was killed in the riots. These articles, books, and pieces of information are like suture points after the stitches have been taken out. They are a great collection of scars on the island's body, and I'm connecting the dots, aiming to discover what caused such a wound in the first place.

I've been here in Goviyapana Junction for over a month and, though I've enjoyed the coconuts on the white sand beaches and the trips to temple, it's almost time to go north, to see what is happening with the Tamil Hindus and the Sinhalese Buddhists and this ancient quarrel they've decided to keep lit.

I've spent the morning on the phone, running from the hotel office to my room and back, asking for help dialing phone numbers. I've gotten hold of the most visible people as well as the least known. Of course my first thought was to interview Vellupillai Prabhakaran, the head honcho of the Tamil Tigers. Prabhakaran is a strange figure, a fan of Clint Eastwood movies who has cited Hitler, Napoleon, and Che Guevara as his inspirations. To many of the impoverished Tamils in the northeast, Prabhakaran's a savior, and he has the cult following to prove it. Prabhakaran built his following by hand training each of his recruiters and sending them to local high schools. Recruiters promise $35 per month plus food rations to the families of recruits. "You will have to die one day," recruiters are instructed to say. "If you die fighting, you get a hero's death. But if you die naturally, you die a coward." Once the recruiter has the audience's attention, he flips on a videocassette of a Rambo movie and hands out juice.

But Prabhakaran has only given a few interviews in his lifetime and, despite my efforts, I've been told by Anton Balasingham, the LTTE's media-relations head, that an interview will not be an option. Balasingham tells me via e-mail that I'm welcome to come up to the northern city of Jaffna, and perhaps we can try when I arrive. A meeting doesn't sound likely.

I've also tried to reach Colonel Karuna, one of Prabhakaran's top brass. No luck there, either. He seems to be hiding in the jungles, terrified of suicide bombers appearing as reporters. A terrified terrorist, but someone who has had a significant impact on the war.

Facing these dead ends and no-shows, I take the search up a level, to the people who founded the LTTE, who then left and started other organizations. Perhaps it will be the people who founded the movement who will offer the most insight into what, really, motivates a terrorist. So eventually, with the help of journalists who have interviewed him previously, I am able to contact Dharmalingam Siddharthan, one of the founders of both the LTTE and the PLOTE, and line up a time to talk. Likewise, I am able, with the help of new associates I've met over the past month, to connect with Shankar Rajee, the bomber of Colombo, another founder of the Tamil militant movement. Other interviews are lined up, the last and most notable being with Douglas Devananda, a founder of multiple militant groups and someone who has seen both sides of suicide attacks.

Prabath walks quickly ahead of me and we turn off the railroad tracks and start down a narrow path under some coconut trees.

When I told Prabath that I would be leaving in a few days, going north, he insisted that I meet his cousin, Chamindra. Chamindra works on a navy warship that patrols the waters of northern Sri Lanka. This is not an easy job. He is married and lives with his wife and his sister. His sister's husband died, I think, or left, so now Chamindra takes care of her and her son, Bandula, who treats Chamindra like a father. Prabath makes it clear that Chamindra is a very, very Good man. Chamindra has managed to earn enough money to buy a house down the tracks from Prabath's place. He is a tough guy (you have to be if you work for the Sri Lankan armed forces), and he respects Prabath because Prabath has such a kind heart, and Prabath respects Chamindra because Chamindra is so damn tough.

Chamindra is away most of the time, launching missiles at PT boats, guarding the borders, watching the watery horizon, doing his training exercises, and cursing the militants until he gets his next relatively plump paycheck. Someone who has been stationed for four years in an armada on the northern shores near Jaffna has it pretty hard at times, but it pays if you can live to the next paycheck.

Chamindra knows the village like the sun that watches from above. Most of the village comes to him for advice, whether it's about money, love, work, or what to do with a goat that eats everything in the yard. As soon as I walk up, we shake hands, and he shows me an important piece of paper. It's brown and has Sinhalese script written in columns. I can't understand a single letter.

"These are the auspicious hours." Chamindra points to some Arabic numbers on the page, characters I recognize. They're times of day. New Year's is coming, and everyone has specific duties, and there are things to be done at certain times. He points to the left-hand column and says, "This is what the village people do in the morning. And here is what they will do later, near afternoon. Then it is time to clean the kitchen. And here everyone must go outside at four minutes after two o'clock and then come back in and light their stoves!"

His mouth opens and his eyes widen as if he's a tall baby, fresh from the battlefield, this one, and he pokes me in the chest with his index finger, his palm up, his hand open, and he tells me that I understand. He was almost asking. Surely, his reasoning goes, I would understand, because auspicious hours are part of the nature of the world, and there are simple laws, like gravity or love, that are evident to everyone. What I see in Chamindra's brown eyes, floating behind his retinas like a great buoy of certitude in a sea of doubt, and what he implies as he talks, is the same particular admixture of curiosity, ignorance, and narrow-mindedness that is Prabath's. It is born of living on an island, isolated from the rest of the world, in the jungle even, where things are old and Good or Bad.

Whatever the case, Chamindra, despite being broad shouldered, thick necked, and wide jawed, despite keeping his collection of automatic weapons, missile tips, mine detonators, and grenades on display in a glass case in his home, and despite supporting himself and his entire family by being a soldier, despite all of these displays of power and pride, asks me to take a message with me when I go north. He wants me to deliver a message to the Tamils.

I'm not really comfortable being a messenger who shuttles missives across battle lines, and I tell him as much, but he asks if he can just write it down, and if I take it, fine, but if not, that's okay too.

So Chamindra finishes writing his note, hands it to me, and smiles. I can't read Sinhalese. I put it in my pocket and assure him I will keep the note with me. But as I say this I wonder, Whom can I hand it to? What will I say? Will a letter passed from one side of the war to the other even matter? Can it? This is not a war that is being fought between individuals. It is a war that is being fought between cultures, and both of them are innocent.

New Year's Day comes as I am getting ready to leave. It's double the reason to exchange gifts (at, as Chamindra indicated, the auspicious hour), so I go to the mall and buy new bats and balls for Prabath and Krishan's cricket team, and they give me a necklace of black coral. Black coral is rarer each year, plucked almost to extinction, and I ask them not to give it to me, but they insist. It doesn't matter in the end, since it will end up on the bottom of the ocean anyway. (I will eventually lose it while swimming, which is probably quite appropriate.)

I leave on a rusted and noisy train full of big-eyed, dark, and skeletal people, all of us excited about going to the big city, all of us hanging out the doors, all of us hot and agitated by the action and crashing of the wheels and the rattling of the cars, and all of us hanging onto one another to make sure that no one falls out. As the train rolls by Prabath's house I wave, but I don't see him or

Krishan outside. The last I heard, Prabath was headed to work in a chocolate factory just outside of Colombo. Perhaps, there, he will find his blonde American woman.

Heroin and Saris

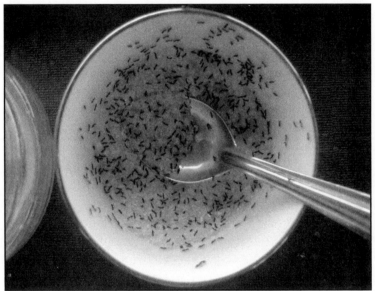

Sugar bowl ant party, Ahangama, Sri Lanka

Terrorists have great job opportunities. If you're an outlaw, then a government prohibition equals a revenue stream, and if you're a terrorist, then you can make some fast bucks by trafficking guns and drugs. The fact that drugs can fund terrorism hasn't been overlooked by American administrations during the Sri Lankan civil war. Though it was Nixon who first used the term "war on drugs," it was Reagan who popularized it, and it was Bush Jr. who fused it with the "war on terror" when he proclaimed, on October 14, 2002, "If you quit drugs, you join the fight against terror."

It has certainly worked for the FBI. In Washington, in 2002, the criminal investigative agency that traditionally busied itself with gangsters and druggies shifted gears to concentrate on nabbing international terrorists and cybercriminals. Since 2002 the FBI's website has listed counterterrorism as its top priority.

But the War on Terror doesn't seem to be going too well for the FBI. The bureau currently has something close to ten thousand people assigned to combating terrorism, or about 40 percent of its agents.[1] According to *The New York Times*, the FBI's Los Angeles offices have had to deal with a number of absurd alarms, such as shady characters taking photos of oil refineries (who turn out to be college students) or a Marriott Hotel under a bomb threat (after the FBI searched the hotel, the man who made the threat called again to ask whether the Marriot had dropped its rates lately, due to bomb threats). From 2004 to 2009, according to the *Times*, the FBI's Counterterrorism 6 (CT-6) squad has fielded over fifty-five hundred counter terrorism leads but not one has yet foiled a terrorist plot.[2]

In September of 2009, attempting to verify this surprising claim, I had several rather long e-mail and phone conversations with the FBI's Los Angeles and Washington offices. More than five thousand dossiers and zero arrests? It was true, the FBI informed me—though that "zero arrests" number only applied to that particular squad. The number of terrorist plots that have been foiled, in total, by the entire FBI, is a classified number that it would not release—but it's only announced about

---

1. The exact number is classified, but this is a rough estimate provided by an agent based in the Los Angeles FBI office from interviews I conducted with them during fall, 2009 and via confirmation of other journalists of similar study.
2. Schmitt, Eric, "F.B.I. Agents' Role Is Transformed by Terror Fight." *The New York Times*, August 18, 2009, www.nytimes.com/2009/08/19/us/19terror.html

two dozen since 2001.[3]

Despite these losses, the FBI is undeterred. In fact, it's expanding its counterterrorism efforts. FBI funding has steadily grown over the past nine years. The budget was $3.2 billion in 2001 and will be over $8.5 billion in 2010.[4] This expansion is part of the "global justice" initiative, which will allow the FBI to take its fight against terrorism overseas.

Since 2001 the FBI has spent more than fifty billion dollars funding its top priority of counterterrorism. This means that, since 2001, American taxpayers have shelled out an average of well over an average of just over two billion dollars for each terrorist plot the FBI has uncovered.

The War on Terror is a losing battle. Even calling it a war helps terrorist recruiters enlist young men who want to be seen as warriors.[5] The term seems to be losing credibility. In March of 2009 the United States Defense Department officially changed the name from "Global War on Terror" to "Overseas Contingency Operation," or OCO for short.[6]

The consanguine War on Drugs also seems to be a losing battle, and one that has had some serious side effects. According to a report by the Pew Center almost one percent of the American population was in the

---

3 This number is based on press releases from the FBI's web site (www.fbi. gov) as well as reports from other media outlets, such as *The Christian Science Monitor's* September 26, 2009, article, "Terrorist Plots Uncovered in the US Since 9/11" (http://www.csmonitor.com/2009/0926/p02s08-usgn.html).
4. Statement before the U.S. Senate Committee on Appropriations; Subcommittee on Commerce, Justice, Science, and Related Agencies, June 4, 2009.
5. Jones, Seth G. and Libicki, Martin C., "Stop the 'War' on Terror." *The Christian Science Monitor*, August 6, 2008 (http://www.csmonitor.com/2008/0806/p09s02-coop.html).
6. Wilson, Scott and Kamen, Al, "'Global War on Terror' Is Given New Name." *The Washington Post*, March 25, 2009, http://www.washingtonpost.com/wp-dyn/content/article/2009/03/24/AR2009032402818.html.

big house at the start of 2008. Most had been incarcerated for drug-related offenses.[7] According to the United States Department of Justice, all major forms of crime—including property, violence, and firearm-related—have declined in the last five years, save one: drug offenses.[8] The War on Drugs has produced an increasing number of incarcerations each year since 1971, when Nixon first announced the opening salvos. The casualties of that War on Drugs now account for about 55 percent of the prison population, or about one of every two hundred Americans.[9]

Wars on terrorism and drugs are fought in the troughs between the high grounds of moral vagaries. In a globalized world, wars against such profitable activities as drug sales or militant uprisings are impossible to win because the warfare lacks defined terms and moral clarity. In Los Angeles, a dangerous militant carrying dangerous drugs might mean a gangster with a reefer, or, if you happen to be in Kuwait, it might mean a Christian with some cognac. There is no pan-cultural consensus about what qualifies as a dangerous drug or weapon; these things are nearly impossible to define in any context other than that of a small group of people living in small region under narrowly defined codes of conduct. In most Christian lands, the drugs of choice are coffee and alcohol; cigarettes are on the way out, and heroin is a big no-no. In some of the many Muslim countries, the drugs of choice are cigarettes and coffee; heroin is on the way out, and alcohol is a big no-no. From Wichita, Kansas, to Brydah,

---

7. "One in 100: Behind Bars in America 2008," http://stage.pewcenteronthestates.org/uploadedFiles/One%20in%20100.pdf.
8. U.S. Department of Justice, Bureau of Justice Statistics, "Key Crime & Justice Facts at a Glance," www.ojp.usdoj.gov/bjs/glance.htm.
9. Richardson, John H., "A Radical Solution to End the Drug War." *Esquire*, September 1, 2009, www.esquire.com/the-side/richardson-report/drug-war-facts-090109.

Saudi Arabia, any drug (or religion) other than the local favorites is anathema. The majority religion determines what's right. For that matter, and as a small digression, we might even say that religion is more dangerous than either drugs or terrorism. The war in Sri Lanka can be traced back, in part, to a clash between the religious ideologies of Buddhists and Hindus. This in turn gave birth to the terrorists, who, we have heard, fund their activities through drug sales. But until an inventive politician finds a way to fund a War on Religion, our other wars will continue to extend themselves out onto the thin and melting ether of global ethics.

In any case, as the world outside continues to grow more global, the sunny palm-tree dappled beaches of southern Sri Lanka continue to buzz with imports, exports, and tourists who have left their compunctions about drugs in their own land far away. High-rise hotels are packed with tourists. It's vacation time. This is where the sausage-skinned sand squatters and longhair surf riders wander the beaches looking to score safe substances. Each day, illegal drugs are bought and stolen, some of them driven down from Colombo, some brought by boat, all grown, cooked, bought, smoked, and part of an assumed— and not terribly lucrative—income for thousands of Sri Lankan families.

On my journey up to Colombo, about halfway up the coast near Beruwala, I decide that the landscape is going by too fast and hop off the train to look around for a few hours. I want to slow it down a bit. Plus, I'm interested in learning more about the link between terrorism and drugs, and whether there is even a link. I decide to find someone who can give me some firsthand knowledge on the dodgy subject of whether there are or whether there are not drug-funded terrorists. I figure I'll need to find a

Tamil drug lord, some great cushion-squatting maharaja with a long black mustache and a longer, blacker opium pipe. I'm expecting a gangster of local flavor.

My method of contacting people through other people they may know seems to be working pretty well so far, but drug dealers, as the FBI will tell you, are much easier to find than terrorists, so I wait for a cab (one of the little three-wheel open-door tuk-tuk kind) that has a young driver, pull him over, and hop in. He looks Sinhalese, and we're in the south, so I deliver the Sinhalese greeting of "Suboratria, machang," and he laughs and looks over his shoulder, then asks where I'm going as we pull away from the curb.

I say I don't know.

He looks over his shoulder again, but he stops accelerating and smiling.

I ask him, "Where can I buy some drugs?", and I realize my voice doesn't sound as casual or as low as I'd intended. The word "drugs" came out kind of high-pitched. "That's where I'm going."

"What kind?" he asks.

"Heroin!" jumps out of my mouth. It seems the heart of the beast, the most feared of the class-A drugs, at least by Westerners. The most profitable, the most used, especially in a place where people are looking for an escape from their war-zone homes. Cocaine would be better in Mexico, but here, in Asia, opiates are the way.

The driver nods once and says, "Winston."

He says it like a name, but it might be a distance. Whichever it is, I'm feeling my neck tightening with paranoia and fear. It's all so absurdly easy that I am now worried that Winston will be a cop, or that this cabbie's a cop, or he's at least going to get some kind of reward for bringing me to the cops. Or maybe the cops are watching. Or maybe that's far-fetched. Maybe I'm just being a scaredy American. After all, Sri Lanka, like most of Southeast Asia, is happy to offer what is asked.

My driver pulls over next to a parking lot. Without saying much he points, from a distance, to a small man sitting on the beach by himself. This is what a cop does, I tell myself, but I don't really know. Still freaked out about this whole arrangement, and having no interest in spending time in a Sri Lankan prison, I look at the driver, but he reassures me and smiles one of those marvelously warm Sinhalese grins, and so I walk down to the man and introduce myself. I won't get arrested for saying hi. This skinny old man stands up and shakes my hand, says, "Hello, yes, it is very nice to meet you," in punctilious and perfect English, and so I point to the driver, who waves back, and the man waves back, and off the driver goes.

Though the man has a five-word Indonesian name, he does, in fact, go by Winston. Like his moniker, he's surprisingly British, Western, and a bit of a geek. He speaks perfect English and is about sixty years old. After almost three decades of failed practice as an alternative healer/yogi, he tells me, he started to apply his medicinal knowledge to people who were searching for rather alternative, if illegal, forms of medication. His skin is wrinkled from sun and strange travels. Spry, quick to laugh, and living more poorly than Prabath, his hands shake and his eyes are a little watery and gravy colored. He still practices yoga daily, sometimes on opiates. I'm sure that's relaxing.

He was born in Sri Lanka, received his undergraduate education in England, and picked up a PhD in the medical sciences at a prestigious school in Colombo. Thirty years later he was broke. Not having a family or friends to help him out, he took up selling brown, black, gray, and white—dope.

We walk slowly back to his house. I still haven't told him what I'm looking to buy. We stroll under the coconut trees and up a little hill, through a tiny jungle path, and to the teeniest shack with corrugated roofing. I guess this is how Sri Lankan junkies live. It sort of fits the part.

Winston is jittery. He was in Colombo the night before, driving all night to get there and back, to buy several grams of China white. Now he's looking pale gray, with tiny beads of sweat growing out of his forehead. He's as jumpy as a spider on caffeine but manages, with a twitchy skull and shaky bones, to pull out a sheet of old tinfoil stained brown and yellow with liquefied opiate droolings. His fingers become long and graceful now, like a magic-user. From his pocket he takes a packet and removes a black shiny gob of dope about as big as a housefly. He sticks it on the sheet of tinfoil, pops a little straw in his mouth, and heats the underside of the tinfoil with a lighter. A coil of delicate blue smoke rises from the foil. Winston slurps it out of the air with his straw, then reloads the tinfoil and hands it to me. We smoke off the same piece of tinfoil with the same straw, as if we were sharing an offering plate to Shiva. It tastes acrid and has a mustard flavor to it, and in about ten seconds I feel my limbs loosen. We ease back into the sofa. We talk. The drug is clear, a little milder than being drunk, and not as sloppy. Old, old drugs are the opiates. The popular favorite in Asia.

Winston steps outside and comes back with a coconut, which he hacks in half with a machete that I hadn't noticed. He's small but fierce. After some coconut juice we agree, for our peace of mind and the guarantee of our ongoing liberty, to spend our time talking in a local café that is in plain, public sight on a plain, public beach. Winston likes to live simply; he shirks what responsibility he can, and he has one or two things he really, sincerely still enjoys. Looking at his large eye sockets and his chiseled face, skinny from clamped bowels and a loose appetite, I think I know what it is, and I think that he also has a hard time just staying alive. He lights a cigarette with yellow fingers. His skeleton glows through his skin. His smile is sincere. He feels good, and we step outside, talking as we stroll. We decide to head to the local café, and I ask if I can pull out my recorder. He asks what the recorder is for. I tell him I'm working on a book. He looks at me and I realize that I've scared him. I apologize and offer to buy him a juice.

It turns out that Winston was in Colombo during the big riots in the '80s, the same time that the Tamil Tigers got off to a serious start with their terrorist tactics. In fact, the riots and the terrorism were directly linked. He tells me that during 1983 about a dozen Sri Lankan army soldiers were killed in an LTTE ambush. The LTTE did it so as to incite riots in Colombo, which worked, and the rioting eventually grew to such a scale that several hundred Tamils were killed, ultimately starting what the Tamil Tigers termed the "First Eelam War." Winston watched Sinhalese rioters bind the wrists of a Tamil man. He saw them pour gallons of gasoline into the street, light the gas on fire, and toss the man into the flames on the asphalt. It's been decades since he's seen this, and it obviously still shakes him up, despite being high. He looks over his shoulder again, nervous we're being watched.

"The Sinhalese were afraid of the Tamils. They were afraid that there were . . . but I saw twenty or twenty-one people with sticks beating a Tamil man. They were smashing houses. But I was just helpless. I didn't know what to do. I couldn't change any of this, so I went to the police to ask if they wanted eyewitnesses for any of the crimes that were happening. But nobody came forward.

They just sent me home. The next day the police finally came, but everyone was gone, of course. The Sinhalese had gone home, and the Tamils had all gone to their *kovils*[10] for shelter. It wasn't fair. It just wasn't right."

I ask him if he knows of the Tamil Tigers bringing down drugs from southern India into northern Sri Lanka for distribution to the rest of the island. He tells me that he's familiar with a weekly ferry service.

"I think it's still in operation. It runs from Tamil Nadu to Jaffna. They bring in heroin, opium, and saris mostly, I think."

I'm newly confused. What's the connection between saris and opiates?

"These are just the things that people need," he replies matter-of-factly. "But the LTTE is to blame, not the Tamils themselves."

"You mean the militants, not the ethnic group?"

"Yes. Around the mid-'80s."

It might be a habit, but he leans in closer, drops his voice to a whisper, and looks over his shoulder. "That was when I got started."

The Dutch and British colonialists both regulated the use of opium and taxed it as a means of making money. By the 1960s, these drugs were illegal, but the increase in violence between Tamils and Sinhalese was accompanied by an increase in demand. Sri Lankan nationals started smuggling drugs in the 1980s, mostly from India, and by 2006 the Sri Lankan government announced that it had made almost fifty thousand drug-related arrests in those two decades. A quarter of them were for heroin, the rest were for pot. But law enforcement was flexible. Opium was okay with the federales since opium and hashish are both often used as part of the indigenous

---

10. Hindu temples.

ayurvedic medical practices, easily found in government hospitals. These drugs were officially illegal but culturally approved.

By the time of the riots of the 1980s, heroin had quickly become popular and the drug had moved from urban Colombo out into the farms and fields of the Sri Lankan countryside. Perhaps people needed a little relaxant during such times, and the LTTE was happy to help out. In the years between 2005 and 2008, Sri Lankan Tamils working for the LTTE were arrested, tried, and found guilty of transporting heroin. But they were very anxious to get back to work, because they considered themselves key support personnel for generating revenue for the LTTE. They were selling drugs for politics, not cash. *The Times of India* found that drugs were being shipped from Rajasthan and the Punjab border and sent down via lorry to Mumbai, where the LTTE would pick them up and bring them to coastal towns in southern India.[11] From there, the drugs would be shipped via boats and small pangas down to the northern coast of Sri Lanka under the watchful eyes of the LTTE. Meanwhile, everyone from the CIA to the DEA seemed to be in agreement that a large sum of money was being made by the Tigers, primarily because the LTTE did not sell the drugs on the street but rather acted as a distributor, selling in quantity, sometimes to other militant organizations as far away as Australia.

"What happened in Colombo? How did you end up here?" I ask, raising my tone of voice and begging him with body language to quit looking so damn suspect. I'm getting worried that the cops will come over to us just because Winston is hunched over, not even because of

---

11. "LTTE Fall Will Alter Drug Trade in India." *The Times of India*, May 30, 2009, http://timesofindia.indiatimes.com/news/city/mumbai/LTTE-fall-will-alter-drug-trade-in-India/articleshow/4595554.cms.

anything he or I might have done. For him, sneaky is natural.

"Well, Colombo was in ruins," he tells me. "People mistook us Malays for Tamils and smashed our houses. Some of my family left Colombo, and I later lost contact with them. I lost contact with my friends, I was fired from my job, and eventually I started to run out of money. It was all because of the riots. So I started teaching yoga and just wanted a place to practice my massage therapy. I came here, but things haven't really worked out." He looks at his hands.

He goes into a long story about how his luck had turned and how his last resort was to sell heroin at a beach resort. Not bad if you want a permanent vacation. Winston seems desperate, certainly, but he's also made a few friends over the years. A generous Spanish man sends him cash from Madrid, he has a new girlfriend who's been clean for two years, and he's put some hours into helping a guy build a house up the road.

"If you want to know the truth of it," he confesses, "the drugs have nothing to do with the terrorism. It's the support from other governments, such as the United States and India, that allow terrorism to happen."

Truth is found in strange places and there was much in what Winston, my new yogi junkie buddy, had to say. Government-supported terrorism has a long history that includes Robespierre's reign of terror during the French Revolution, the Soviet Union's 1930s politburo surveillance techniques, Germany's Nazi regime, the Khmer Rouge of Cambodia, and many, many others. Up until 1990, India helped fund much of the Tamil militant cause in Sri Lanka. They provided both training grounds and arms for the LTTE and others and redirected proceeds from arms sales to support the Tamil rebel groups in Sri Lanka. It is worth nothing that, like India, the United

States also has a history of shady relations with its southern neighbors, redirecting proceeds from arms sales to support contra rebel groups in Nicaragua, or to provide the training that Osama bin Laden received in the 1980s to fight the Russians in Afghanistan.

Maybe the War on Terror itself can be considered state-funded terrorism. As I scratch my chest and look at the beautiful beach outside, feeling cool like Steely Dan, and high enough to have a perspective, I think to myself that maybe the War on Drugs can be, too.

Chapter Three: Colombo

"Civil strife is worse than war,
just as war is worse than peace."
—Herodotus

The English Equation

"Eats" Vendor, Colombo, Sri Lanka

On calm days, the waters of the Indian Ocean gently touch the white beaches of the island before the foam rolls back into the sea. Birds flock from one palm tree to another, the wind caresses the tall fronds, and the island seems an idyllic jungle world, utterly at peace. The coast is a stunning, fertile green, a large cloth of viridian velvet that some four-armed god tossed onto a still sea of lapis.

Along the west coast, about a third of the way up, is the capital, Colombo. In the clearly discernable center of this metropolis, the city has two identical towers and a series of large shopping malls that frame a small harbor. The distinctive Beira Lake just beyond the towers sometimes hosts small regatta parties, as the British did in the 1800s, and as college students and the Sri Lankan elite do today. But Colombo is no country club. Home to over a million people, and consuming nearly thirty miles of the coastline, Colombo is the combustion point for most of Sri Lanka's political fires. Sinhalese and Tamils and Malay and Burghers and Chetty and Bharatha and Chinese and Thai—and hundreds of other groups from India, the Middle East, and the rest of Asia—all live in close quarters. It's a spicy stew of people from nearby Asia with an occasional white blob of Dutch, American, or Portuguese thrown into the generally dark broth of the city. But despite being well blended within her borders, Colombo is still quite isolated from the outside world, relative to a place like New York or Paris.

The city exists as a delicate series of collisions, with the lines of tiny canals, footpaths, rivers, and roads tangling their way in every conceivable angle, testimony to an ancient city with no development plan beyond webs of footpaths. Pumping in and out of the city are hundreds of thousands of bicycles, motorcycles, mule-drawn carriages, buses, lorries, honking cars, and stray animals, all trying to find their way through the mass of bodies and machinery in front of them while in the alleys and oddly angled passageways slither the steamier truths of the city.

Colombo, were it a person, would be a woman in her late fifties, haggard, mean, worldly, and foulmouthed. The opposite of Prabath. Her vanity is all that's left of her beauty. The buildings here are crushed into each other and densely disorganized, like an ugly version of Jerusalem, and there's no room to walk without stepping in a pothole, trash, or a brackish puddle. Stinking meats swing, like fly strips, from the gables in alleyways, and four-legged mysteries that look like rats scamper from the gutters, coughing up blood and scraps of plastic. The steaming streets stink of fish blood, dogs pick their way through overturned garbage, cows meander between furiously honking cars, and everyone slaps at flies in the hot and smoggy sunshine.

The streets are shitty, but most distasteful is the pollution from an interminable line of diesel-farting machines that arrive from all directions at once. So Colombo has a grayish tint on her, a sooty, stained, skin-pop blush, and she's not as old as she looks. Colombo is as Colombo can, but it doesn't make her a pleasant city. Compared to the beauty of the rest of the island, Colombo looks a blemish of mismanaged industrialism and automated manufacturing.

Despite being draped in gray pollution and living under the overcast skies of civil war for so many decades, the people of Colombo are kind and considerate and somehow find a way to shine bright. Despite terrorist attacks, mob riots, and public lynchings, the people here—the Tamils and Sinhalese both—get along fine. Which is fortunate, because as I walk through the streets, I can't tell them apart. It's not like, for example, Angolan and Aborigine, or Kuwaiti and Bangladeshi. Tamil and

Sinhalese is a distinction that's nearly invisible to my Western eye. From what little I can tell, Tamils are taller, with thinner features, slightly darker skin, and longer fingers. But beyond that I have to look for Hindu signs, like a bindi on the forehead, to tell the difference.

Colombo still strains for success in a curiously Western style. Her natural preference for cacophonous and densely clustered bodies, a state of affairs found in most Asian cities, is tempered increasingly by other lifestyles. Between the English, the Dutch, and the Portuguese, Colombo has been trained to be quasi-European, but her population remains Asian. After all, the city spent over six centuries under imperial rule. Businessmen have traded their sarongs for suits and their villages for skyscrapers. Lawn parties are still hosted in gardens built by the British, where gin and tonics are served as horses canter on display. Upper-caste members of that time still rule the caste systems today (though few Sri Lankans will admit to it) and all the while the filthy stories of Western imperialism are repeated. If Colombo is anything, it is a self-contradiction; Occidentals are considered filthy, yet they are admired.

In another example of the Western touch, in downtown Colombo, adjacent to the army barracks, stand two matching skyscrapers. They are the Colombo World Trade Center, and they're the spittin' image of the former World Trade Center in New York, the one that was flattened on September 11, 2001. These two towers stand some forty stories high. Like those of the WTC in New York were, they are precisely identical to one another: a challenge to nature, a statement of control and discipline, and a celebration of technology and commerce. And, like the World Trade Center in New York, these were bombed in 1997.

I'm standing in front of the entry to the army base,

about twenty minutes early for an appointment, my hands in my pockets, staring up, my mouth open wide.

I am here to tour the city a bit, learn the history, and meet with the man who set the bombs in Colombo back in 1984. He still lives here. I want to talk with some of the people who started and worked with militant groups such as the LTTE (also known as the Tamil Tigers), and I want to meet some of the people from the other sides as well—civilians and military both. After twenty-five years of agitation, terrorism, freedom fighting, politics, and civil war, Colombo has both military and police permanently stationed in the streets—one of the only cities in the world with such an arrangement. It may seem excessive, but it is part of a cultural memory; in the late 1980s, there were more Tamil militants than there were members of the Sri Lankan army and police force combined.

Over six hundred years ago, Colombo's maiden name was Sinhalese: *Kalan-totta*, meaning "ferry from the Kelani River." This was what it was called when the Chinese invaded. Then the Arabs kicked the Chinese out. The Arabs too had problems pronouncing the name, so they changed it to Kolambu and yoked the town with enough trade prerogatives that it became, effectively, a part of the Arab empire. In 1517, the Portuguese stole the reins from the Arabs and then later named it Colombo, after the cheery memory of Christopher Columbus. One hundred and thirty-nine years later, the city was taken from the Portuguese by the Dutch, and then the Dutch were chased out by the British, in 1796.

The English, occupying both Sri Lanka and India, believed that in order to rule a country, the memory had to be beaten out of it. They specialized in an invasion of at least two fronts: military and cultural. I will call this the English equation (we can't hold them entirely responsible, because they learned it from the Portuguese and the French, but the English have taken the concept the furthest). The approach was to beat the snot out of the country, then, while it was stunned, cauterize the brains to burn out the memory and, as the country began to recover from the beatings and burnings, teach it something new to distract it from recovering its old patterns of cultural and political behavior. This is how imperialism works: Bash it physically, control the mindshare to gain power, collect the capital to move on ahead, then cauterize the culture and the local media.

First, we have the beatings. This is the military portion of the English equation. In 1919, there was a great deal of concern in the British government that German and Spanish insurgents would cause disruption in India. The English government drafted wide-reaching legislation called the Rowlatt Act, which allowed searches without warrants, arrests without trials, and trials without juries. Of course, visiting Germans and Spaniards were not the only ones subject to the Rowlatt Act; the Indians were, as well. One of these Indians was a well-heeled gentleman named Mohandas Gandhi, who protested this system with peaceful sit-ins he called *satyagraha*. Gandhi, protesting the Rowlatt Act, led a group of almost ninety-five hundred protesters to the town of Amritsar on April 13, 1919. Folks sat down around the fountain and gardens at the temple to make their opinions known. About two hours later, British troops arrived, blocked the gate, trapped the people inside, and started firing into the crowd, killing almost four hundred people and wounding another twelve hundred in ten minutes of rattling steel and wailing voices.

Though this was not the first time it happened, this was the first part of the English equation: Physically beat the people into submission.

After the beatings come the burnings. This is the cultural portion of the English equation.

For some two thousand years, Sri Lanka was considered the home of "traditional" Buddhism. Most Sinhalese belong to the Mahavihara sect of Buddhism, which takes what the Buddha said literally. So literally, in fact, that the monks decided to write down (contrary to the Buddha's recommendations) what the Buddha said. The Aluvihara Temple, in the middle of Sri Lanka, is where they kept these writings, long wood-bound books made of ola leaves (flattened and treated palm fronds) that were handwritten in an ancient derivative of Sanskrit named Pali. In 1948 the British made a trip south, walked into the library with some lit torches, and in three days left the fifteen-hundred-year-old library a mess of ashes and black cave walls, destroying the best-kept record of the Buddha's teachings in that part of the world. It was the Buddhist equivalent of losing the great library at Alexandria.

This is the second part of the equation: Burn the cultural memory from the country. The equation, in the 150 years the English occupied India and Sri Lanka, was tried in a few different ways: Beat then beat, beat then burn, burn then beat, et cetera. But eventually the countrysides of old Ceylon had been bruised and embittered, and the people, over the decades, began to lose the memory of who they were and where they had come from.

After 544 years of colonial rule, in 1948, the English decided to end their occupation, and Sri Lanka was handed her own head back, which she promptly screwed on backward.

It had been six centuries since she had been self-governing. Though she still had an elephant's memory, the memories were of beatings and burnings. So the colonized turned into colonizers, mimicking their former masters. But there was a difference this time. Now it was the Sinhalese majority who did the beatings and burnings, and it was the Tamil minority who took the heat.

With this new head screwed on so strangely, the government was blind, deaf, and off-balance.

The civil war started with a question: "Now that the English are gone, what language do we speak?"

The British had the habit of building English-language-based systems in their colonies. In Sri Lanka, this system was imposed on everyone: Tamil and Sinhalese, Buddhist, Hindu, and the sprinkling of Muslims and Christians alike. But before the British showed up in the eighteenth century, nobody really cared much about English. Despite diverse invasions from the Portuguese and Dutch, they still spoke Tamil and Sinhalese, didn't worry about what Christ did on the cross, and had plenty of their own fights to keep them busy. The island nation of Ceylon maintained an intense correspondence with India, but otherwise the influence that previous colonizers had on the island was superficial. Many people neither knew nor cared who sat on some faraway throne wearing a crown. But the arrival of the Brits changed the political climate, and a trip to London to be educated and inculcated in Occidental customs was the ticket to a governing seat in Ceylon. The English, after all, were the best imperialists on the planet, and they had gotten pretty good at setting up social hierarchies.

By the time the English went home and a new Sri Lankan government was being established, the Buddhist monks who had always held much of the power over the island, despite colonial rule, were getting very upset about the power of imported elitists, specifically people such as the new prime minister, Don Senanayake, a "Brown Englishman," as they called him, who had been educated and groomed for governance at Oxford, flown back to Sri Lanka, and propped up in power.

By 1948, the monks had built up a great wad of discontent and complaints about Occidental culture as a whole. After six centuries of problems, Westerners were no longer welcome. But the monks found themselves facing an avalanche of cultural change that brought much more than the English language to Sri Lanka. Bohras, Sindhis, Parsis, Muslims, and Christians were all appearing daily, and at an alarming rate, bringing different languages, foods, and customs to the island. The monks, as Sir Thomas Maitland pointed out in a letter of 1810, had long enjoyed a healthy influence over the Sinhalese government, and, despite their vows, they, like most humans, didn't like to share, when it came right down to it. The British had known this and manipulated this power balance for some time, but when the vacuum of the empire began to form, and the ancient ruling class of Sri Lankan monks faced losing their long-held power, one chamber of the gun was loaded.

But it takes two hands to clap, and the Tamils were not pleased with the turn of events either. Even though Tamils comprised only 23 percent of the island's population, Tamil officials demanded a 50 percent representation in the government, which, of course, didn't make the Sinhalese very comfortable, since they then comprised 70 percent of the population. Seventy percent is a majority, so they should run things, they argued. Thus the second chamber of the gun was loaded.

By 1955, the monks, the Tamils, and the Sinhalese were all at odds with one another, each of them claiming rights to a little more than either of them deserved. In an effort to settle this dispute, the new, and of late quite unpopular, prime minister, Sir John Kotelawala, held some meetings. First he visited with Buddhist monks and collected their opinions. Then he traveled to the northern part of the island, where the Tamils lived, and collected theirs. Then he held a public meeting and, hands in the air, cheerily said that he would give equal linguistic representation in Sri Lanka's new constitution to both Tamils and Sinhalese. The Tamils were happy with this proposal. But the monks, and specifically the conservative Mahavihara sect, were not pleased with these events. With a marketing spin on the message, they told Sinhalese students that they'd be forced to study Tamil (which may or may not have been true; it had not yet been decided). The students got upset about this and some started protesting, and some started protesting quite violently.

But it wasn't only the students who were rioting in that fateful year of 1955. Sir John Kotelawala put in place several unpopular reforms. Suddenly the people of Sri Lanka, hefting the newly found weapon of mob mentality over the head of government insensitivity, rushed into the streets with a violence that the country hadn't seen before. The growing feeling of unease and distrust was shared by all quarters—Tamil and Sinhalese alike—and rioting quickly became a national pastime.

Appeasing the majority seemed the best water to throw on the fire so Solomon Bandaranaike, another "Brown Englishman," in a 1956 bid to claim the office of prime minister, offered to make Sinhalese the official language. He felt as though it was the only way to avoid the dispute; after all, in a democracy, the majority rules. Or at least that was his reasoning. Acting quickly, he proposed the Sinhala Only Act, a decree stating that Tamil would not be used in schools or in government institutions. Twenty-four hours after he proposed the legislation, it narrowly won, with fifty-one of the ninety-five available votes, and over a million Tamil taxpayers became officially illiterate. The majority of Sri Lankans had been appeased, but the eighteen-hundred-year-old differences between the Sinhalese and Tamils had not been erased. History aside, the passing of the Sinhala Only Act meant that from then on, Sri Lanka would distance itself from both its English and Tamil populations. This meant that Ceylon would be a Sinhalese country, as opposed to a Tamil and Sinhalese country. History has shown it to be one of the worse decisions made, because it incited the civil war by denying dialogue with the Tamil minority.[1]

The year of the Buddha's 2,500th birthday also brought the first Tamil-Sinhalese riots to Colombo. As you or I might mark the passage of any year by holidays, the citizens of Colombo marked the passage of 1958 by riots. Houses were torched, shops windows were smashed, stores were looted, cars were overturned, people were crucified on street lamps, mothers and fathers were tied down as they watched their children being tortured, neighbors were burned alive on the hoods of cars, women were raped, men were raped, children were raped, families were killed, and Tamils throughout Colombo decided it was time to move out of the neighborhood. Most of them went north, to Jaffna. After all, other Tamils had been living in Jaffna for nearly 2,000 years, so it seemed to be the best available solution.

The Tamils were being driven from Sri Lanka, where they had lived for millennia. After almost thirty years of conflict, in 1977 the TULF (Tamil United Liberation Front, a moderate Tamil group from the north) was asking for a separate state. Their reasoning was, "If we can't get along, let us live on our own up here." But the new Sri Lankan government didn't want to let go of revenues from the north and, four years later, more riots broke out, and more Tamil groups splintered off from the main charter of a separate Tamil state. And each one

1. India, meanwhile, was adopting English as a secondary language.

became more extreme and more determined to make a difference.

Despite having chosen a language, there was still no dialogue.

In the last twenty-five years, Sri Lanka has been swatting at a swarm of militant groups (EPRLF, TELO, PLA, etc.), agitators (GUES, TNT, ENDLF, etc.), freedom fighters (PLOTE, EROS, TELF, etc.), terrorists (LTTE, PLOTE, EROS, etc.), counterterrorists (EPDP, PLA, TELO, etc.), anti-terrorists (Black Butterflies, Yellow Leopards, Black Cats, etc.), and terrorists whose job it was to terrorize the anti-terrorists (LTTE Black Tigers). This cast of characters includes rare guest appearances by the Indian Army (IPKF) and foreign intelligence groups (RAW, CIA, and FBI) alongside militant Palestinians (PLO and PFLP), who helped show these guys how to detonate a bomb, load a gun, and build a propaganda platform. Probably the best known of these are the Tamil Tigers, or the LTTE (Liberation Tigers of Tamil Eelam), founded and ultimately commandeered by Vellupillai Prabhakaran. This group alone did more to help and hinder the Tamil cause than all the other groups combined. In 2003, they had an estimated fifteen thousand Tamils in their army and over two thousand Tamils in their jails. Yes, Tamils. Though that number decreased over the years until the Tigers's demise in 2009, Prabhakaran, who was killed on May nineteenth of that year, and his crew consistently targeted Tamils as frequently as Sinhalese.

All of these groups scrambled and reassembled in 2009 and, as of this writing, many are now obsolete, some are officiated as government bureaus, and the landscape of course changed with the 2008 to 2009 Sri Lankan army's northern offensive, when the LTTE was effectually brought down and the leaders that did not surrender were either killed or captured.

During the 1980s, as war heated up and bodies gathered like bugs on a bumper, the Sri Lankan government got harder and harder on the north, effectively enforcing an embargo on the Tamil territories of that region. The LTTE was able to use the local hardships to its own nifty advantage. It neatly turned poverty into profit. First, since kids in their teens were pissed off about living conditions and wanted someplace to vent their anger, the LTTE could count on fresh recruits showing up at its door. Second, the members of the LTTE itself, under the same financial pressure, had more reasons to cry victim, removing themselves from an accountable role, arguing that they were simply trying to gain equal access to the ability to make money. This argument furthered their cause in courts and legislative battles. And, third, there was the tightening of families and communities that wars seem to engender, the ceremonies and memorials, the patriotism, nationalism, jingoism, racism, and tribalism. But fourth, above and beyond all of these reasons, the LTTE was masterful at using the media to gain exposure and credibility; also, by using a system of symbology and strategy, it portrayed itself as a victim in need of restitution, which, perhaps, it was.

The fundamental formula is the same on every continent: The imperial power leaves, and in its vacuum a disturbance is created that causes internal conflicts. These conflicts are not monitored by the imperial power that previously assumed responsibility, so the conflicts increase, a civil war erupts, and decades are spent getting back to a precolonial level of stability. It has happened in Mogadishu, with the Italians. It has happened in Iraq and Burma, with the English. It has happened often in the last two hundred years in a wide array of countries and cultures and it may happen again in Iraq.

As I stand in Colombo, hands in my pockets, looking up at their twin towers, it occurs to me that 9/11 was important because of what those towers symbolized, not because of the number of people killed.

In fact, if you're an American, you're seven times more likely to be killed by your own mother than by a terrorist.[2]

According to the U.S. Department of Health and Human Services and the U.S. National Center for Health Statistics, about 500,000 of us will smoke ourselves to cinders this year. That's the leading cause of death. Another 250,000 of us will bite the dust due to obesity. About 200,000 of us will check out as a result of medical errors (misprescribed drugs, misplaced procedures, and runaway hospital-found infections). Workplace infections are dangerous too. Infectious coworkers, computer keyboards, doorknobs, stair railings, dollar bills, mosquitoes, or the fork you ate with last night in the restaurant are all significantly higher threats than a terrorist. And try to avoid breathing, while you're at it, as microbial agents are just as deadly. Be very afraid of the sneezing fellow in the airplane seat next to yours. About ten times more people than the 3,100 who died in the WTC attacks will commit suicide this year, or have sex with the wrong person; 20,000 will tune out from illegal drugs; and about 16,000 of us will be murdered, probably by a peer or family member who has no affiliation with militant groups interested in political change. Occupational trauma will get about 5,000 of us, and another 4,000 will drown. Twenty-five will be zapped by a bolt of lightning

---

2. On average, according the U.S. Department of Justice, about 100 infanticides, in which the mother is the offender, occur in the United States every year. See http://www.ojp.usdoj.gov/bjs/homicide/children.htm and http://www.fbi.gov/ucr/cius2008/offenses/expanded_information/homicide.html for more.

and twenty will get snacked upon by sharks. Then, last on the list, we have terrorists. According to the U.S. State Department, an average of fifteen Americans have died annually from terrorist attacks since 2002, all of them in the Middle East.[3]

Terrorism flourishes on disproportionate media representation, and nothing represents disproportionately better than digital media by which a single person can yell, "Don't Tase me, bro," and have his voice broadcast around the world in a matter of hours. Digital technologies do a better job of transmitting information than any other media. And, therefore, of transmitting fear as well. Soon, cyberterrorists will develop the capability of influencing all of us simply by attacking a few of us, creating a need for computer-operator licenses and cell phone identities. Lawrence Lessig, a Stanford Law School professor, has said that he came to a similar conclusion after a conversation with former federal counterterrorism adviser Richard Clarke. Clarke evidently had written much of the Patriot Act well before September 11, 2001, and was considering a similar proposal aimed at protecting against a cyberterrorist attack. Lessig predicted that such an event would occur within the next ten years.[4] This direction of thinking was confirmed when, in August of 2009, the U.S. Senate proposed empowering the president to disconnect private-sector computers during a "cyber-security emergency."[5] If terrorism is primarily a media event, then soon it will be downloadable.

---

3. Note that active servicemen and military personnel are not included in these statistics, nor are U.S. civilian deaths in war zones.
4. Fortt, John, "Futurists: Feds to Squash Online Freedom." *Fortune's Techland* blog, July 23, 2008, http://techland.blogs.fortune.cnn.com/2008/07/23/futurists-feds-to-squash-online-freedom.
5. McCullagh, Declan, "Bill Would Give President Emergency Control of Internet." Just Get Us There blog, August 28, 2009, http://justgetthere.us/blog/archives/Bill-would-give-president-emergency-control-of-Internet.html.

But the Twin Towers? That mighty symbol has cost us dearly since the attack—especially in airports. Their destruction was a fantastic spectacle, perfectly suited for television. Never has the mainline drug called news been so important to so many, and never have ideas—toxic or otherwise—been broadcast so far, so quickly. For terrorists, this is a good thing. This globally slung muck provides the single commodity they most need to achieve their goals: attention. After all, without gaining attention, there is little point to terrorism, to freedom fighting, or to pricking the elephant with something sharp.

I'm scheduled to meet with a several people while I'm here in Colombo, among them a Sinhalese general and several Tamil terrorists (as defined by my own government). The first, the major general, is one of the most decorated commanders of the Sri Lankan army. After decades of dodging bullets and watching soldiers die, Sanath Karunaratne is now the army's media director and military spokesman. The second person I will meet is one of the fathers of the Tamil militant movement, Dharmalingam Siddharthan. Third will be the man who set the bombs in Colombo, Shankar Rajee, the one who exported suicide bombing to the Middle East, and the man who imported bomb building to Sri Lanka. Last will be a chameleon of a man, now at the top of the LTTE's hit list, named Douglas Devananda. Devananda, like Siddharthan and Rajee, also worked with the LTTE and has since taken a bitter distance from its approaches.

I turn my back on the twin towers of Colombo and walk toward the army base nearby.

The Major General

Major General Sanath Karunaratne, Colombo, Sri Lanka

Major General Karunaratne has been hunting Tamil terrorists for most of his life. Joining the Sri Lankan army in 1976 and receiving his training in India, Pakistan, the United States, and the United Kingdom, he bobbed up the ranks, eventually serving in the northern region of Sri Lanka as a chain-smoking, blood-spattered, hot-muzzled, no-nonsense Sinhalese major. Having led dozens of invasions into Tamil Tiger (or LTTE) training camps, he's seen more action in Sri Lanka than anyone, three soldiers told me. He prides himself on being something of a MacArthur for Sri Lanka, or perhaps for the Sinhalese; it's hard to say which.

We're supposed to meet in about twenty minutes.

The general was someone whom Chamindra had first suggested I speak with, as he had headed a number of important sorties, the most famous being the first Battle of Elephant Pass. This particular battle was one of the bloodier and more dramatic skirmishes of the war. His fame came garnished with whispered words of respect from a number of Sri Lankans I spoke with who all saw him as someone with an inside view of the conflict, the history of the island, and the Sri Lankan armed forces. After a series of phone calls, e-mails, and visits to the foreign affairs office, the Sri Lankan military finally gave me a phone number to the general's office. Now, two weeks later, recorder in hand, I'm en route.

Flipping the corner, I walk down a street, cross a plaza, and arrive at the Sri Lankan army's front gate. I am literally in the shadow of the twin towers as a young man dressed in green fatigues and an automatic rifle slung casually across his chest asks me my business. I tell him I am to meet with the major general. His manner immediately changes. His back straightens, his chin tucks in, and his tone of voice switches from bitter to creamy.

"Please come with me, sir."

He leads me across a short driveway, and we step into a green army tent. It's hot inside and smells like canvas and oil, but it's shaded, and that's what counts. Several desks are set up where young women dressed in green are writing things on ledgers. I am shown my seat and handed a cup of tea.

Five minutes later, a van pulls up, and two new escorts show me the way. We bump though the base and stop the van at the foot of a marble staircase—not large by Washington standards, but large enough to make the point that this is the entryway to the sanctum sanctorum. Six guards flank the hallway inside. They snap to attention and stand in silent stiffness as we walk past. My guides don't acknowledge them. The job of the military, regardless of country, is to waste heartbeats.

Another row, another stairway, another column, and I am ushered into a plush office with a mahogany desk. Behind it sits a small man with hard eyes and a black mustache. He stands up to shake my hand. He is crisp, like all generals.

A television blabbers in the corner, squirting out national news. Newspapers are scattered around the office, as well as magazines, notes, booklets, and pamphlets. A couple of posters with plaster backing still attached have been peeled off some alley wall somewhere in Colombo, rolled up, bound with rubber bands, and set here for the general to see. All of it has been organized with care.

My van-driving escorts stand near the door as the general and I sip tea and begin a three-hour talk.

The general begins with his most famous battle, at Elephant Pass, which involved a kind of secret weapon the Tamils had devised: a sand loader stolen from a nearby cement factory. The Tamils had soldered the cab with a steel-plated armor, turning the John Deere backhoe into a tank, plating it up to protect the driver and loading it with guns. This contraption was brought out against the Sri Lankan army late one battle night, and only the heroic self-sacrifice of one of General Karunaratne's soldiers stopped it from wreaking substantial damage. The soldier, a corporal, climbed onto it and, despite being shot in the back three times, managed to throw a grenade into the cab. The cab exploded, and the homemade tank rolled off the road.

Our talk moves from bullets, and I ask about something that confuses me: "What's the difference between a Tamil and a Sinhalese?"

When the general talks to you, he looks straight into your eyes as if to pin you down. "If you look at me and a Tamil, you will not see much difference. Who is Sinhala and who is Tamil? Everyone came from India. We look the same: the hair, the complexion. We have the same roots, the same region, the same features, hair, et cetera. The biggest difference is, biggest difference is . . . "

He pauses and I check to make sure the recorder's still running. Green light. Okay.

The general continues to think. He has a sense of integrity, and he wants to be honest in each answer. As he pauses, I wonder if I've asked him a question I shouldn't have; maybe it's outside his role as military spokesman. He taps his pen on some paper on his desk, a piece of paper he was using to detail the Battle of Elephant Pass, then looks at me with a sincere proposition.

"The biggest difference is that the Sinhalese are proud. We have a better history. Our language is from Latin, and we have Aryan roots. So there is a great difference, culturally. We have twenty-five hundred years of history, and the Tamil race does not have this. Inside we are very different."

I'm trying not to raise an eyebrow, and I wait for a punch line, but he's not kidding. He just looks at me and taps his pen again, in punctuation.

"What do you mean," I ask, "by 'a better history'? How can one history be better than another?"

"The Sinhala population is eighteen million, and we have many people all over the world, and we have a home. But the Tamils do not have a home. In Sri Lanka we have many victories. In the Tamil race, there are not victories like this. But in Sri Lanka we have the ancient things, the old things we have made here. There is a richness here."

From my ignorant side of the table—and I must say that I cannot know as much as the general, here, can—I can't help but find what the general has said to be the same as what Prabath told me about Good men and Bad men. Tamils and Sinhalese have been building the island of Sri Lanka, largely together, for over eighteen hundred years. Their history is shared, so I can't understand how one can be "better" than the others.

The general is weary, and the lines of his face are a diagram of shrapnel and smoke, human limbs flying in the air, and men screaming. The general, exhausted, hateful, professional, keeps his head high.

I ask him, in part, to change the topic. "What makes a terrorist?"

The general licks his lips, says, "LTTE," then says it again, then folds his hands on the desk in front of him, thinks for a moment, and again picks up the pen. This man is a media professional. His face changes and I see him look at me, and he takes a different tack.

"Tamils are universally recognized for their mathematics, science, poetry, history, etc. All over the world they are recognized. All over the world." He draws a circle on the piece of paper, and it sounds as if he's getting ready to explain how sex works to a thirteen-year-old. Apparently there is a reaction on my face.

"But this terrorist group, the LTTE," and he taps his pen on the page in front of him, "you see, they still live within a caste system."

The question seems to be going back to race. Nothing accurate can be said about Sri Lanka's caste system. Though the Buddha rejected it and the British outlawed it, the system still serves a function here. Money, power, race, and class are intertwined like strands of a rope, weaving different parts of Hindu and even Buddhist society together. There's still a dowry system, for example, that dictates marriage procedures. Marrying a teacher or a clerk will cost a woman's family a little over two million rupees.[1] Civil servants and doctors demand between four and five million rupees. An IT pro or a businessman can bring in a one hundred million rupee dowry.

And as I think of these things, I realize why I was given the chair at the devil dance, and why Prabath's family made a dinner especially for me, and other things too.

The general redraws his circle. He's not thinking about a circle but about a recurrence of events.

"The poor people of this system do not have any other options. Becoming terrorists is their only solution. They are poor, and because of that, they could not pay their daughters' dowries. The daughters don't have dowries, and the boys don't either. So first they are jealous. Second, the boys like guns. You see, Prabhakaran, he had a lot of discipline for these groups. 'Don't join the Sinhalese, because you will die a thousand times,' he tells them. 'If you join the Tigers, you will die only once.' You know, they have the cyanide pills" — he's referring to pills the Tigers wear around their necks, as pendants — "so that if they are captured, they can kill themselves. But there were many people born out there, and they had seen nothing other than the Tigers; they had never been to Colombo, for example. And [the Tamil Tigers] offered them a solution."

The general is telling me that terrorism is poverty's first child. This seems a bit like Miles's account. It has nothing to do with notions of "hating freedom" or religious battles. The general is willing to leave politi-

---

1. Or about U.S. $20,000

cal, ideological, and personal reasons outside in the cold. From his perspective it is about money. This I can believe.

Major General Karunaratne is involved in two wars, and only one is fought on a military front; the other is waged in the media. They're similar. Both involve appropriate positioning, a sufficient number of warm bodies, meeting technical requirements, and speed of transmission.

"The government has realized, Sri Lanka has realized, that the world community has a significant value. We were not open to world media. LTTE was different. They were better at this than we were. They were trying to tell the world that we were killers and racists and barbarians and that we will not allow their women to come out of their houses without killing and raping them. They started their propaganda machine, and so the armed forces started ours. Even today, they have six websites to talk about their cause. And we have ours, as of January, 2000. People went to the LTTE website, and so I thought, 'I will do it this way too.'"

As if he were pulling his favorite gun from his holster for me to see, the general turns to his computer and opens a Web browser.

Since reputation and attention are the core commodities of media, Karunaratne's job is to get his version of the story to Reuters and the Associated Press before the Tamils do. After decades of battle, Karunaratne knows that if there is a battle somewhere, the wins or losses are reported in the media, not by what really happened on the battlefield. And so his second battle with the Tamils is one of speed and spin—marketing events to alter public opinion, and since public opinion determines funding, the general makes sure his side is the one that's seen, before the Tamils.

"Faster, faster, faster," the general chants, pressing his fist against his desk. "There is no other way of getting the government working. You have to get your version there first. The Tamils have their story, and we have ours. The Tamils are not responsible for what they put up. They have no accountability. I still have to get approval on what goes up. I can't use the word 'terrorist' since the memorandum of understanding was signed. Since that day, I cannot call LTTE 'terrorists.'"

"When was that?"

"Two thousand and two. February 14, 2002."

He looks at me with a resigned expression.

The Terrorist Who Thinks
It's All Unnecessary

Dharmalingam Siddharthan, Colombo, Sri Lanka

In 1980 the People's Liberation Organisation of Tamil Eelam (PLOTE)† originated as a Tamil militant group focused, like the LTTE, on the dream of a separate Tamil state in the north of the island. The PLOTE was cofounded by a bear of a man named Uma Maheswaran. Prior to starting the PLOTE, Maheswaran was the chairman of the LTTE and had received training in Lebanon and Syria with the Palestinian militant group PFLP. When he returned in 1980 and got into a shoot-'em-up rivalry with Prabhakaran, Maheswaran left the LTTE and, with Dharmalingam Siddharthan, formed the PLOTE.

Today the PLOTE is led by Siddharthan and is a

government-recognized political party that often coop-
erates with the Sri Lankan government on behalf of the
Tamils and, in particular, the national army. Part of what
it's done is help the military locate not only LTTE sympa-
thizers, but also expose new tactics that the LTTE might
use (such as LTTE cadres dressing up in Sri Lankan army
uniforms, then firing at unarmed civilians to put false
blame on the army). Part of the reason the PLOTE is so
good at sniffing out devious guerilla tactics is because,
back in the day, those very tactics were invented by the
group itself.

On May 31, 1981, at a public meeting in northern
Sri Lanka, three Tamil men unexpectedly opened fire in
a public square, killing two Sinhalese policemen before
disappearing into the jungle. These three men were part
of the young PLOTE, and what they wanted to achieve
by killing the Sinhalese policemen was to incite more
anti-Tamil riots in Colombo, further dividing the population and bringing attention to the Tamil cause. It worked.
In the following days, anti-Tamil riots shook Colombo to
pieces and sparked further riots. The PLOTE's methods
were effective enough that within the four years that
followed, their membership swelled to about nine thousand. Most of these people were in southern India, in
the state of Tamil Nadu, based in camps, learning battle
skills. These camps followed the standard Indian training
regimen: members learned to shoot straight, crawl around
in the dark, smoke cigarettes, detonate bombs, talk dirty,
and use a compass. But the PLOTE added a few twists to
the usual rigor, such as teaching members how to walk
on hot coals. They also threw in a few extra elements
of discipline, such as killing members who decided to
leave without written permission. These camps, scattered throughout the Indian state, drew great suspicion
from Sri Lanka and the international media. Of course

the governors of Tamil Nadu, when asked about these camps, denied their existence. But the camps were there, and they continued to grow. Part of this growth was due to the PLOTE's powerful propaganda machinery, which even included a Tamil- and Sinhalese-language radio station run out of India for several years. Since the countryside of Tamil Nadu is a viridian patchwork of poor farms, ox-drawn carts, and hundreds of thousands of very poor people hoping to find a better life, the PLOTE's recruiting strategies were so successful that its training camps filled quickly. Unfortunately, its coffers did not. Many of the PLOTE troops were unarmed and itchy fingered, walking around camp holding sticks in the air, with one eye squint closed, pretending to fire: the militant's air guitar. The PLOTE needed money so it could get more weapons. If it had more weapons, it could get more money. Then it could get more troops. It was simple economics.

By 1984 the PLOTE was running into problems. With almost ten thousand members to support, it was a little short of change, so it robbed Kilinochchi's main bank in northern Sri Lanka, carting off 27.5 million rupees (about U.S. $275,000) worth of gold, which it promptly melted down and sold, using the profits mostly for marketing (or propaganda, depending on your perspective) and for training more recruits.

The PLOTE's financial problems didn't go away, and so it held on to its methods. On the afternoon of October 21, 1984 (the day before the major bombing of Colombo), at a magistrate's court in Kilinochchi, business was slower than usual. The security guards were playing cards, the rest of the building empty, when four men toting sawed-off shotguns stormed the building and, at gunpoint, herded the court guards into a closet and locked them in. Stuck in the dark, the guards, ears at the door, listened while the assailants hauled a load of booty to a getaway car idling in the street. When the guards finally broke out of the closet, they found that the invaders had taken seventy-two shotguns, several .303 rifles, and uniforms, and had raided the drawers of legal documents, scattering papers everywhere in their haste.

At this point the PLOTE was growing more powerful, and that did not go unnoticed. The Sri Lankan government knew that the PLOTE was accumulating money and weapons at an alarming rate, as did the Indian government. The PLOTE had also been playing footsie with the Chinese, the Russians, the Palestinians, and the occasional expatriate from Vietnam, all the while avoiding the occasional gaze of the CIA, which was watching developments in southern India with growing suspicion.

But by their fifth year of existence, in 1985, the PLOTE was forced to rethink its tactics, mostly for financial reasons. On the second day of April, about five months after the raid on the magistrate's court, a large-capacity container ship arrived in Madras (now Chennai). Madras harbor customs agents searched the vessel and found a container nearly the size of a train car, marked "used periodicals," stacked high with over fifteen hundred Chinese-made rifles from the 1950s, three hundred handguns, and several radio sets from Japan. The materiel had been purchased by the PLOTE for about U.S. $300,000 from a black-market arms dealer in Taiwan. The Madras authorities, knowing the situation was a bit complicated, asked the state governors of Tamil Nadu and even took it all the way up to India's prime minister Gandhi to learn if the PLOTE had previously reported the contents of the container to the customs agents who found it. Gandhi said no, so India simply kept the weapons.

This was a major setback for the PLOTE. The training camps, still full of soldiers eager and ready to fight but without the guns to do it, were forced back to the idea of an honest day's work. So three weeks later, on April 25, 1985, PLOTE commandos raided a police station, shot a policeman, and carried off twenty-four shotguns, twelve rifles, and a submachine gun. They took the keys to the bank and promptly went over to help themselves to a withdrawal of over six million rupees. Then, apparently to slow their pursuers, or perhaps for spite, they set fire to a gas station and disappeared into the jungle.

This solved some of the PLOTE's problems, but with ten thousand troops, you need more than a few dozen courthouse rifles. A few months later, another U.S. $300,000 went to a Palestinian who was supposed to secure a new load of weaponry. The Palestinian disappeared with the cash. It was a crippling blow to the organization and one that led to increasingly terrifying actions.

Maheswaran, still the PLOTE's primary leader, caused deep divisions among the PLOTE management. He or his lackeys killed more than thirty-eight members of the PLOTE. Such murders were generally accomplished by telling the victims to dig their own graves, commanding them to climb in, and then summarily tossing a grenade in with them. There were also members of the PLOTE who would just disappear. If someone asked where they'd gone, Maheswaran would dismissively answer, "Oh, they took a boat ride to India," or "They went for a trip up north," only for their corpses to float up on the beach a week or so later.

In a 1986 interview, Maheswaran said, "We have liquidated some individuals who betrayed our cause. Such things are inevitable in politics." Six of their victims were found with large cuts over the lengths of their bodies, their skin peeled back and their genitals removed.

"Politics" and terrorism were quickly blending.

Since my time down south I've been on the phone a lot, scheduling appointments and following up on the leads to leads that I need to meet people here in Colombo. One of the appointments is with Siddharthan, one of the men who raided the magistrate's court, and one of the men who muzzled and finally subdued Maheswaran. These days he lives in Colombo. He is a man who has traveled across the worlds of politics, militancy, terrorism, and now back to politics.

It is four o'clock in the afternoon, and a cage full of parakeets cheerfully discuss the events of their small world. Ours is not such a cheery conversation.

A bashful man shuffles into the room and sets two glasses of juice and some crackers on the table. He steps backward toward the room's exit.

Sitting across from me, Siddharthan quietly thanks him in English, picks up his juice, and leans back to heave an exhausted sigh. He is fifty years old. I notice that his skin has a waxy shine to it that's far from either healthy or glowing, and underneath his skin, pulled tight across his skull and creased around the forehead and mouth, something seems to be boiling. The muscles on his face squirm in strange configurations and his expressions suggest nervousness or pain. He is resistance embodied. His fingers are constantly clicking and calculating on an invisible abacus. He turns to look at me, and his eyes, far down in the wells of his eye sockets, seem soft and doughy. He lives in a state of childlike and constant prayer. Even eyes that have seen the worst of the pain in Sri Lanka remain innocent. It's the nature of this island.

Wiping sweat off my forehead, I flip on my recorder with my thumbnail. I'm not interested in misquoting him.

He seems the opposite of the general. The general,

who had hard eyes, seemed to be in command, the author of his environment. Siddharthan is soft down deep, and in a long-endured psychological torment. He is a man who has found himself in someone else's world. As soon as I recognize this difference, this opposition of their personalities, I decide to ask Siddharthan the same question I asked the general.

"I can't tell the difference between a Tamil and a Sinhalese. Can you please tell me, what is a Tamil?"

He laughs a little and nods.

"The Tamils are mixed in among the Indians, mixed in among the Sinhalese, and mixed in with other nations as well. But the line is political. The line around Tamils is political. Language, yes, the influence is there but . . . "

He's having a hard time with the question too. He pauses for four or five seconds, and just as I think his face will ease up and he'll relax, I see his shoulders, incredibly, fold into themselves and his face become an oily canvas covering a pool of electric eels, all working to get out through his eyes. " . . . the whole struggle is unwarranted and unnecessary. Perhaps it is just because I am growing old that I see this. Personally, I think it is all unnecessary. If you ask a Tamil, he will tell you that a Sinhalese man is the better man. If you ask a Sinhalese man, he will tell you that a Tamil is the better man. So it is all political. The culture of the Tamils is different from the Sinhalese by language, mannerism, and, I guess,"and here he smiles, "the curries are different. Yes, the curries are definitely different," and he chuckles again, and his face relaxes and his shoulders uncurl.

Siddharthan is a Buddhist name. Dharmalingam is Hindu. Like much of Sri Lanka's population, he has both Buddhist and Hindu roots. But he has chosen to follow a Hindu method of living partly because, like many of Colombo's residents, he no longer has faith in the motives of the Buddhist monks. He points out that in those loaded days of political sit-ins, the bikhus, the higher-level monks, had a significant say in political affairs. They still do, he tells me. But in those days, the monks wanted Buddhism to remain a Sinhalese power.

"Buddhism belongs to the whole world. Let's face it: There is not a lot of difference between Japanese Buddhism, Thai Buddhism, Indian Buddhism. I can't see a lot of difference. But if you go to a Buddhist temple today, you see a lot of Hinduism mixed in with the Buddhism, even the Roman Catholic influences. It's lots of little differences. None of them matter . . . in any Buddhist temple you can see Tamil ghosts."

Behind him on the wall are the posters of Ganesh and also Kali, Shiva, and Gautama Buddha, multicolored, delicate embroideries, and posters of gods with many arms, floating in the midst of their weightless mansions, smiling like brilliant cherubs. For a man as dark and as concerned as Dharmalingam, these ghosts might help ease the difficulties of his day by reminding him of what is eternally important and what is temporary and insignificant. But I realize, as I notice a small collection of military dog tags on the shelf behind him—reminders of friends who have died—that Tamil ghosts haunt him as well.

The very first Tamil terrorist was a college student named Sivakumaran. His story is well known among Tamils. In the fall of 1969, five friends met at their professor's house in the small town of Valvettithurai, the coastal village in the north that gave birth to the Tamil militant movement. One of these five friends was Vellupillai Prabhakaran, who later used gas, poison, and gunpowder to start the machine called the Tamil Tigers. Another was a local radio operator. Two were local thugs looking for adventure. And the fifth member of the study group was Sivakumaran, the man who, with the help of the other four, founded the Tamil Liberation Organization, the first Tamil militant collective.

Sivakumaran was, in American terms, a scholar and an athlete. He was respected and loved by many people and was infamous for his late-night discussions at Jaffna University, where he spouted the necessity of armed resistance. But Sivakumaran was more than another loudmouthed academic. In September of 1970, he made assassination attempts on a Sri Lankan deputy minister, Somaweera Chandrasiri. A few months later, he tried to kill Alfred Duraiappah, the mayor of Jaffna. By 1974, he had a warrant out for his arrest, a group of followers, and a reputation for being a charismatic leader. But Sivakumaran knew about methods of police torture in those days and, at the gentle age of seventeen, decided that death was better than imprisonment.

One summer evening in 1975, Sivakumaran was robbing a bank when several police trapped him. He calmly pulled a necklace out of his shirt, removed a cyanide pill, and swallowed it, dying on the spot. Thus the Tamil cyanide culture was born. From that time on, Tamil Tigers wore cyanide pills around their necks for the same reason, and many—probably hundreds of them— have died in the same way.

In the 1970s and the 1980s, the Tamil cause was considered from many sides. Some, on the political right, said that militant means were needed; only military might could make the law. Some, on the political left, said that dialogue was needed; only negotiation could do it. Then, in between, were the moderates who were most likely the only ones that could bring about the compromises both sides would need to make.

Siddharthan's father was a moderate and one of the founders of the Tamil United Liberation Front (TULF), the political group that first called for a separate Tamil state in the north, near Jaffna, in the 1950s. Unlike many of the other militants of the day, the TULF wasn't shooting off guns; it was composed of moderates that had at least a tacit willingness to engage in dialogue instead of battle. They would have been the Sri Lankan government's best bet for a group to negotiate between the rising blood tide of Tamil militarism and the snake pit of Sinhalese politicians. Neither side was happy and each needed a moderator. Siddharthan's father, tall, soft-spoken, and respected on both sides, was known as being good to his word, fair to his people, and a brick-solid negotiator. Young Siddharthan, looking for a way to get the politics of the day out of his system, joined his father and other TULF members out in front of the Kachere, the Jaffna federal courthouse. Following Gandhi's lead, they organized peaceful sitting demonstrations. They would block the gates and sit quietly, working to make their point until the Sinhalese police appeared with batons, just as the British had once upon a time in Amritsar, where peaceful protesters were likewise beaten with batons.

Several months after the TULF was founded, a coworker of Siddharthan's father was gunned down in the street. It was a symbolic killing carried out by other Tamils who wished to make it clear that the TULF would not speak for them or be recognized as the voice of the Tamils. The killing, an act of terrorism, was symbolic.

Then, a week later, several young men drove up to Siddharthan's house and asked for his father. His mother recognized them as neighbors, invited them in, gave them seats on the sofa, and served them lemonade. She asked them to wait until Siddharthan's father returned from work, but the boys who were sitting on the sofa with the lemonade didn't say much. Since something bad seemed to be in the air, Siddharthan's mom sent a cousin up the road to fetch his dad. A few minutes later, when he came down the road on his bicycle, the guys abandoned their lemonade, threw Siddharthan's father in a car, and drove off. His body was found two days later in the nearby town of Thavili. This was the first killing of a moderate leader in Jaffna. And it was done by other Tamils.

Across the table from me, Siddharthan is now older than his father was when he was murdered. I watch his strange face torque and twist under the pressure of his steaming brain. "I think this killing was done by LTTE. But I don't know for sure. They were not against him personally. He was very close to Prabhakaran. Prabhakaran used to visit our home to eat, and he was friendly with my father."

Prabhakaran got not only the idea of a separate Tamil state from the TULF, but his elimination methods as well. The TULF, despite being moderate, was known to say, "Traitors do not die natural deaths." And the TULF was also one of the groups that helped initiate the militant cause. They never suspected that, like most militants, or governments, even, that their lessons would be used against them.

Siddharthan points out that his father's killers wanted the same thing his father did. His father's death led Siddharthan in a new direction.

"By 1982 the movement had grown, but slowly. There were four or five main militant groups. The LTTE, PLOTE, and EROS were among them, but there were only about a hundred and ten people. But, suddenly, in 1984, LTTE had six hundred."

"What was the recipe?" I ask.

"Prabhakaran would train them and then send them back and ask them to recruit other people for him. His success was his steady approach. And his mystery. Tamils love a good mystery, and Prabhakaran was just that. One year later, in 1985, there were forty-five hundred people. Now, nobody knows this, but Prabhakaran left the LTTE for a while. When he came back to the LTTE, that's when the killing started. He started eliminating members of other groups. You don't know what it's like in there. Today all you hear about are child conscriptions, extortion, but the LTTE doesn't care. They know how to do one thing well."

I nod. We both take a sip of juice.

As I look at him over the rim of my cup, I realize that this terrorist has become a pacifist. The violence he's lived through has steered him, with the strong hand of revulsion, down a different road.

"I'm going to tell you the truth. I don't think Prabhakaran was a Tamil nationalist. He was just a criminal. What happened, at the beginning of the Tamil problem, was that the militants got used. People like him were used by the politically motivated people. You understand? He was used. He was a criminal. For him it was an adventure. But Prabhakaran couldn't put his gun down. He had no choice. He came from a poor town."

He wipes his forehead again, takes another sip of juice, and looks at me, his eyes smoking deep inside his writhing face.

The 1980s saw the major split between Tamil militant groups, and it was then that Siddharthan's own group, the newly formed PLOTE, became desperate. Aside from robbing courthouses and making deals with shady Palestinian arms dealers, they were also striking up talks with the Indian government. The PLOTE had become the largest of the militant groups, so India began to support them with significant weaponry and a place to train; India did not want Sri Lanka to become a military rival, and the militant factions would ensure that didn't happen. Though it was not the official policy, the Indian government gave the militants small arms, rocket launchers, handguns, and mortars, but only about one to two hundred rounds of ammunition.

But even with the help of India, the PLOTE, like other militant groups, simply could not round up enough training facilities to build an actual army. To solve this problem, select members of the PLOTE received training in Damascus via the Palestinian group Fatah. Another Sri Lankan militant group, the EROS, made the introduction. The People's Front to Liberate Palestine (PFLP), setting aside all ethnic divisions save one, said that it would be willing to accept any number of people from any organization, anywhere—the exception, of course, being Israel.[1] The deal was relatively simple: "Send us your boys, and we'll train them and put them on the front line for two months. Then we'll send them back with skills, training, and, if they're good, some ammo." For groups like the PLOTE, it was the offer it needed. After all, while there was some access to military knowledge among Tamil civilians, building an army is not a small job, and it requires education.

But the PLOTE and the EROS had worked together for years. So in 1982, with the assistance of the EROS, Siddharthan visited Damascus several times and worked with the PLO and other groups of the region. He has seen the inside of terrorist organizations and has worked with

1. Founded in 1967, the PFLP, designated as a terrorist organization by the United States and the European Union, is a paramilitary factional group associated with Fatah and the Palestinian Liberation Organization (PLO).

and for them. He has helped organize them. After all, the man is, according to multiple lists written by multiple state departments, a bona fide, capital-T terrorist.

"What do you think of terrorism as a political tool?" I ask him.

He turns his palms up in a simple posture.

"Terrorism is simply targeting innocent people. It is targeting people who have nothing to do with your struggle. This is regardless of whether it is by an individual, a group, or a state. Everything else fails. You cannot convince them to join you, and you cannot convince the government to change. We decided that Sinhalese people had to understand our suffering. When we bring the war to Colombo, we are hitting economic targets. We are weakening the economy and making it feel our struggle. And by doing so we gain the attention we need."

The PLO-Trained Munitions Consultant from London

Shankar Rajee, Colombo, Sri Lanka

Two days later, I'm standing in Colombo's second district, in front of the city's main Hindu *kovil*. It's 10:00 AM, and Colombo has lurched into the workday, the roads now clogged by the beeping tuk-tuks and the circus of brightly decorated motorcycles carrying families, chickens, and stacks of wood. The high concrete walls of the kovil are painted in garish red-and-white stripes, and the smells of cinnamon and myrrh mingle with those of cow shit and exhaust, filling the air with a song of Ceylon. I'm near a gateway that opens into the courtyard of the temple. Inside the ancient courtyard, a massive column of squirming, dancing, singing, fighting, screaming deities stretches up through the gray pollution of the city. Diesel fumes, like fallout snowflakes in a Hindu diorama, drop past the ancient gods as they cling to their column of concrete in the sky. All is holy and profane, and the world here seems built of meat and dreams.

Shankar Rajee, also known as Nesadurai Thirunesan, is the leader of the militant group EROS and the man who bombed Colombo on October 22, 1984. He asked me to meet him here at ten o'clock. As I look at my watch (10:01), a taxi pulls up directly behind me.

It's not entirely fair to say that Rajee was the man who bombed Colombo, because it was a group—the EROS—that planned, wired, and detonated the bombs. Rajee has himself made a long list of contributions to the Tamil cause, not all of them violent. Since the 1960s he has been a hub of the Tamil movement, politically, philosophically, and militarily. He has also been the link between Tamil and Palestinian militants. He has been trained by some of the most wanted and feared men in the world, and now, in Colombo, he has been leading the EROS on its quest to free Tamil Eelam.

He is the perfect terrorist specimen I've been searching for.

Or so I suppose.

Out of the cab steps a fat-faced, doughy man in a white button-up shirt. He glides over and, with a gentle smile, a nod of the head, starts politely shaking my hand. I think this might be Rajee's driver. I stumble over my first few words as I come to terms with the fact that this small, well-bellied, balding buddha in front of me has lived his life high on the CIA's most-wanted list for decades.

He's too pudgy. Meeting Rajee, in fact, is a visual disappointment. I was expecting a hardened war criminal, some chiseled Indian version of a Clint Eastwood gunslinger–cum–Hindu James Bondlike electronics hacker. But Rajee is soft-spoken, articulate, and graceful. He speaks slowly and selects phrases carefully. He has pudgy hands, and he uses them to wipe his chin often, as if he were drooling. He has a wife and children. He doesn't talk about them much.

In January of 1975, a group of Tamils living in London formed the EROS. The group, which feels like the unnatural progeny of London intellectuals and PLO-trained munitions consultants, found a niche as a liaison between the PLO/PFLP and Tamil organizations such as the PLOTE and the LTTE. Not that there was a shortage of this sort of Palestinian-Tamil interaction; after all, *The Tamil Times* reported in June of 1984 that there were almost sixty members of Israel's intelligence agency, the Mossad, living in Sri Lanka, all there, presumably, with the intent of tracking Palestinian militants.

But the EROS was different from the PLOTE and the LTTE. It never, for example, robbed banks to buy weapons. It claimed to be different because it had higher ideals. Rather than rob banks, it bombed cities instead.

We get out of the tuk-tuk in front of his office. Rajee says something to his driver. As we exit the cab the driver shuts down the engine and follows us. We walk up to the door, past a couple of rigid guards holding automatic rifles, past a heavy steel-plated door built into a steel-plated wall, down a hall, and into a cool, whitewashed room, modestly set with a few tables and chairs. A traditional Malaysian carpet is in the middle of the floor. The curtains move slightly in a breeze of jasmine or something gentle, like musk. A coffee table has some newspapers on it. Near the sofa is the obligatory cage of parakeets. A fan spins overhead; that's where the breeze is coming from.

Rajee waves his hand at a couple of chairs. I take a seat and pull out my notebook. He leaves the room, and

I wonder, briefly, if I'm in danger. But why would I be at risk? After all, as Siddharthan put it, attention is what's wanted. No one is going to walk into the room and shoot me. No, I offer them what they need. But there's always kidnapping. Maybe that could do them some good.

His driver walks into the room carrying a tea platter. He sets a cup down on the table in front of me, and with it a little cube of sugar, and a spoon. Then for Rajee he does the same but puts down three sugar cubes. Then he leaves the room.

Along the far wall are two desks with very different chairs and piles of paper and posters. Some of the posters promote the PLOTE. The EROS and the PLOTE are still closely linked. The battle, it seems, has been divided. One part of the battlefield is owned by the LTTE and Prabhakaran; another part by the EROS, the PLOTE, and several other groups. A third part of the battle is owned by the Sri Lankan military. Prabhakaran, as he often does, sits as the fulcrum of the political balance.

Stirring my tea, the clinking of the spoon seems really loud. I resist the desire to look around and remind myself that my fear comes from media experience more than personal experience. And anyway, what kind of kidnapper takes three lumps of sugar with his tea?

Rajee walks back into the room, smiles at me, and sits down. He puts his reading glasses on. Aloud he reads a blurb from the newspaper and grumbles about the LTTE. He and Siddharthan both like the LTTE less than they like the Sri Lankan government.

"Tamils should not be doing this to each other," he mumbles, shaking his head as he holds the paper. He slaps the paper with the back of his hand and rolls it up on his knee. He looks at me and takes off his glasses with a sideways swipe.

"So. Where do we start?"

I flip on my recorder and start my survey.

"What is a Tamil, and how is he different from a Sinhalese?"

His eyes are sharp and focused, he doesn't blink often, and he speaks with the diction of a switchblade.

"Tamil is a language. Tamil, which is supposed to be the mother of all Dravidian languages, dates back through several thousand years of recorded history. And the people who speak this language have particular traditions, cultures, way of life, heritage, and thinking. Note that the Kurds are the largest population of people who do not have a homeland. The Tamils are second."

Having no homeland is the tie that binds Rajee to the Tamil cause. Rajee's parents came from Urumpirai, a village in northern Sri Lanka near Jaffna. Like most educated, middle-class Tamils, he and his siblings were born in the north, but his father moved the family down to Colombo, where he worked as a rubber analyst. Rajee started attending grade school in Colombo. His mother worked around the house. The whole family were good friends with the Sinhalese neighbors; during holidays, his mother would invite them over for meals. Rajee's family had a car in their garage, and they had, if you will, a chicken in their pot.

"It was a lovely life, you know. We had a very happy family, and I was the eldest of six of us. It was a normal middle-class life, really. My father had a vehicle, we were going out on holidays with friends, things like that. Most of our holidays weren't in Jaffna unless it was a wedding or a funeral or something, and my parents would go. The sort of holidays in which you take presents along. So the family enjoyed the kind of local village atmosphere and friendship with people in Colombo. That was the mid-'50s. Things were different then."

The year 1958 was a watershed for Rajee. In June,

everything slammed to a crash when racial violence flooded the streets of Colombo. Rajee's family's suburb was ransacked for three days straight. By the third day, when a mob of over a hundred people attacked a neighboring house, his father realized that his shotgun wasn't sufficient protection for the family. His mother proposed they move to the south of the island to live with some friends. They decided instead to move in with a neighbor for a few days until things cooled down. Rajee was nine years old.

"Was your neighbor Sinhalese or Tamil?" I ask.

"He was Muslim . . . I don't remember his real name, but we called him Uncle. The next day we moved to a refugee camp that was set up near the college, as our house was set on fire that night. And we lost all our possessions.

"My only worry at that time was that I had a big tricycle, and I was day and night thinking about this tricycle and what could have happened to this. I begged my father to take me to the house the next day—I just wanted to retrieve my cycle, or see if it was still there, or see what had happened to it. My mother wouldn't let us go. She said, 'That sight is so unbearable that I don't want you to see what happened to all our possessions.'"

He takes the newspaper off of his knee and puts it on the table in front of us, then purses his lips.

"So there I was in the refugee camp for two weeks, with nothing except my shorts, my trousers. Nothing on top, nothing on foot. Having to stand in the never-ending food line for my bread and dahl for breakfast, lunch, and dinner. As my brother and sisters were too small, I had to stand in line for them also.

"Two weeks after that, we were taken to the harbor for military escort. Between the buses that brought us there were these armored vehicles, and the place was under curfew when we were moved. There we were as citizens of this beautiful island. We cannot move from one part of the country to another part. We had to be shipped by several shipping convoys, and it took four days, since they were not moving in the night, fearing danger. So off to Jaffna we went. The trip wasn't, I would say, enjoyable. It was just a cargo ship, temporarily set up for this."

The 1958 riots were the first island-wide riots that targeted Tamils, only ten years after Sri Lanka had gained independence. The riots lasted for five days before the military stepped in. Then two more days of rioting followed, by which point most of the Tamils living in Colombo stepped aboard one of six European shipping containers that were secretly commissioned to carry them up the coast, eight hours to the north.

"When we got to Jaffna, we didn't have a place to go. It was the first time I would meet my relatives. And while, of course, there were temporary refugee camps set up in Jaffna, our relatives couldn't bear to see us live there, and they suggested we live with them. So for a while we were a burden, by then, with our relatives, until we settled down in the village some time later. Even though things in the south seemed to be turning back around and some people were returnin, I think that the experience and the pain and the trauma never allowed us to think of returning."

There were more than a few reasons for this. By that time, a special government order had admitted Rajee into the public school system in Jaffna. Since he had been reared in Colombo, though, among Sinhalese, he spoke Sinhalese better than Tamil, so he was knocked back a couple of grades. Suddenly his new home didn't appear so homey, and the education system, which didn't want him either, seemed undesirable as well.

Meanwhile, Rajee's father had been given a grant to do rubber research in the Soviet Union. He and his father kept in close contact, and it was through these letters that Rajee began to learn about politics and his view of the world became increasingly international. The letters had a massive impact on him and introduced him to ideas about politics, life, and the Soviet people. He eventually concluded that most of his problems had come from the 1958 riots, and so he began to organize demonstrations and marches protesting government decisions and anti-Tamil racism in Sri Lanka.

He pauses and looks at me for a moment, pulls on his chin, and says, "This gave me the outlook of being a Tamil nationalist."

In 1966, Rajee's family decided that he should move in with his father, who had returned to live in Colombo. Meanwhile, in Jaffna, political temperatures were rising.

"The student movements and political activities were getting more and more prominent. Then came the final straw—when they brought out the education standardization for university admissions. This gave a clearly weighted advantage to the Sinhalese."

Rajee looks at me with a wry smile stretched across his face. He waves a hand in the air and shrugs. Imagine being in a school where your scores are automatically going to be lower than they would be in another school, if the same test were given in both buildings. In essence, the government was awarding bonus academic points to Sinhalese students simply for being Sinhalese.

"That took me to London. I decided, 'Well, at least they speak English there.'"

He looks away and chuckles into his shoulder. The irony of going to England to find educational equity that could not be found in his home of Sri Lanka—largely because of the lingering impact of English rule—has never been funny for Rajee, but he laughs again anyway.

In London, he majored in agricultural engineering and minored in automobile engineering. He wanted to continue in economics, systems analysis, and agriculture. His father was a source of inspiration, and Rajee was planning to follow in his path.

"But this," he almost sings, "was not to be."

During the years Rajee was in London, the United States was busy in Vietnam, and bullets from other countries were hissing through the streets of Luanda, Maputo, Cape Town, and, of course, Gaza. People from all of these countries made their way to London, and Rajee was happy to find himself surrounded by other refugees. After all, not having roots puts you at a great advantage when it comes to making new friends. And his new friends had ideas as radical and as diverse as the lives they led.

"There were several Palestinian students in London, and there were people from Africa there, organizing and mobilizing, and much of it was about the Palestinian cause. The draconian policies of the governments—this was also a great deal of interest to us. The internationalism and imperialism. The enormous energy of the movements of the late '60s and early '70s inspired us. Baader-Meinhof, the French radicals, on one side. And they were all fighting against imperialism and neocolonialism."

It was a heady time for Rajee. Far from his little island of racism, he'd entered a world of international politics. One of the first people he met in London was a Sri Lankan man named Eliyathamby Ratnasabapathy, popularly known as Ratna. He was central in bringing together a study group, which eventually came to be known as the EROS.

Ratna had an eclectic set of connections that

included Sri Lanka's finance minister, Sri Lankan leftists, Palestinian guerillas, refugees from Mozambique, refugees from Angola, and guys with a television and a videocassette player. The group would get together in the evenings, pop in a tape, study their problem in comparison to other problems from around the world, and draw parallels. Since they all came from small groups that were being oppressed by larger national forces, the questions were simple: What is the source of the problem? Where is the solution and how do you fund it?

These study groups were fertile ground for the recruitment and indoctrination process. Representatives of political organizations would come and speak and answer questions in quiet tones after the talks. The study group organized fundraising and networking functions, coming into contact with progressively more radical groups. The cause was often the same, regardless of the country or region—political change wasn't happening and so alternative methods had to be invented, usually militant. The ends, as the argument goes, would justify the means.

One day in 1977, the Palestinian representative in London, the late Said Hammami, came to give a talk. He and Rajee formed a fast friendship and spent the evening talking. And during this conversation, the second major rash of riots was spreading in the Sri Lankan streets. The next morning, Rajee read the news.

What he read was that the TULF was asking for a separate state. Rajee was convinced it would not work; the TULF was too moderate, too patient, too compromising, and too complacent with the Sri Lankan government. After years of discussion and endless efforts, all of which seemed to be met with neither progress nor any terms of improvement, Rajee and others decided this approach would not achieve the goals of a separate Tamil state.

As he put it, "We decided that the only way was to arm ourselves."

Shankar Rajee had found many things in London. He had found a reason to die and, therefore, perhaps, a reason to live. He had found, for the first time in his life, people like him: refugees who had no avenues of escape. He had found a radical point of view that would throw him into a life brimming with violence and secrets with life-or-death consequences.

There were logistics involved. Imagine, dear reader, that you decide to take up a weapon against your government. There are certain challenges before you. You need to know what kind of weapon to use, you need to know where to get it, and you need to know how to use it. Answers to these simple questions are kept from the reach of most of us, even in the United States, where the right to bear arms is constitutional and where the application of that right is, at best, blurry.

But the PLO, via Said Hammami, offered Ratna's group access to a new kind of school, one in which Rajee and two other Tamils could learn not only what kind of gun to shoot but what kind of war to conduct.

Rajee and his pals had some misgivings.

"Among the study circle, we were a little nervous. Are we really going to find this out? Are we serious, you know? So, three of us decided to put ourselves through this training, and all the others were simply waiting to see if the three of us would come back."

Rajee snickers, closes his eyes, and wipes his chin.

The first step for them was to collect visas from the Lebanese Embassy so they could enter. Since Rajee and his two colleagues didn't want to stir suspicion, they claimed to be from Bangladesh, and they claimed to be journalists. The visas were issued and accepted with no problems. But the day before they were to board the plane, they realized that they had another factor to consider: making nice with the militants in the Middle East. They decided to bring along a gift of some sort.

"We took some tea as a symbol, as a gesture to the Palestinian people, picked by the Tamil people, as if to say, 'This is our sweat and blood, this is the only thing we have to give.'"

Armed with their boxes of tea and newly burnished political views, the three "Bangladeshi journalists" climbed onto a 747 bound for Lebanon. Rajee recalls how nervous he was, sitting in the plane during takeoff, a student suddenly bound for bombed-out Beirut. It is one thing to be a student in a study group that watches videocassettes in London, but 1977 Beirut would be a different kind of classroom, where demerits would not be marks on paper but bullet holes.

They arrived in Beirut almost an hour late. The PLO contingent that was supposed to meet them was nowhere in sight. Rajee and the other two students began to wander aimlessly around in the airport, kicking at the dust. It was when airport security began to wonder why three young Bangladeshi journalists from London were carrying so much tea and so few cameras that their PLO contact miraculously appeared, thanked the security guards, piled them into a Red Cross ambulance, and whisked them away.

"Actually," Rajee recalls, "I never knew that an ambulance could be used for any purpose other than medical. That was my first sight of war, when the ambulance, with sirens blowing, crossed roads, avoiding bodies, burned cars, burned armor, until we reached the so-called Green Line, where things were a little easier. This was in the camp.

"We were taken to the PLO office in the camp, assignments were given to us, and we handed over the tea and performed these pleasantries, and we were told we would be met by the officer. So after a while we were driven by the military vehicles, without lights, along a mountainous track up over long hills in the night, and finally we reached a place in the Bekaa Valley. I forget the village . . . but it was six or seven kilometers from the Syrian border.

"Before we had even settled down, the delegation came and we were interviewed by the military commander of that time, Abu Jihad. He briefed us and told us we would be put through a program and told us where we would stay. It happened to be in the stables of the brother of the king of Jordan. So there were lots of beautiful horses—I love horses, those thoroughbred Arabian horses—and some little huts around. Then we were moved after a couple of days to a camp in Damascus—to a PLO camp called Hamooriya, mostly for international training. There were Nigerians, Germans, everyone. It took place in either English or Arabic, and we were put in our group."

And so their training began. They were put into different classes that included war tactics, weaponry, device improvisation, explosives recipes and methods, and then a host of special techniques such as letter bombs.

"For example," he explains, "we learned about the design of detonation devices for a dead tree or a live tree, a tree of different sizes, a building with round pillars or square pillars, the thickness of a wall, the area to be detonated, the range of destruction. We had mathematical approaches for these different ways to calculate all of this. It was a thorough, comprehensive class. And we had small, practical experiments dealing with various types of detonators and setting up explosives, trying them out, and all that. Then was the other class. It was titled 'Kitchen Explosives.' The problem posed is this:

You are in an urban area, and how—with the materials in the kitchen—how would you go about building an explosive? Then, of course, the device, the configuration mechanics, triggering devices, time delays, and lectures from other people who had done their own in the past."

There were other courses as well: machine guns, grenade construction, enemy weaponry, the use and targeting of anti-aircraft guns, surface to air missiles, blowpipes, et cetera.

"A funny story," he continues. "One time while shooting at the range, I got a five-out-of-five shot, and the group commander lifted my hand in the air and screamed, 'The Bangladeshi hit five out of five!', and the whole camp cheered. I thought, 'Wait, I'm not Bangladeshi!' But then I realized that I didn't know where all those guys were from either. Some of us knew, but most of us didn't.

"There was another time when we were all told that someone important would be coming to visit, and we were sent into a small room and told to face the wall, which we did. The person then walked behind us and quietly congratulated each one of us, but we couldn't see who it was. Then, after he said something to you, you were to put your hand behind your back with your palm up. He gave us each a sweet. I later found out it was Yasser Arafat. After he left, they told us that.

"Then we went back to London. There we were with all the confidence and all the knowledge. And we took"—he laughs—"all the various types of weapons and ammunition back in our bags: a lot of ammunition from the camp, and things like automatic machine guns. And a lot of ammunition: the various types . . . the white-tipped ones, the red-tipped ones, the green-tipped ones. We had an enormous quantity of all of this in all our baggage.

"And in Paris, at Charles de Gaulle, we were intercepted. And the customs guys asked us what we were doing with all this. And we said we found it on the streets, that it was a souvenir. And they said, 'If you share some of this with us, we'll let you go through customs.' And so when we had spare ones—the exploding types, the heat-generating types, for example, we had a lot of them—we gave half to them, and we took the rest. And they let us go!"

Rajee's really laughing now, and he leans forward and takes some tea.

"We were bringing these back to show our people. This was kind of a demonstration, to show them that this was available. It was a very interesting time. As I look at it now, I think it was crazy; but at the time, it made sense. Of course, after the training we were put in the front lines [in Lebanon] for a fortnight to help with the battle. To help with operation duties and all that, to learn how to do this. I mean, we were right on the front line. And at this time there were some people who had been in communication with LTTE, and we wanted to build a working relationship with them."

What followed was that Rajee presented the weapons to Prabhakaran, who, oddly, seemed unimpressed. The automatic machine gun seemed to raise an eyebrow, but otherwise he at the very least put on a show of utter nonchalance. Rajee never understood why, but Prabhakaran was not interested in what they had learned or in what they had brought back for the Tamil cause. Over the years the relationship between Rajee and Prabhakaran curdled, but Rajee points out that on several occasions when he met with Prabhakaran, the LTTE honcho was growing increasingly interested, like an addict, to larger and more dangerous weaponry.

I ask him about the bombing of Colombo on October 22, 1984.

"What happened? What's the story?" I ask. I'm trying to get to my core question. I want him to make me understand what motivates a terrorist to kill people and, even more troubling, how a terrorist justifies it.

"Technically, I was in charge of that incident. Activities were carried out with my second in command, with whom I was in constant communication. We realized that the war was not producing the desired effect. We wanted the government to negotiate, and they were ignoring this call. We set up a dialogue between the parties, and there was an agreement that the conflict should be taken to the door of the parliament. At this point, our conflict had become page-nine news. Things were going almost normally in the south. We realized that we needed to make the ruling class and the bureaucrats feel the pressure and tension of the war. We needed to make them listen to our grievances.

"With this in mind, we drew up an action plan. We suggested to the general command, the GC, that it should be S&S—sabotage and subversion—to bring about a start to this with a bang, so to speak. A lot of thought was given to selecting the targets. We selected the targets that would have minimum casualties. I was in Colombo at great risk, and the team here sanctioned locations in which, over a span of three hours, we would have different well-timed explosions. These would be symbolic explosions that would be designed to create enough panic and, well, terror to make the government realize that they were not as powerful as they thought.

"I believe it was the continuation of this strategy that enabled India to persuade Colombo to return to the negotiating table. This was what really started the talks. And from then, the government began to listen. The bombs in Colombo had a cumulative effect: 'If you don't deal with us now, then there will be a real problem.'"

So it was evident that terrorism was working. The detonations had of course drawn not only attention but also each of the important parties needed to negotiate. The goal of the terrorism was to generate conversation.

"How did you determine the locations?" I ask.

"Preferably a location would be near security or military installations. Two, it should be in the vicinity of a lot of public movement, just in the vicinity, but we did not want to affect the public. We wanted to create public attention. We hit commuter centers, for example, where there was a lot of movement. And then it should be spread out in such a pattern that, while they were dealing with an explosion in south Colombo, there was a bomb going off in north Colombo. They literally didn't have time to deal with it. By the fourth bomb, they didn't have enough people to deal with it. I think this was the message: 'Things are going to get worse. We cannot be ignored.' The selection of targets minimized casualties, so it was clear that this was not an act of revenge. We wanted to highlight the weakness of the civic structure."

"And what," I ask him, "do you interpret the messages of September 11, 2001, to be? It was similar in its ability to draw public attention, but it was also different because that was intended to maximize casualties. What do you think Al Qaeda was saying?"

"This isn't a political message. It's past that. It's a message of revenge. The only message is 'We can also show our destructive capabilities. The U.S. homeland is not safe.' And I think that it was intended to show the pain and frustration of the Arab brethren who were going through with that act.

"They wanted to point out that the Americans are insulated, that all that matters is their 'American way of life' and their living standards. Americans are not paying attention to the pain in the rest of the world. For the

Americans, the end justifies the means. They do not care. But they hypocritically hold a high ground—a moral high ground—and cause the deaths of thousands of people to sustain their quality of life.

"This will be the end of the [American] way of life. It may mark the collapse of their regime, and it's a target that [Al Qaeda] has had. That is the world they see. But now, with Iraq, it will take decades for America to rebuild her past reputation."

He pauses for a moment and takes a sip of tea.

"What could Sri Lanka have done fifty years ago to avoid all of the problems here? They should have stuck to what they said. Instead, it was too little, too late. There were pacts that were signed but not followed.

"See, when you become a superpower, the arrogance with which you exercise that power should be considered. All the great empires and all the great powers of the world have perished because of arrogance."

Rajee died, apparently of a heart attack, in Colombo on January 10, 2005. Since then, Rajee's son, Thirumal Thirunesan, or Nesan Thirunesan, has ordered that his death be investigated as a murder by the LTTE.

I met with Shankar Rajee three times during my visits to Colombo, and our final meeting was in a small café. The week before, I'd e-mailed him the transcript of the interview to allow him to make any necessary changes or corrections. He looked good when we spoke, and he seemed engaged in his life. His last sentence to me had to do with his family and how much he cared about them. It was a touching moment somehow, and in the time we spent together he impressed me as a man who was articulate and compassionate, with a wry sense of humor despite his time in refugee camps, prisons, and Lebanese training camps.

He was one of the founders of the Sri Lankan Tamil militant movement, a primary witness who'd fought with, but mostly against, the LTTE. During the final years of his life he had largely withdrawn from the spotlight, splitting his time between Chennai in Tamil Nadu, India, where his mother lived, and Colombo, where he worked as an agricultural consultant.

Terrorist? He said so himself, but such a personality in a terrorist was not what I'd expected to find.

The Mahout of Social Services

Douglas Devananda (center) and colleagues, Colombo, Sri Lanka

I step out of the cab and look at the leaves overhead. It's a nice little neighborhood, green, with a few three- and four-story reddish-brick old-school buildings sagging out over the street. A clothesline hangs from the curved trellis of one of the structures. My cab drives off and some kids kick a ball past me. One of them throws a handful of leaves that fall at my feet, and they scream. The trees are dense here. I check the address scrawled by Shankar Rajee in my hand.

This building in front of me has a big silver wall. No, it's a huge metal garage door . . . framed by two towers. No, wait: It's a metal garage door, framed by two towers, with big bearded men holding machine guns glaring down at me from inside their nests in the turrets. The men are wearing identical hats. The metal garage door has a little eye slit in it. This is goddamn medieval.

I have to take my eyes off the guys with the guns so I don't trip over the kids, who are running around my legs again. Rajee suggested I come here and was kind enough to make a phone call. He handed me the phone, I spoke to the secretary, and two hours later I'm here in front of this massive metal fortress. If you're Douglas Devananda, the commander of the Eelam People's Democratic Party (EPDP), and one of the most-hunted people on the island, you need a spread like this.

Devananda grew up in Jaffna in a tough family of hardworking Marxists, union leaders, and fast-talking intellectuals. As a teenager in a poor country where serious discussions about ethnic cleansing and labor ideologies were the typical dinner-table conversations, he was influenced by his father's political views. In 1974, at the age of seventeen, he traveled to Colombo and found himself wading through the volatile swamps of anti-Tamil discrimination. Nearly killed in various street fights and even riots, he also faced the same problem that Shankar Rajee faced: If he lived long enough in Colombo to eek out an education, it would receive demerits based on his Tamil background. A few years later he became a founding member of the Eelam People's Revolutionary Liberation Front (EPRLF). Thus began the young militant's strange career.

Slowly walking up to the door, I stand in front of the peephole for a second, expecting it to slide open. It doesn't, so I look up at the two machine-gun fellows overhead. They are both craning over a bit, keeping their hawkish eyes on me. One of them nods over his shoulder to someone on the other side of the wall. The little gate at eye level still doesn't open, so I figure they're waiting for me to ask to come in. I give a single one-knuckle rap, just to say, officially, "I know you know I'm here." The peephole slides open and a yellowish eyeball glares at me. This makes me feel like saluting, so I hold my pen up next to my own eye, ballpoint in the air, to declare my weaponry. Raising an eyebrow, I feel tugged between pathetic and proud to have a pen for a gun. The door unbolts with a raspy bang.

In 1978 Deva, as he is sometimes known, went to Lebanon to train with Fatah, as did Shankar Rajee and others. He trained for six months. Fatah ran the school, much as they did in Rajee's experience. Devananda didn't like it much. They made him wear his boots day and night, the food stank, the juice was stale, and they weren't allowed to leave the camp without an escort. But he got the training he wanted, and he returned to Sri Lanka to change things with the new tools he'd acquired from the PLO's largest faction.

The door slowly slides open, small wheels grinding over what look to be real railroad tracks, and I step into an open courtyard where some five or six guns are pointing at me. They've got me surrounded. Still holding my pen near my temple, I move real slowly as I step into this rather spooky party, and two more large bearded hawks of men, completely kitted out in body armor and grenades, shuffle toward me, kind of crouching, hands forward like they're each pushing invisible beach balls through the air toward my stomach. I decide it's safest to stand there with my pen at my temple.

By 1985, in southern India, Douglas Devananda was at the depths of his wildness. He was living in the jungle, buying and selling arms, starting and quitting militant groups, and he had become a senior leader of the LTTE. He founded the EPRLF, which stayed together until 1991, but it was in 1987 that Devananda had a change of heart and a massive falling-out with Prabhakaran and the rest of the LTTE elite.

Now that I've been thoroughly searched, I'm led into the building—two guards in front, six in back—down a short windowless passage, past a desk, and to a small remote-controlled door. No one touches it; we just stand there. About twenty seconds pass and I decide I can put my pen back in my pocket. The door clicks and something on the other side hisses.

By June 1986, EPRLF, PLOTE, EROS, and LTTE (as well as others) had become something of a superhero team, fighting side by side, guns ablaze, racking up one victory after the next. Their adventures included storming forts, fighting off Sri Lankan army helicopter raids, and selling pickles and stamps when they couldn't find a jeweler to knock off for some extra cash for ammunition. The militant groups made a fierce and pragmatic team, and it appeared as if this would be the power formation that would establish the state in the north. Administrative offices that shared power began to form, and the rivalry seemed to balance the collaboration. But their bond disintegrated under the strain of a single important question: "Which comes first: military strength or political strength?" The answer to this critical question would determine the island's future.

We step through the door, and in front of the two guards leading the way is a small fountain. Walking around the little pool, I see large koi, all orange-and-white spots, snuffling around the bottom like aquatic swine. Lily pads float on the pool, with water sprinkling in from the side. A guard mumbles something to a woman, and she writes something down, and we all slowly walk forward down the passageway.

On November 1, 1986, in Madras, members of the EPRLF got into a fistfight with some locals. An AK-47 was fired in an attempt to cool things down, a man was shot, and the Madras crowd reacted violently. Devananda, then the head of EPRLF military operations, and his cadre jumped on a roof and faded back into the jungles of India. The next day, Madras newspapers were infuriated by the presence of militants with automated weaponry in their town, despite official government assurances that they weren't there. Three days later, at 4:00 AM, Indian commandos raided thirty-four of the militants' training camps, confiscating antiaircraft weapons, some very familiar-looking AK-47s, revolvers, and grenades. Members of the PLOT, the EROS, the EPRLF, and the LTTE were taken into custody, photographed, and fingerprinted. The next day they were sent home. The Indian government then had to admit that it had, in fact, known of these groups—otherwise it could never have rounded them up so quickly. The LTTE, in a moment of genius, went on a hunger strike, claiming betrayal by the Indian government. This somehow, by means my Western mind cannot grasp, made the Indian government feel bad enough not only to give the LTTE back the confiscated weapons, but also many of the weapons that had been confiscated from the other groups as well.

The seven of us shuffle down a series of steps

and enter what seems to be the sanctum sanctorum of the EPDP headquarters: a windowless room painted a pus yellow and holding four or five large desks covered with papers, a large map of Sri Lanka on the wall to my left, a counter with some coffee and a couple of plates of half-eaten dahl, a smell of perfume, and a sitar leaning up against the wall. Where is Miss Moneypenny? Where is M? I start to mull the possibility that this may be the home of a very sick mind, and, as if on rehearsed cue, here is Devananda, sitting casually on a desk, one foot on the floor, talking with a man who is seated at another desk. He's tall with a large beard, bespectacled, wearing a nicely pressed white shirt with starched collars and short sleeves. He's charismatic, broad-shouldered, and younger than I had expected.

The December after the fight in Madras, in 1986, the same question continued to plague the militants: "Which comes first: military strength or political strength?" The LTTE, newly possessed of most of the weaponry, summarily answered this question by shooting members of other groups and, stating that they were in charge of all the militant groups, rounding up fifteen PLOTE soldiers under the pretext that they were harassing Muslims. The PLOTE withdrew from Jaffna. The EROS did as well. The EPRLF was the last faction of militants preventing Prabhakaran and the LTTE from dominating the north of the island as well as the Tamil militant movement in general. Having seen enough inter-Tamil fighting, the EPRLF brought recent events to public attention. Tamils across the island were shocked to learn that more than two dozen Tamil militants had been killed by the LTTE. The LTTE was outraged. On December 13, 1986, the EPRLF was attacked by the LTTE and almost half of its military branch was killed. But Devananda escaped, fading into the jungle, and, knowing the LTTE's inner workings—who was in charge, how they functioned, and what they needed to survive—became the LTTE's primary Tamil target. I sit down to wait on a posh leather sofa and am handed soda crackers and a Coke. I am also handed a packet of paper. The guards stand behind me and it makes my scalp tense. The packet has a nice cover with an intro page and a couple of paragraphs. The next page is a dark black photocopy of Devananda's CV, then on the next page a couple more CVs of people he is working with at the EPDP, then after that is an overview of his organization and a statement of their goals. It's reminiscent of Silicon Valley investment brochures. A media packet was not what I'd expected to find when I walked through the medieval front door. Militarized and mediated: That is Devananda. That is terrorism.

In a 2007 terror report, the U.S. State Department points out that Devananda has survived at least eleven assassination attempts, most by the LTTE.[1] There was the day when the LTTE drove by his Havelock Road residence in Colombo and opened fire from the van, killing four of his bodyguards.[2] There was the day in June, 2004, in Kalutara Prison, when Devananda was invited by four prisoners to give a lecture on his own life in prison and, on his arrival, was attacked. One of his attackers drove an iron rod, a piece of rebar, into his skull. Fortunately the Sri Lankan medical personnel on duty saved him (but not his eye). One of the attacking prisoners, Kandasamy Lingeswaran, was a member of a prisoner-exchange program that Devananda himself had initiated as a means of building examples of forgiveness

---

1. "Country Reports on Terrorism 2007,"
    http://www.state.gov/s/ct/rls/crt/2007/103709.htm.
2. Those guards were, for heroism's mention, Balan Selvakumar (from Vavuniya), Asaipillai Mohanadas (Jaffna), Uthayakumar Krishnapillai (Mullaithevu), and Arasanth Uthayananth (Trincomalee).

between Tamils and Sinhalese. Then there was another assassination attempt, only about two weeks after his prison run-in, when Devananda was at the Hindu Affairs Ministry on Galle Road and a rather sketchy woman who refused to submit to a security search detonated a suicide pack she had under her sari, killing four policemen and injuring eleven others.

Devananda stands up from the desk he's been sitting on and the man he was talking with also stands up. A third man joins them. As they walk across the office they strike me as an odd trio. Flanked by one squat, squishy man in a blue shirt and another who is mildly chinless, Devananda seems all the more healthy and charismatic. In any case, they all seem quite nice and friendly and introduce themselves, and as soon as Devananda addresses me the gun toter behind me lets out a small sigh and disappears. All is again calm in James Bond land. We sit down at his desk and niceties are exchanged. At this point he asks me if I would like more crackers, and I am about to say no, thank you, when I am reminded that this is how an elephant is trained.

After I switch on my recorder, I ask him my opening question: "How are Tamils different from Sinhalese?"

His answer is quick. "We are a distinct nationality."

It seems significant that he has first noted the nationality, not the ethnicity, race, or culture. His fight has been a fight of nationalism.

He continues, "We have a different language, culture, and way of life. We also have equal rights and privileges, such as privileges to education and financial facilities."

"You seem to indicate that the nationality is founded on the language and culture." And with Devananda's nod I continue, "So where does the culture come from?"

"From the language, and it hinges on the government. The federal government has been a source of discrimination against Tamils since 1947. As far as the peace process goes, we feel that we are no longer holding talks with the government. Every time the peace negotiations have failed, if there is one sector to blame in all talks, LTTE should shoulder that blame. They are not genuine. They are not interested in changing. From the beginning, they have said they would not change. Prabhakaran uses violence as negotiation. LTTE has not given up violence."

Seeing that Devananda is a politician adept at steering conversations, I go with him.

"Why not?"

"The killings continue," he replies. "They bump off whoever is opposed to them, and they even have their own police and judicial offices. People are tried, but they take other people from state-controlled areas as well."

"So what's the solution?"

"The war in Sri Lanka has continued for decades. A generation of Sri Lankans have been raised in a war-torn environment. Eight hundred thousand Tamils have left the country because of fear or economic reasons. Five hundred thousand Tamils are displaced internally, and the majority of the children born in the north and east are undernourished. No responsible party can be blind to these problems. We have prepared a program to address all these problems faced by the Tamil people in parallel with a program of political resolution of the ethnic problem. On the political front, we are working towards autonomy for a single region comprising the northern and eastern provinces, through devolution of powers, and the sharing of power at the center."

Despite his reckless beginning, Devananda gave up the military path in 1987 and is the only Tamil politician from Jaffna to have reached the rank of senior minister. Having occupied the cabinet post for more than a decade, he's maintained good relations with three Sri Lankan presidents: Premadasa, Kumaratunga, and Rajapaksa. Devananda is now the minister of social services. His path from militant to politician has gained him both the hatred of many people and the love of many people, and his travels have taught him the wily art of politics. But, really, he's a mahout. He's a terrorist gone politician—one adept at training elephants.

Original coat of arms, Dutch colony of Ceylon

Chapter Four:
Kandy

"A jug fills drop by drop."
— Traditional Buddhist saying

The Bomb of the
Temple of the Tooth

Entrance to Temple of the Tooth, Kandy, Sri Lanka

Kandy is high-caste. It's commonly said that the race here is superior. In this world where caste runs the show, the Kandyan Sinhalese are often considered, by the Sinhalese in particular, better bred, clearer featured, smarter, and more cultured.

The notion has more to do with the legacy of the British Empire than with Singhalese blood. The story is that at the turn of the nineteenth century, the queen's government set up a rather complicated competition between two agricultural castes, the Govigama and the Karava, each of which had ambitions to move up the sociopolitical ladder. Local British governors told both groups that the queen herself had demanded a competition to see who could produce more crops over a period of two years. When the Govigama, by virtue of living at a higher and more fertile elevation, handed over a few more dozen pounds of food, the queen gave a noble nod of the head to the victor.

Having apparently won the queen's blessing, the Govigama then set about convincing the rest of the island that being from a higher elevation also elevated your caste. The messaging stuck for a couple of centuries. During that time the mountaintop town of Kandy grew into Sri Lanka's capital and cultural center. I suspect much of it had to do with British governors coming up with creative excuses and inventive means to milk the locals for exports that could be sold back in London, but whatever the case, the idea that people from Kandy are from a higher caste is solidly embedded in Sinhalese mentality.

I decided to go see the place. Getting there presented something of a problem, since I would normally hitchhike. But Sri Lanka has a very different relationship with the car than, say, Germany or the United States. Even though Sri Lanka is one of the most densely populated countries in the world, Sri Lankans have fewer cars per capita, as well. So I rented a motorcycle.

I'm normally a rice-rocket kind of guy, but this is not the place for a low-slung and high-tech piece of equipment. I'll be driving on dirt roads more often than not, across rice fields, perhaps. If there are gunshots and no road, I might have to make a creative exit. I need something all-terrain, so I find a small dirt bike, a little Honda 250 trail bike that will get me across ditches, through streams, and over the potholes that, along with bomb craters, broken glass, rubble, and rebar, make up the ground plane of most war theaters.

The goal is to go north into Kandy, to see the Temple of the Tooth that the LTTE bombed. From there I'll continue up to Jaffna via Kilinochchi to visit the war there, see what it is like, learn what the effects of it have been, talk with people I meet along the way, and see other small villages that are linked with the civil war—to go into the land the Tamils call their own. Once I hit the north end of the island, I'll turn the tip and angle back south to Colombo. I'm not sure what to expect, since most of northern Sri Lanka is still a hot war zone. I don't have much of a plan. But north is the direction to take, if I want to learn about what happened here and visit the terrorist breeding grounds.

The drive into Kandy is a pure winding and windy road of joy. Once I'm out of the city, I get used to driving on the left side of the road. It meanders through low-lying foothills and pockets of small villages. The countryside is green and dense with strange birds orbiting thick leaves and a couple of elephants walking by and smiling people waving, all a blur of bright color and broad smiles as I try my best to keep from getting hit by oncoming traffic.

At first I think, "Oh, how nice! Look at the beautiful people waving. Sri Lankans are so friendly!" And, yes, the Sri Lankans I have met have been friendly. But then it occurs to me that not everyone stands on the side of the road and smiles and waves. Something is peculiar here. Along the winding mountain curves, I see literally thousands of people on the side of the road. They're carrying food and water, building houses, sitting on the front porch with a glass of arrack and a hound dog. But these people are not smiling and waving, though they're certainly watching me. They're giving me the big bug eye. Everyone stops to stare at the white guy. I stand out like an Afro at a rodeo. No, it's far more extreme than that. I stand out like a minotaur with an Afro at a rodeo. Cricket games stop, conversations halt, cars hit their brakes, and people run to doorways to get an eyeful of the ghost flying through town.

Race has a strange role everywhere in the world, but here in Sri Lanka it takes on mortal importance—such importance that a civil war is being waged over it.

But the curves and the cradles of the road ride well, and the smells and scents of old Ceylon blow around my head. And while the traffic is aggressive, surging rivers of cars and lorries and carts and motorcycles, the ride is beautiful. After some four or five hours of flight and fright, I arrive at the gates of an ancient city named Kandy.

It is as precious as a fairy tale. The city is a crown on the highest mountain. In the middle of the town is a glassy lake. In the middle of the glassy lake is a perfect little island. In the middle of that tiny island is an ornate and curious little hut, painted bright red and gold, with a slanted roof and frilly gables where kings would store secrets, such as prisoners, fortunes, and harems. It's mythic. Pink petals fall from the trees and cover the delicately cracked sidewalks. The city is a gentle silk princess resting on a mountain bed of blossoms. This is the public side of Kandy, her famous side, and her most ancient and elegant angle.

But between the flowers and the gold-painted gables, I begin to see, even from the blur of the motorcycle, the smaller, meaner faces of Kandy: the bluish sewage water drooling from a neglected house, the spiked gates, the gilded paths for tourists that are so different from the sidewalks the Kandyans themselves use. There are those familiar, hawkish eyes of poverty staring out at me from grass huts. I almost run over a dog as I look back, hypnotized from the wealthy seat of my motorcycle. The damn gangly dogs are everywhere—sitting in gutters, furiously scratching their mangy necks, trotting across the road in front of honking cars, nosing around in trash. The Sri Lankans have no idea what to do with their dogs.

The windows of the city are barred like prison cells. I decide that Kandy, despite being a princess, is also a criminal. She'll pick the pocket of the tourist who has come to ogle at her gussied-up corset of flowers. As in the towns down south, which I'd passed on my way up, of Unawatuna, Midigama, or, most of all, Hikkaduwa, the criminals follow the tourists. The locals despise the differences they're forced to feel and so crime takes its place at the table of wealth.

Maybe Kandy is just a normal mountain crime town with a fairy-tale tourism center tucked into its navel. I swerve around another dog on the road. Maybe this happens to all great fables: They eat themselves and turn mean.

To my right, a pack of forty sand-colored cats are leaping along the terracotta rooftops, jumping fast from one building to another. I do a double-take and realize that this herd of galloping cats all have human faces—mean little dark faces of tiny men and frowning women with babies on their backs.

As I brake, the tribe of forty macaque monkeys slow their gallop across the gables and eye me, also, with disturbingly identical curiosity.

Monkey see, monkey stop. I want a closer look, and so do they. I put the kickstand of the motorcycle down, hop a small gutter, dodge a few cars, and walk underneath the little band. Eighty or ninety black eyes, piggish and mean, ogle back at me. Mothers with babies dangling from their bellies, matted-up and greasy little things, eye me with suspicion and surprise. Certainly they've seen people before, so, like the dogs that bark at me, they too must notice my skin color. Even the infants have question marks in their eyes. A couple of granddaddies itch fleas, and one of them loosely holds a flower in his mouth while another one pulls at his pecker. I'm looking at a mobile village, it's looking at me, and we both find the reflection disturbing.

A large male pounces off the roof, saunters along a fence, hops onto a wire, and tightropes his way directly above me. His balance is perfect, far better than any Olympic gymnast's. He is as comfortable on a draped telephone wire as I am standing on the sidewalk. But something weird is going on. I can't tell if it's because I'm looking at him that he's looking at me, but we have each other's undivided attention.

He's a little man, with filthy fingers and suspicious eyes rimmed pink with hatred. He's got an "I'm gonna kick your ass" saunter, dirty and vicious. He's been eating trash and pulling girls' hair for his entire miserable life. He has sharp little pointy black ears, like a diseased imp. But the humanity of his face isn't a mistake; he's my relation, all right. His expression isn't a mistake, either: He doesn't like me. I don't like him much, either. He reacts first. The hair on the top of his head moves back, his ears tighten, and his teeth roll out from under his lips in a gummy, macabre, grimy grin of aggression. He'd make a four-armed midget carrying switchblades and machine guns look cute.

He hunches down, tightens his shoulders, and lets loose with a slobbery hiss that sounds more like it came out of his back end than his front. He's about to jump on my forehead and tear my face off.

Monkeys are little thugs. They're bullies and thieves and dumpster divers. It occurs to me that the bars on the windows in Kandy have been installed not because of human criminals but because of monkey criminals. They're there to keep the shitty little bastards from wrecking everyone's homes. Kandy has its problems, but, in the larger perspective, these monkeys remind me that we humans are maybe okay, evolving as we are. People are healthier than monkeys. We're cleaner. We have things like language, art, and history. We're nicer. Sure, we make civil wars from time to time, but at least we can't hiss like that anymore.

Since I've come to Kandy to see the Temple of the Tooth, I leave Mister Hissy Fit on the wire and turn the bike toward our human version of civilization. I park my bike, throw my bag over my shoulder, and wade through the swamp of tuk-tuks, people, bicycles, and cows, past all the vendors selling eats, through the market of spice sellers, around the beggars and businessmen, across a small plaza where a Domino's and Burger King advertise familiar brands in an unfamiliar language, and over to the Dalada Maligawa, or the Temple of the Tooth of the Buddha.

At the entryway of the temple, I'm greeted by a man named Naranj Wijeera, the temple's custodian. We take off our shoes and walk up some stairs together.

He's a little bald on top and has a round face with chubby cheeks. He's Sinhalese, he points out, and he's a Kandy resident. Which is to say he's of clarified caste, no question about it. But the reason I want to talk with him is because he was at the temple the day the bomb went off.

It all started in the hills some distance away, on a small road through the jungle, in 1983. A school bus full of young Buddhist monks was slowly lurching its way down a hillside. Everyone inside wore the traditional saffron robes and had the neatly shaved heads. Some of them carried parasols. Most of the monks inside were teenagers—disciples who had been sponsored to take on the public honor and duty of studying Buddhism and who had dedicated their lives to the philosophy. A truck stopped in the middle of the road, and the bus was forced to hit the brakes.

Ten hours later, in the morning sun, the newspaper photographers found the thirteen young monks neatly lined up next to the bus. Their shaved heads now had bullet holes in them, and their saffron robes were a darker shade of red. They had been mutilated with machetes.

The Buddhists—Sinhalese and otherwise—were outraged. The LTTE claimed responsibility. Since most Sinhalese are Buddhist, it was considered a racial rather than religious attack. This stirred the hornets' nest, and Colombo was on the verge of breaking out into anti-Tamil riots again.

In 1983, the country had been convulsed with riots, each of which motivated counter-riots. However, just before this shooting there had been a short period of peace, and the intent of the shooting was clear to anyone who gave it some thought. The obvious intent was to generate another riot. Another riot in Colombo would bolster the terrorists' cause, helping them in the long run and bringing them media attention. Maintaining their martyrdom required the LTTE to incite the supposed oppressor. The LTTE gambled that the reaction to their act would be more extreme than the act itself. The end result would be to paint the Sinhalese as the villains.

But while Colombo was tense, it didn't reply to the violence with violence. As General Karunaratne had put it, the popular conclusion was "These are not Tamils; these are terrorists." This fouled up the terrorists' plans. So the members of the LTTE, not getting the response they wanted, went to Anuradhapura. They walked up the path to the Jaya Sri Maha Bodhi, a fig tree that was brought as a gift from India and planted in 250 BC by King Devanampiyatissa. This bo tree is one of the key relics of Sri Lanka's Mahavihara Buddhism tradition. It is said that the tree is sprouted from a branch of the tree that the Buddha sat under when he achieved enlightenment, and so thousands of Sri Lankans visit the tree each year, on a kind of pilgrimage. The Tamil Tigers showed up one afternoon at this temple with machine guns and sprayed bullets into the tree and into the backs of those unlucky worshipers meditating beneath it.

By now, the would-be rioters in Colombo were confused. How could they respond when their response would certainly be used against them? It was clear the LTTE wanted more rioting, but that would only support the LTTE's cause, proving that the Sinhalese were as bloodthirsty, merciless, and unfair as the LTTE wanted them to appear. On the other hand, how could they not do something? The LTTE had to be stopped, and physical force was clearly the only thing that would do it.

Then things got exceptional: Several days passed, and the LTTE carried out a third assault on a third symbol of national pride.

Naranj Wijeera and I are standing on a small bridge that crosses a moat. It leads into the most sacred Buddhist shrine in Sri Lanka. He squats down and puts his fingers on the floor of the bridge. Families, tourists, monks, and photographers pour past us. People walk by in socks or bare feet, their shoes left out front.

"See this?" he asks. I nod. It looks like marble. The clean white stone has been carefully hand carved with decoration and inlays.

"Okay, now come and look at this." He leads me up some stairs, down a hallway, and around a corner into another hallway. It's the entrance of the central chamber. Now he puts his fingers on the wall: "Look here." This is the same kind of marble as outside, but immediately next to it is an older, darker marble that is cracked and fissured. It is where the rebuilding of the temple stopped after the bomb was detonated. In the last twenty years, over fifty thousand tons of new marble have been carried into this old temple.

We walk back out to the entrance and stand again on the bridge. Naranj waves an arm at the bottom of the stairs, where a crowd of about fifty people mills. I can see seven or eight temple guards. Beyond them, on the main road, a three-meter-tall spiked gate made of metal bars is set up on an elaborate wheeled transport mechanism. Approximately fifteen or twenty guards stand out there, automatic weapons across their vests. The entire temple perimeter is a secure compound. A guard, far away, waves back.

In 1998, war had broken out in the north and east, but despite that there were only a couple of guards at the temple, since terrorist attacks were simply not expected there. At six o'clock in the morning of the twenty-fifth of January, a white pickup truck slowly maneuvered through a small crowd out in front of the temple. There was nothing suspicious about it to the two guards on duty.

But the truck looked a little different to a woman working there at the time. As a guard, she was sensitive to what kinds of people visited the temple and when. As a Sinhalese, she was sensitive to the riots and, most of all, to the attacks that had taken place in the weeks before. When the beat-up white pickup truck stopped in front of the driveway and didn't have any old people or monks inside, but instead three very healthy-looking Tamils dressed in quasimilitary uniforms and small necklaces, she ran to close the iron security gate. But the passengers whipped out handguns and rushed her. The gate closed, several bullets went through her, and the truck stopped short. People who had heard the gunfire turned as a man in the truck hit a detonation switch, igniting 250 kilograms (about 550 pounds) of dynamite. A bolt of lightning crawled through the building's foundation, cracked the base of the walls, bent around the corner, split the stairs up the middle, dug lines into the ramparts, and shook the building's roof so hard that tiles rained into the newly expanded moat below. The cracking from the truck bomb continued into the inner areas of the temple, splintering the foundations of buildings that had been resting there for over thirteen hundred years. People fell to the ground from the impact of the blast, and many of them never got up.

After this third attack, the public alternated between screaming for retribution, silently chewing their fingernails off, and publicly demanding that the government do something, all the while knowing another riot was not the answer. The papers were guarded, the government held its tongue, and everyone knew who had done it and why.

Despite what came after, this was a key moment in the cycle out of terrorism for Sri Lanka. Somehow the public chose patience instead of terror. Symbolic terrorism is nurtured by a violent response. Sri Lankans chose to let it lay still.

The LTTE's goal had been to gain attention by destroying public symbols. But Sri Lanka knew that, like Gandhi, it had to wait and endure the beatings. Sri Lanka knew that things could get worse.

And they did.

The Couple with Broken Glass and Good Karma

The good-karma couple, Kandy, Sri Lanka

This man's English is better than mine. He wears a snappy corduroy cap and a mint green pressed chemise. He habitually licks his lips in a genuinely happy manner as he shows me the construction he's doing on his house and the hotel that he's built behind it. He is so refined and proper that he seems gay. But if he is, he also has a wife, who's also weirdly talkative and chirpy, prim to a doll-like point, yet still round and buttery. She dresses in two white gauzy shirts with delicate silver necklaces and earrings, the jewelry as copious and as sparkling as her smiles. Constantly smiling, then nodding at each other, then giggling, they invite me into their house. It is immaculate. They run a hotel in Kandy and have lived here for over fifty years.

I don't understand why they're so happy, but I'm eager to try the tea they offer. Of course it's time for afternoon tea.

I unlace my muddy boots, and we walk into the house. Of course there are doilies everywhere; little blue and pink paintings of puppies; tchotchkes in glass, tchotchkes in silver; little harps that can be played but never will be; tiny animal figurines carved out of at least fifteen different kinds of wood, as well as onyx and ivory; decorative candles; sculptures of Ganesh; enough vases to start a floristry; and little napkins kept neatly in little holders, all in line with the edges of the tables on which they rest. Nothing, save for the table and chairs, seems useful. But it all seems beautiful in the way that figure skating seems like a sport, or how Mae West would have lived if she hadn't been so famous, only richer.

"Oh yes, oh yes," the woman nods, her eyes wide. "It was terrible, terrible, like thunder you know. Like thunder, wasn't it?" And she looks at her husband, who stops smiling but doesn't stop nodding. They remember, together, that morning in 1998.

"We knew right away what it was. There had been the other terrorist attacks, the shootings, you know, and so when we heard this happen, we knew right away what it was. Even though it was, what . . . ?" and she looks at her husband again, who is still nodding, then continues, "three kilometers away?"

He turns and looks out the window into the broad valley below, where some herons slowly flap through the afternoon sunlight. Mist drifts from the jungle below.

"The birds all flew up, I remember seeing that, and then I remember the windows broke, and glass fell everywhere," and she waves both arms toward the floor, "all around here . . . and here."

"And over there, too!" her husband pipes. "The dishes all fell off of the counters, there, and, oh, these tiles we had just put on fell off the roof."

There is a pause, then they both, as if rehearsed, say in unison, "Oh! Oh, it was horrible!"

Then they begin to smile at me, now silent, with the word "horrible" hanging in the air. I take a sip of tea. They are so happy, even a tragedy cannot dislodge them. They are so happy-go-lucky, so sri, that even a bomb in their village will not cause them to respond with anger and hatred. How can they be so happy, living through such things? Is it just time? Is it just that these are the happy days, nearly a decade later, sitting and sipping tea and looking back at The Day? Sniffing around, hoping to uncover some insight into the public opinion that kept the rioting and the violence from happening, I ask them what they thought afterward. How did such a couple respond?

"Well," he says, "we thought at the time, 'Let's just wait and see. These terrorists have already done damage, and perhaps they will do more, but we need to wait and see.' That was what we thought, you know. Action is not always needed."

The woman nods and the man continues.

"LTTE didn't get what they wanted. Much of it has to do with karma. They have not come back, and now things are getting better."

They may be right. Maybe they have good karma because they waited. After all, this idea of karma is an old one and a popular favorite. So perhaps, like the evolution of a crocodile or a shark, it has stood the test of time. Karma. Happiness. Bombs. Smiles. Tea.

I take another sip.

In the eyes of this outsider, Asia is an illegible mystery, like a faucet that you turn, but instead of water, music flows out the tap, visible, physically tangible music that pools in your hand and becomes a proof of an alternate universe where all the rules of physics and the soul are different.

Might, we are taught, makes right. Law, we are told, needs enforcement. But here they are, this cheeky couple, smiling proof of the power of karma.

Buddha statue, between Kandy and Sigirya, Sri Lanka

Chapter Five: Sigiriya

ஆழம் பார்க்காமல் காலை விடாதே

("Don't jump in the river before you know the depth.")
—Tamil proverb

Karma, Part I:
The King Who Drowned in the Earth

View of the rock, Sigiriya, Sri Lanka

Karma is everywhere in Sri Lanka. It is a concept held dear by both Buddhists and Hindus. There's also this concept of dharma, which is a righteous path, a holy direction, and can be interpreted to mean "that which keeps us going" or "that which supports us in our journey."

My dharma is, as I mentioned, rented. It's a Honda XLR 250R Baja trail bike. It's a single-cylinder four-stroke with a little chain drive that I can flip fast through its six gears. Hopping fast over the bumps, the thing weighs only about one hundred kilograms, and if I'm feeling punk (and nobody's watching) I can pull a short wheelie on it. It claims to be air cooled, but I don't understand how that can possibly be a functioning feature here in this hot weather.

I love my hot dharma.

Pulling over, I slow it down, put my left foot on the asphalt and feel the twenty-eight-horsepower engine letting heat off near my left calf. Swinging my other leg over the seat, I pull off my bandana and stop to take a look around as my flesh gradually reattaches itself to my bones.

The road north, so far, has been a collage of blurred dapples of orange and green, chalk-white temples, proud little farms, waving people on bicycles, lorries overloaded with hay, and an elephant or two. Hanging over it all, the sky is a gentle robin's-egg blue (not that hard blue, up high, like in New Mexico or the Italian Alps, but a gentle, creamy blue).

On the horizon, framed by that blue, is an orange block of stone. It is shaped like a gargantuan elephant— one that has just been killed, head on the ground: a god-elephant, big as a mountain. I've arrived at the Sigiriya rock citadel. It's round and lumpy and as old as the Mahavamsa, the ancient epic poem that tells the tales of the kings of Sri Lanka.

Once upon a time, over thirteen hundred years ago (long before Dutch traders, English imperialism, and Portuguese clipper ships), there was a Sinhalese boy-king named Dhatusena. He and his family lived west of the capital because a Tamil king named Pandu had recently invaded the country and had exiled the royal families. Since it seemed that Dhatusena would never be king, he became a monk. It was said that one day while he was meditating at the foot of a tree, it began to rain. A king cobra fell from the tree and covered Dhatusena's head with its hood, protecting him from the rain—the same thing that had happened to the Buddha. A priest who saw this, one of Dhatusena's enemies, became jealous of the omen and apparently shoveled a good deal of dirt and rubble on him, disturbing his meditation and scaring off the benevolent cobra. It was whispered that the cobra's presence was an omen and that Dhatusena's death would be like his life. Karma works like this.

Pandu was very nervous about this. If Dhatusena were an incarnation of the Buddha, Pandu would lose his new power. So Pandu sent an assassin to murder Dhatusena. But that night the monks in Dhatusena's temple dreamed about the threat before the assassin arrived, and they shuttled him out of the temple early in the morning. That afternoon, the envoy sent to kill Dhatusena couldn't find him and returned to Pandu with news that Dhatusena was missing.

Dhatusena decided that if the cobra wanted to shield him and Pandu wanted to murder him, a great destiny must be in his future. So he hid in a tent in the hills with some friends and swore that he would reclaim the country from the Tamils. Over the following sixteen years, he gathered an army and planned.

When he returned, he killed Pandu, then he killed the Tamils who were living in Sri Lanka, then he killed any Sinhalese who had intermarried or invested in the Tamil kingdom. Once these things were done and the government was changed, he turned his attention to other concerns. He wrecked all the Hindu kovils, built new Buddhist temples, and reinstated Buddhism as the national religion. Then he got to work on more pragmatic items, and began repairing the irrigation tanks of the island.

The Tamils who had been driven out believed, as they do today, that the island was Tamil property and it was the Sinhalese who were the invaders. Dhatusena would have to be deposed sooner or later, and they would reclaim the kingdom for their own.

One day, Dhatusena was supervising the improvement of the Kala Wewa water reservoir, walking along the edge, inspecting the work that had been done. One of his engineers came to report a problem: A monk had been meditating in their work zone for some days, and they couldn't make progress with him sitting there. They had tried to disturb him but could not. They had picked him up and moved him, even, but he did not come out of his deep meditation. So the workers, in a land where meditating monks could change the government, asked Dhatusena what to do. Dhatusena himself tried to disturb the holy man but got no response. So he ordered his builders to continue with the work as if he weren't there. They heaped dirt upon the meditating priest, burying him alive, sitting upright, into the shores of the Kala Wewa reservoir.

By now, Dhatusena was in the autumn of his life. He had two sons and a daughter. One of his sons, Moggallana, was the rightful heir to the throne. The other son, Kassapa, was illegitimate, and he would be lucky to be a minister when he grew up. Dhatusena's daughter, meanwhile, had married her cousin, Dhatusena's nephew. These things were all relatively normal for those days.

But neither the days nor the decisions were to remain normal. One day, for example, Dhatusena's daughter showed up with blood on her skirt, complaining that her husband (Dhatusena's nephew) had beat her. Dhatusena decided not to punish his nephew but, instead, to punish his own daughter, and he had her burned alive. Dhatusena's courtly decisions grew stranger as the days accumulated. He seemed to be losing his mind. Soon, fed up with it all and in a mood for revolt, Dhatusena's sons decided to overthrow him. Moggallana talked with Kassapa and proposed the idea, and the two went and imprisoned Dhatusena. But as soon as their father was in jail, Kassapa double-crossed his half-brother, and Moggallana was sent into exile—to the north, with the Tamils. The kingdom belonged to Kassapa.

The Sinhalese people didn't much care. They continued with their lives and weren't too upset by this, since Dhatusena had a rather nasty reputation, and many people thought they might be a bit safer if he was locked up. Moggallana, meanwhile, was furious about his exile, since he was the rightful heir to the throne. He traveled to India to gather an army of Tamil warlords who would lend a helping sword.

Kassapa sent his father into interrogations, hard ones, to learn where his wealth was hidden, but the old king wouldn't say a word to his bastard son. When Kassapa finally relented, the wily king said to him, "Take me to the Kalavapi River, and I'll show you the treasure."

When they arrived at the river, Dhatusena jumped in with all his clothes on, climbed out dripping wet, and said, "This is all the treasure I have!"

Was the king serious? Had his years of work on the

water reservoir been his main investment, and Kassapa just hadn't understood? Or was this some kind of joke?

Kassapa ordered his father to be killed. He had Dhatusena stripped naked and chained to a wall facing east. Then a wall was built around him, and he was buried alive.

Some say it was his karma for killing the monk.

Karma, Part II:
The King's Son
Who Drowned in the Earth

Just as his father had done before him, Moggallana was building his army.

Kassapa had become worried because his half-brother, Moggallana, would be able to gather a substantial army out of the north, and he would feel vindicated coming back to take the throne. But there seemed to be no other contenders. As long as he could keep Moggallana away, all would be well. The Sinhalese farmers and villagers offered no complaints, and since he had both money and an army, all he needed was a well-defended position.

He went to Sigiriya, an enormous boulder that rests on top of a hill.

Since he was trained as an architect when he was young, Kassapa went to work building a citadel on top of Sigiriya—not just your normal run-of-the-mill citadel, but a citadel with two purposes. First, to fend off an attack by Moggallana. Second, to give himself a luxurious lifestyle. Then, he decided, he would rule the country.

It took two decades and thousands of people. Workers began by splitting boulders in two by a process of heating and cooling. The boulders were cleanly cloven and then courtrooms were chiseled from the smooth, flat surfaces. Bricks were baked and stacked around the upper perimeter, ventilation systems were devised to keep food cool, and pumps were installed to bring water from the crocodile-filled reservoir below to the cool baths on top of Sigiriya. Lumber was cut. Luxurious gardens soon sprang to life, cooling the hot head of the rock that was so close to the sun with calming green and sweet-smelling courtyards. Paintings called "The Beautiful Ladies" were stenciled onto the walls, and, true to Kassapa's decadent form, the subjects of said paintings would dance by the hundreds in the party chambers upstairs. The nights were filled with music and dancing, the days with bathing and eating.

Throughout the days, the sentry towers signaled to one another the confirmation that there were no invaders on the horizon. And so the village of nearly fifteen thousand people lived for nearly two decades. Finally, Kassapa finished one of the greatest palace-fortresses ever built, with technology that exceeded Europe's best by hundreds of years. He was perched like a hawk on one of the highest overlooks on the island. If his brother came, he would know.

But having killed his father and thrown his brother out of the house, he was becoming knotted and worried as the years passed.

The rock is, even today, impossible to climb without the stairs. The rock is easily defensible, and Kassapa had a large enough army to keep most any invader at bay. Even supplying the citadel with food and water for months would not be a problem.

Once his castle was finished, he didn't go out

much. He stayed at home and commissioned Buddhas to be carved. He built some nice ones with glittering eyes and sent them to local monks. A few of the temples that received these gifts, such as the Mahavihara, were less than enthusiastic about accepting presents from a mountain-brigand father killer, so they respectfully declined. Kassapa insisted. They replied with a classically Buddhist shrewdness by taking the statue and saying, "It is the property of our teacher."

Kassapa went on like this for years, plagued by guilt and a desire for redemption. He poured vast wealth into alms, statues, meals for the monks, new robes by the hundreds, paintings, and prayer after prayer after prayer. Lots of prayers, since he knew that Moggallana was still out there, and Kassapa knew he would be back. But until then Kassapa had his dancing girls and his bathing pools and his paintings and his guilt and his prayers. But these things did him no good.

One morning a messenger arrived and told Kassapa that Moggallana was camped out just a few hours' march north with twelve Tamil nobles and their armies.

It was the moment Kassapa had been waiting for. But he seemed, at the same time, confused. His life seemed to get easily bogged down. At birth he was close to the throne, yet far away. He killed his father for the power but hesitated for the money. He liked the ladies but prayed like a sinner. He asked for forgiveness but knew it was too late. He had spent eighteen years and hundreds of lives preparing an utterly defensible citadel, waiting for his half-brother's return, but then, at that last moment, he threw it all away in one final, murky decision. He screamed, "I will eat him!" and ran from the castle, grabbed his weapons and armor, clambered onto his battle elephant, and led his hastily organized army out into the field of battle. Why did he leave his carefully constructed defense behind? Perhaps after two decades of half-hearted meditation, he changed his mind. Perhaps something could be decided in melee. Perhaps it was a question of honor. Perhaps he thought he could easily defeat his half-brother.

While monks stood on top of the rock shaking their shaven heads, Kassapa's army followed him north through the forest, weapons clanking and animals grunting, to the battlefield where Moggallana and the twelve Tamil armies waited. Kassapa could see the campfires burning. He led his troops across a small field, intending to split the ranks and then flank his opponents. They crossed the field, the smoke in sight, but suddenly heard troops coming through the woods toward them. Suddenly, Kassapa realized that they were walking into a muddy swamp while being surrounded by the Tamil armies. Kassapa was the first to enter the swamp. As he looked down, he saw that his elephant had gotten stuck in the mud.

As I listen to this story from The Mahavamsa, told to me by a guide and local interpreter, I look out over the landscape from the west side of Sigiriya rock. I'm sitting in the eroded stone lookout where a guard once sat over a thousand years ago and watched for Kassapa's army. The man telling me the story points to the field, far below us and a good twenty or thirty kilometers away, where Kassapa died. I have my chin near his shoulder, so I can see, specifically, where the fateful wrong turn occurred. The wind whips the shirt on my guide's arm back and forth in the sunlight, and I can smell burning coconut husk on the breeze.

There are a couple of versions of what happened to Kassapa. Some say that when he tried to turn his elephant and get out of the mud, his troops thought he was running away, so they ran back to Sigiriya and left him there to die. Some say that when his elephant got bogged down, he killed himself by cutting his own throat. Some say that Moggallana stood next to the bog and fleeced him with arrows. Others say that he threw himself down to drown under the heavy feet of his pachyderm steed.

You can see so far from the top of Sigiriya rock that an overactive imagination might make out India to the north. Also running north are the paths trod flat by the feet of thousands of Tamils who have come south, or Sinhalese who have gone north, each side traveling to bring down a companion or consort from the other side—a Tamil traveling to bring mercenaries up to India, a Sinhalese traveling to invite thieves to Sri Lanka.

Each side is guilty of bringing war from across the fence into its own backyard, and each side continues to do it today.

My guide looks at me and says, "Karma follows you like a shadow."

Chapter Six:
Aluvihara

පනිත්ත පෙර සිතා බලනු

("Look before you leap.")
—Sinhalese proverb

The Monk with a Gun

Traditional Buddhist offering, Aluvihara, Sri Lanka

Nothing is more dangerous than gossip gone gospel.

Just as a Baptist minister clings to his bible, so too do Sri Lankans cling to theirs. The old texts such as the Mahavamsa (which details the previously mentioned history of Kassapa, Moggallana, and the Tamil kings) and the Dipavamsa are documents that anchor the history, knowledge, memory, and culture of the country. They are Sri Lanka's decision-making road maps. These documents are their practice and their prayer. They are also a pretext for prejudice and dubious claims to purity.

Texts like the Mahavamsa were transcribed by Buddhist monks. Stories were passed down in Pali some thousand years ago. Since then, a rather radical group of librarians—an erudite group with that peculiarly anti-septic and cloistered taste for preservationist aesthetics—has taken up the job of translating the texts over into Sinhalese, Tamil, and English. The monks who do the translation come mostly from the school of Buddhism known as Theravada. They have considered it their job to gather each syllable that trickled from the mouths of the Buddha's first disciples and map that philosophy upstream, to its source. After some twenty-four hundred years, Theravada is known as the most conservative school of Buddhism in the world. And some Sri Lankan monks have told me of prophesies, or perhaps ancient rumors, that Sri Lanka will be the last place where pure Buddhism will survive. Sri Lanka is the primary roost of Theravada. This makes for a group of ferociously serious monks with a stiff purity fetish.

But these monks weren't just sitting in libraries and humming into their books. They have also enjoyed plush seating in the deepest chambers of Sri Lankan government for the last two thousand years. About one thousand years ago, at the time of the greatest number of invasions and negotiations with Tamil kings, they were the government, and Sri Lanka was a Theravada monarchy. Throughout all the subsequent changes of regimes and even after the colonial invasions, the Theravada monks kept a tight rein on power. As Governor Maitland of Matara discovered in the late 1800s, it was the monks, behind the scenes, who were actually running the show.

Theravada has also started to gain a reputation as a less-than-peaceful religious orientation. Theravada as practiced by Khmer adherents in Thailand, Cambodia, and Laos, and, of course, as practiced in Sri Lanka, has caused more than a few people to tug their goatees and ask themselves why overzealous nationalism has so often sprouted from areas of Asia with roots buried deep in that school of Buddhism. Whether these approaches to Theravada are the cause of terrorism or the effect of colonialism is hard to determine, but, like a large bird near a new corpse, it is there.

Theravada Buddhism hasn't only concerned itself with philosophy and fundamentalism; blood has always been important too, and, like the religious practice, the blood must be pure. Historically, only members of the highest caste were allowed into this bookish and bald aristocracy. The Manu Smriti, the original caste breakdown, was written three thousand years ago by priests who pointed to their own position as the highest possible level to be achieved. Members of lower castes were simply forbidden to enter the ranks of the enlightened. This was contrary, oddly enough, to what Buddha had said. Part of his rejection of Hinduism in the first place had to do with a rejection of caste. Then about two hundred years ago, Theravada went through several ruptures over this question of origin and purity. Arguments started. Splits and compromises were made. New robes with new colors, signifying new philosophies, appeared on the streets of Sinhalese society. Change sparked new fires, but the reverence for purity, like the reverence for documents, remains intact.

On June 8, 1956, in the town of Galle, a Theravada monk jogged up a small hill. Several hundred Sinhalese carrying wood planks and cricket bats followed close behind. The collection of farmers, mechanics, and academics led by this holy man scuttled around a bend in the road and staggered to a halt in a courtyard of the local equivalent of the civic courthouse. There they saw nearly three hundred Tamils quietly sitting in protest of the Sinhala Only Act. They were protesting as Gandhi had taught protest only a decade earlier.

The Sinhalese crowd, with Sinhalese cops in the mix, jumped into the courtyard and proceeded to beat, kick, and spit on the Tamil sitters. It was an exact repetition of the British response to Gandhi's protests. In this case, however, the Tamils were not the majority group, as Gandhi's crowd had been, and so the peaceful protest tactic didn't have the same weight. And anyway, who was watching? The Tamil leader of the protest, Chelvanayakam, called it off, and people ran out of the courtyard leaving scarves, protest billboards, and a considerable amount of blood. The Sinhalese Buddhists claimed they'd won the day.

In another incident three years later, on September 25, 1959, in the town of Colombo, a different monk walked up a different road, approaching President Bandaranaike. The president had recently managed to pass several compromise and therefore controversial laws within parliament, most significant being a bill that allowed limited use of the Tamil language. It was a hard bill to pass, requiring heavy behind-the-scenes political muscle to get it through parliament. The power manipulations, it was claimed, did not take place solely within the official government but had extended into the Buddhist clergy, cracking the very heart of an ancient system. On that September day, the monk who stood in front of Bandaranaike quietly pulled a handgun from the folds of his rust-colored robe and shot the president in the stomach. Bandaranaike died in the hospital the following day.

The blades of the rumor mill started going round, flinging out the heavy accusation that the murder of Bandaranaike had been an order originating high up the politico-religious chain. Regardless of what the monks had really said to each other, Sri Lanka had witnessed its first political assassination carried out by a Buddhist monk.

Both of these monks were students of Theravada Buddhism. Both monks were students of "purity."[1]

A couple of hours north of Kandy, outside a green and small town named Matale, I pull the bike off the highway, feeling mildly rattled, and park next to a guy dressed in a plaid shirt, probably made in Chennai. He's selling little Mickey Mouse dolls, manga comics, fluffy blue Care Bears, stuffed Teletubbies, and cans of Coca-Cola. Behind him a stone staircase stretches up the hill to the temple of Aluvihara, tucked up in the clouds. Aluvihara, part of the island's tourist track, is about smack in the middle of the country.

My ass is vibrating, my face is covered with dead bugs, my teeth are shaken loose from their normal arrangement, and my forehead feels like it's been under a blowtorch. I'm exhausted. All part of the high-speed

1. I asked a friend of mine, an ordained Buddhist monk, to review this material. He had many helpful notes to add, prime among them being that these were exceptional acts that can be found among any group and that "non-harming is a clear and straightforward tenant found in Theravada."

happiness of a two-stroke on a sunny day. My back aches and my arms are heavy, but I'm feeling fine.

"Hello!" he shouts at me. Friendly.

"Hello!" I shout back.

"Would you like a Coke?"

I walk up to take a look at what he has to sell. He's there for the tourists, and, sure, I'm a tourist, and, sure, I'll probably buy something cold to drink.

"What's your name?" he asks.

"Poya." I smile at him.

"Where are you from?"

"Kandy," I answer.

He narrows his eyes because it is as clear as my white skin that I'm not from Kandy. But he smiles a bit anyway.

"How much for a Coke?" I ask him.

"You drove this motorcycle from Kandy?" is his answer.

"From Colombo."

He looks at the bike, makes a silent assessment, determines what it says about me, comments on a bike he has driven, comments on this one, and then offers me a discount on my drink, despite not having listed prices. Friendly commerce.

If I were to visit God, I assume I would find him living at the top of a long flight of stairs like these. All important things are up stairs: national courthouses, monuments, temples, churches, and the Buddha's very own library. These are serious stairs, more a street inclined up the side of a hill with pockmarks for footholds. And it's more of a boulder than a hill, thrown by a titan and stuck halfway into the earth. And the guardrail, I suddenly realize, is carved out of the face. An elaborate and ancient wall that runs on either side contains the walkway. There are smooth slopes in the top of each step, where thousands of years of soft foot traffic have sanded away the stone. Hundreds of polished square tongues.

At the halfway point, I turn around and stretch my eyesight across a quilt of broad valleys. South of me is Kandy, and I can see the mountains that frame it pushing up like knives that threaten to pop the green velvety fabric. The shadows of two mountainous clouds slide over the tiny shacks and patchworks of fields decorating the earth. Scribbles of coconut smoke lift out of the jungle. Under the hot and golden sun, the landscape evaporates and steams and waits for the cool night to come to it again.

At the top of the stairs are a complex of round boulders, each about as big as an apartment building, all connected via a series of passageways and subterranean chambers. Each boulder has been chiseled and chipped by thousands of hands over thousands of years. Tiny staircases weave in and out, each step a disk engraved into the face of the boulder, suggesting the footprints of some little god who walked up to his home, but also leaving the impression of the stockinged toes of thousands of silent monks. The stairs lead to porches and intimate gardens, also carved into the stone, long chiseled lines that trickle down from the top of a boulder to the dirt ground, swept neat, and to a quaint little door in the face of the stone wall. Opening it, I find underground passages, cavities, and cramped winding hallways that intersect and lead deeper into the temple's vaults.

Architecturally, Aluvihara hasn't changed for fifteen hundred years, and it will stay like this for just as long again, barring some massive detonation or earthquake. Ducking, I step into a particularly well-known room where a Buddha reclines. Innumerable niches, each containing little saucers filled with coconut oil and burning wicks, surround the sculpture with a wreath of flames. A monk sits nearby, cross-legged. In front of me the massive sculpture, the size of a school bus, reclines in his underground bedroom, all vermilion, gold, and deep lapis lazuli. His eyes, half-lidded, are delicately painted—alien eyes that seem to smoke with intelligence—and as I step closer and look into them a strange wind seems to envelop me and strip me of thoughts, leaving me empty, lightheaded even, yet whole and confident. The curious sensation causes me to step back. My heel hits the wall behind me, so I put a hand against it and look to the monk who is sitting nearby, thinking he might have something to say about all this. But he looks at me without smiling and I can't tell if his expression signifies humor, disdain, or understanding. Confused, I pause for another moment to look into the eyes of the Buddha, then flee, slowly, into the sun.

In another room, I find a teak bench lined with sendal and taffeta, also decorated with Buddhas who sleep a dream of eternal mindfulness. Each Buddha is plump yet ferocious, each room rich enough and old enough that I cannot comprehend any of what I'm looking at, and so, crassly, I stumble ahead until I find myself outside again. The leaves rattle as the wind flies, carrying with it evidence of the spice garden nearby, sharp flavors of ginger, cardamom, coriander, and lemongrass. I rub my forehead and try to get my bearing.

A series of steps writhes up to an overlook at the top of the hill, at the very tip of the temple's complex. They dive down again inside, to a courtyard with a small natural fountain and lotus flowers drifting in a pond and a big brass cylindrical bell, which was a gift from Thailand in the 1960s. It is the archetype of an Asian temple: peaceful, balanced, clean, cared for, and austere. And though the architecture here is the same as it was over a thousand years ago, the key ingredient, and the reason for the place in the first place, has changed. Now it is something of a tourist destination and a place where worship is remembered and to some degree still practiced. However, it was not always like this.

Aluvihara was inhabited thousands of years ago, but the architecture itself was finished when the Tamil kings from the north occupied much of the island and the Sinhalese were in decline. Sri Lanka has always been balanced in this fluctuation between Tamil and Sinhalese predominance. When the Sinhalese regained power, they became the new guardians. Meanwhile, various visitors came and left marks of their own upon the culture, and engraved them here in Aluvihara. As well as Hindu and Buddhist art, the temple contains Tibetan landscapes, Chinese dragons, and Dutch inscriptions.

In the first century AD, a Tamil invasion that swept the island caused a group of concerned monks to flee into the hills, where they spent several hard decades in hiding, discussing and memorizing what they knew and reciting the lessons of the Buddha so as to burn them into their memories, and somehow into the world's memory, too. Then they decided that, despite the Buddha's wishes, these important parables needed to be written down. They also decided that Anuradhapura was not the place to do this work, as it was too much a potential target for future invasion. They picked Aluvihara and wrote the Tripitaka.

Five hundred of them gathered up their pens and set to work. This tiny army of monks passed hot afternoons busily transcribing Buddha's every word into books they made here at the temple. Different versions of the story disagree about the beginning, ending, and overall time frame of this transcription period, this portion of the Pali canon, but the stories agree as to the process. The monks would build each book the same way. Two narrow pieces of wood—cut quite thin, sanded, and varnished—made the covers. In between these two slats was sewn a fan arrangement of ola leaves. The leaves, sewn together, made a collapsing kind of interior page arrangement. Like the bellows of an accordian, they could be folded out and read without making a big maplike mess and unhinging everything.

With a small metal quill, the pages were engraved, then wiped with black ink. The excess ink was then wiped clear, and the pages were treated, sealed, and dried before the books were put on a bookshelf to sit for hundreds of years and occasionally referenced. It was the most precise transcription of the Buddha's words in the world.

After some seventeen hundred years of careful study, discussion, transcription, and storage, the British army appeared one afternoon in 1848 with a pocketful of matches. Naturally, because the Pali canon was made of leaves, a little bit of ink, and dried wood, they burned well enough to cauterize a cultural lobotomy.

The British burned much of what had been categorized and reduced Aluvihara's libraries—many of the primary (most "pure") teachings of the Buddha—to ashes. In talking with one of the administrators about it, I asked how much was left, and as a response he raised the palms of his hands and shrugged. I discovered later that some few texts were reclaimed, and then hidden, but the vast majority were lost.[2] Which was the British intent. Doing so softened up the Sri Lankan cultural memory and, therefore, reasons for resistance to the British invasion.

But this fact isn't mentioned in the guidebooks,

---

2. Some of the texts have been restored over the last fifty years, and some of these have been digitized. A slightly modernized version of some of this work, in Pali and Sinhalese, can be found at: http://www.bodhgay-anews.net/pali.htm.

at least not the ones published in the United Kingdom. We English speakers, after all, have our own traditions to protect.

The Brit with a Book

Tamil Curry

It is, again, time to talk with a terrorist.

From behind her lunch, The English Woman, perfumed and blinking fake eyelashes, announces, "I hate these people. They're all alike; they all just want something from you." Her Anglican Afro, pale and brown, scrubs at the air as she shakes her head. Writ large on her skin is a lifetime of harsh collagen correction, powdered appliqués, youth-restorative potions, and a recent and very unfortunate facelift that stiffens her upper lip, giving her face a canine snarl. Signs of "high-class" in some cultures.

She has been chugging full-fall down the Ceylon tourist track. Most tourists get locked into the same route, one that starts in Hikkaduwa, goes to Kandy, then Anuradhapura, and back to Hikkaduwa again. It's a circuit that cuts a curl through the island's center, a conveyor belt that starts in the sunny south, then takes the visitor up through the mountains, past the most historic parks, and back to the south again, all the while managing to steer short of the invisible line south of the war zone. The Cultural Triangle, as it is known, is a beautiful trip that gives an historic overview of the southern part of the island. The Sinhalese take credit for it (mostly), even though it is also a showcase Tamil culture. This tourist track includes it all: World Famous Beaches, Exotic Botanical Gardens, Picturesque Waterfalls, Beautiful Hill Country, and Ancient Cities. Despite the conveniences and entertainments and trinkets, what's left out—as from all tourist tracks—is the reality of the country: the families and their home-cooked food, the teas and the spices, the dreams of the people as they work, the flutes that can be heard deep in the full-moon jungles; all these are missed. The war is too. A country's disagreements and poverty are not of interest to people on vacation; they have enough of that back home. The tourist track keeps the exotic marketable. It also keeps the tourists separate from the native population. This is of utmost importance since the population's civil strife is bad for business.

The English Woman holds up a guidebook, then pulls out another, and says that she went only to the places that were given the thumbs-up by both her guidebooks (she opens her eyes wider and raises her eyebrows as she says "both"), and though she has been waiting to be entertained, so far she has been only displeased.

"Maybe your guidebooks aren't right for you," someone patiently volunteers.

No, no, she berates. The problem isn't her literature; it is the country and the selfish people who live here. "Regardless of where I go, they're constantly making demands. Usually they want money, or they want to sell me something. They refuse to leave me in peace. Even the guides are like this. They have no sense of personal space whatsoever."

It is true that the locals aren't exactly Calvinist, and concepts like "space" and "privacy" aren't understood in the same way as they are in, say, Woodland Park, Colorado, where the skies are not cloudy all day and where walking onto someone else's property can land you in some deep cow pie. In places like that, we walk far apart from one another, and the famously discussed personal space boundaries are proportional to the general population density. After all, the entire country of Sri Lanka is as densely populated as the city of Los Angeles.

A tourist is, for Sri Lankans, a cash cow that they would be unwise not to milk. But what most tourists don't recognize is that once you stop shielding yourself from it all, the interaction changes. A Dutch surfer I met, a guy named Phillip, pointed out that if you were to offer to sell them something, things would change. It's all about equality.

The English Woman then softly claps her hands and continues, "But the beaches are beautiful. We've had a simply marvelous time there. However, it is impossible to leave the hotel. Fortunately, they have a private beach, and that's been brilliant."

Someone asks her how she likes the service at the hotel.

Plastic red, her lower lip sticks out. She adjusts her flowered blouse and pokes at her curry with her fork.

She's a landslide of disappointment. She came looking for paradise, but it's tainted by the people who live there. She's a touristocrat.

Tourism (or, rather, the peculiar version of it practiced by the wealthy Occidentals one can find frying on the beaches here) is an industry like dairy farming. The tourists are there to excrete excess cash. They are led down to the beach to be fattened on mai tais, after which they wallow out to the sand and sit in the sun. Their fat, it seems, melts a bit so that when they ascend to their high-rise hotel complex, it can be drained, siphoned, and poured into the coffers of the smiling hotel managers. Sometimes there is overflow. Sometimes the tourists will spill some of their fat in the street, buying local products. Other locals see this, and they become more and more aggressive attempting to capture those few random droplets that the hotels don't manage to siphon themselves. The tourism industry says to the tourist, "We'll give you the prime cut of the local land." It says to the locals, "We'll bring you the fat of the foreigners." So the knives are sharpened, the pumps are primed, and the hawkers come to pander, sell, and barter as only Asia knows how.

Sri Lanka is changing under the weight of these tourists. Tourism is the fastest-growing industry in the country. High-rise hotels are springing up along the beaches and edging out the palm trees. Rental car (and motorcycle) agencies couple up with Internet cafés so you can catch up on your e-mail while you wait for your driver to bring your car. Dive shops, glass-bottom-boat tours, and surf schools conduct competing marketing campaigns.

On the beach in Hikkaduwa, a system I first heard about on the beaches of Mexico is finding a profitable welcome. The dealer sells some illegal goodies (low-grade marijuana, mostly) to the tourist. The dealer pockets the cash. The dealer tells the cop. The cop arrests the tourist and confiscates the contraband but is willing to let the tourist off for a small, *ahem*, fee. The cop hands the goodies back to the dealer, who then looks for another target. Dice, slice, and wait for another sunburn to meander down the beach. In the end, one must recognize the reality: It's a local's industry, not a tourist's vacation.

But mostly the tourists keep to themselves, both financially and socially. They rarely circulate outside of their hotel complexes. And they are almost never seen walking along the railroad tracks or hanging around devil dances. This is at least part of the reason everyone has been staring at me. The races just don't mingle much around here; the pinks who come in are either too afraid of cooties or too smart to put themselves at risk of contracting typhoid.

It's the money that matters. Everyone knows that one euro from the continent is worth ten here on the island. Perhaps this is why these pinks are in Sri Lanka. Anyone from the outside world has money. It's a well-known fact that fingers flock where money falls. At Polonnaruwa, I entered the tourist track sort of by accident when a fellow traveler I met invited me to travel with her a bit. As we walked past a museum, we were ambushed by at least a dozen salesmen. They were waiting along the path and ganged up to beat me about the wallet with tiny tin elephants, boxes of beautiful and garish jewelry, bottles of cool water, and eats. These salesmen knew that tourists would walk up this path, so they stationed themselves, guerrilla style, and waited to make a killing. It was their job, and it was mine, as a tourist, to pay them to do it.

With the terrorists, tourists, and imperialists all in concert, singing songs of social change, this strange melody of a high-strung choruses accompanies history's heavy beat. Tourism, terrorism, and imperialism might, in fact, be linked.

The island's tourists and terrorists are not flung far from one another. The woman with the guidebook and the monk with the gun each had the same problem; they were responding to gossip gone gospel. They were led away from their own thoughts and experiences by their books. The books told them that a kind of "purity" could be found, and when it was not where they looked, they turned violent. They had been led astray by their media. Like the French during their revolution, the Israelis in the last few decades, or the Americans after 2001, the terror felt in the society was absorbed and then retransmitted by the population.

This was part of the very reason I had come to Sri Lanka: I did not want my own gossip to become gospel. In order to know what media to believe, we must invent our own. We must see for ourselves.

The frustration and sunburn make her face glow red as she takes another bite of her dinner, shakes her head, swallows, and concludes, "There were twenty people all asking me for my money. They surrounded me and just stood there with their hands out and kept saying, 'Money, money.' Unbelievable. Disgusting. 'Money, money, money . . . '"

She sets down her fork and appears to forget us. She fondles her guidebook, licks her lips, and pulls out a map.

What can she do but continue?

We'd be lost without our literatures.

Chapter Seven: Vavuniya

"The secret of life is to have no fear."
—Fela Kuti

The Red, Red Road to Jaffna Town

Mine-warning sign along Highway A9
(the "Highway of Death"), outside of Vavuniya, Sri Lanka

Staring at my own map at the gas station several hundred miles up the road, I'm certain, absolutely certain, as certain as The English Woman, that I do not want to get lost. I'm at the front door of the war theater.

Since maps and motorcycles mix like convertibles and cocaine, I've been using my compass. It gets me where I need to go, since there aren't many roads. My strategy has been to glance down every so often to make sure I'm still headed north. It's easier than pulling over, and it spares me the indignity of crashing into a tree trunk with a big piece of paper covering my face. The specific road doesn't matter, as long as it goes north.

This is, as the PLOTE, the EROS, the LTTE, and others have called it, the Tamil homeland. Both the Sinhalese and the Tamils wandered down, thousands of years ago, from India, so it's hard to say if this idea of a homeland is a history, a future, or a fiction. The major battles of recent history have happened in the north, that much is clear. Since everyone from Karunaratne to Siddharthan to Prabath has given me a different gospel on the place, I have to see it myself.

Fortunately, I don't have to navigate much. All the roads from the south have been slowly angling themselves into a funnel, a single squeezed-in channel. Like a river that is fed by many streams, this main tributary is getting faster and rougher as I go along. But instead of rapids, there are potholes—more and larger potholes than I've ever seen in my life.

Everyone has warned me that north of Vavuniya is where things get strange, where the Tamil Tigers have claimed the upper fourth of the island of Sri Lanka, where the people are poor, where the diseases fly free, where the people are frightened, and where the torture chambers are buried. South of that, the area I'm entering now, is no-man's-land. The map confirms this. There is only one road between Vavuniya and Jaffna. Checkpoints are in between. There is one little red line that looks like a long stretch of road with security hurdles. So I'm being funneled. And in the heat of northern Sri Lanka, I'm also getting fried. There is nothing to be done except drive. I can't get lost since I can't take a wrong turn. Everything goes north. Everything points to the LTTE.

I'm planning on passing right through Vavuniya, so I don't even stop, just pull out of town, increasing the throttle into the hot wind and past the market, the gas station, and the dark little holes of buildings where obscured faces watch me. Like inverted ghost heads, it's the whites of their eyes that I can see and not much else. I start to head north from town. I get the bike moving and cool off.

The sun is still slowly roasting me, but the wind cools me off, giving me the lovely chance to get simultaneously sunburned and dehydrated. As long as I can find a couple of gallons of fresh water to drink each day, I'll be fine. The road unrolls itself like a magic scroll that gradually becomes more crumbly and gritty the deeper north I go. Cows veer out into the road, huge sacks of leather hanging over bony skeleton machines, ambling, looking for trash to rummage. People dodge out across the road at times, too. There are buildings with oddly gabled roofs, not quite Chinese, and schools with chalk-drawing parties out front in the street, here and there, and a hundred kids surround the motorcycle when I stop in front of one to look at the map. It takes me twenty minutes to break free from their tiny, curious hands. I pull out onto the road and the bikes are everywhere, insanely loaded, really maximized. A family of four on a single bicycle teeters along, loaded also with groceries and laundry.

The road resembles an immense snake that has

uncoiled, like a red river I am following into a heart of darkness. If it is a fascination for abomination that is pulling me north, then it is only my contempt for fiction that is pushing me from the south. The truth of the war pulls me as much as the fiction of the media repels.

The occasional lorry rolls by, decorated with painted curves and dagger-sharp angles drawn into the wood, with rolling clouds of pink painted over an azure psychedelic background, the weird eye or fanged face on the tailgate, the whole truck madly zigzagging the road, avoiding potholes that could hide a small car, the massive bundles on top of the truck swaying from side to side, threatening to fall on the bicyclists below. I pass houses that are little more than heaps of palm fronds over patches of dirt, abandoned pieces of corrugated steel with families of three inside hiding from the sky. The earth is mean, dusty, and scorched to a charred, scabrous red. And the road is getting meaner by the mile.

One thing is clear: A financial line has been scratched across Sri Lanka, dividing the comparatively rich south from the very poor north. Sometimes, in a city, you know when you've crossed into another zone. You see it as you cross the railroad tracks or walk across a street. Maintenance or the written language or the way people speak: Suddenly things change—the shops or the houses or whatever signs you used to navigate wealth and poverty. Here, in Sri Lanka, I have crossed this line, and people's eyes take on a narcotic glaze. They are droopy and slow, as if they're soaked with cholera, or exhaustion.

Sri Lanka is full of apparent dangers. My fears about coming here revolved around guns and bombs and shrapnel-filled mines, or being kidnapped and held for ransom, or being drugged by someone I'd meet only to wake up in a bathtub full of ice with my liver missing.

I arrived in this land with a fear of death, I suppose—mostly anxiety at the prospect of interviewing terrorists, a fear of being held at gunpoint and taken into a dark basement with car batteries. Other, less obvious possibilities of an untimely end arose in my mind, such as the risk of being trampled by an elephant, drowned in a river canal, burned as a sacrifice to a "Hindoo god," or murdered by marauding mobs of monkeys. But, no, these things did not happen.

But the Highway of Death! Highway A9! Here, indeed, did I find, I can say with full force, the one thing that nearly killed me in Sri Lanka: the painted lorries.

One does not drive this highway: One beats one's way up it. In the middle of the highway, there are yawning potholes. How potholes grow to be the size of elephants, I cannot tell. The asphalt, when it is unbroken, is fine and operational, but there is no real shoulder at the edges of the road as much as there is a dissolution of the asphalt into a collection of unstable stones scattered on top of sand.

None of this would be a problem were it not for the trucks. The road is wide enough for a single vehicle, but the potholes occasionally constrict the drivable space down to a couple of meters. Of course, when there is little space there is also, by some cosmic and persistent coincidence, a truck coming in the opposite direction. These lorry drivers neither give way nor slow down. Instead, they shove the pedal to the floor, point the grill of their truck directly at my throat, honk a final death threat as they do it, and edge their huge rig onto my side of what little road there is to see if they can separate me from my motorcycle.

I desperately throw the bike onto the crumbly half-shoulder area, the front wheel skidding madly in the loose sand, pebbles spraying from the truck, spackling my forehead. My eyes squint, and my brain folds itself into a prayer. I grit my teeth and hope that if I fall, it will be away from the truck's tire, that my skull will not land under the wheel. Rocks scatter underneath my tires and the bike lurches into sand with a sickening twist, then pops back up toward the truck, which, in this brief tenth of a second, is nearly past me. I imagine a spray of gas and steel and coolant and bone shards.

Then, somehow, we manage to miss, though I have no idea how (my eyes are still tightly closed). I feel the rear bumper shaving the hair off the knuckles of my right hand because, all the while, we are driving on the side of the road opposite to what I am used to. I open my eyes and soar over a pothole. God, why can't I slow down?

The Doppler effect of the horn and engine leaves me giddy, and here comes another, up ahead.

It's four in the afternoon.

When I spoke with Rajee, he mentioned that there would be both LTTE and Sri Lankan army posts along the way. Evidently there will be an army checkpoint, then an LTTE checkpoint, then another army checkpoint, or something like that. I guess they have to alternate checkpoints since it's a contested zone.

Heavy gray clouds crawl over the horizon. I'm hot, thrashed, dusty, and impatient. A rainstorm rinse might give me enough energy to cross the border of the DMZ and into the north tonight. As I look a little closer, and as the minutes roll beneath the front tire of the bike, I realize that these clouds may not refresh so much as drown. Monsoon. This is the month when they start. The muscular and massive clouds dwarf the mountains. A great curtain dangles from the underside of a brainy cumulus. Not a curtain, I see as I get closer, but, in fact, a wall. But no, not a wall but a cylinder, a black column of water pouring from the shadow mountain on high.

I pull over and double-check that my camera is well-sealed in its ziplock baggie. I start the bike again, watch the cloud. Pull back out onto the road. Accelerate to a comfortable and normal speed. Grope behind myself to confirm that my bag is firmly attached to the seat. Watch the cloud. As it comes nearer, I squirm in the seat a bit. The shadow comes first, and then the water lands on the road in front of me, a wall of water intersecting with the highway, an immediate fuzz and flood, and I slam into it, forced to decelerate to prevent the rain from peeling off my scalp, already tender from the lorry gravel, sun, and bugs.

Half an hour passes in a high-speed torrent.

I emerge from the monsoon cold and wet and driving very slowly. In front of me, some branches and stones are piled up around the highway as some kind of traffic control. A guard shack emerges from the smear of rain. A tree trunk spans the road, a long stick, really, and tires are stacked in columns, and sandbags.

Four LTTE guards are sitting inside a makeshift shack—more of a roof supported by sticks—surrounded by sandbags. Their desk is a card table. I decelerate the bike, put my foot down in the mud, and wait. Laughing and shouting, they're playing cards. Money is on the table, and weapons are lying around like dirty clothes in an American teenager's bedroom. I decide it would be judicious to wait for them to stop rather than to interrupt. In that thirty seconds, I see beer bottles and a couple of AK-something-or-others leaned up against a wall, a lot of paperwork, a magazine with a bikini girl on the cover (in Tamil; I can't read it), and pictures of Ganesh and Shiva on the wall behind them. They stop playing cards and look up.

The big one with the beret waves at me to approach. He has a round scar the size of a dime on his chin. His mustache is shiny and so black it looks like it's made of plastic. He raises his arm, opens one nonchalant hand in the air, says, "Papers," and waits for me to hand them over.

"What papers do I need?"

I had already asked this when I was in Colombo. I knew when I came here I might have to head all the way back down, but nobody in Colombo knew specifically what papers were needed in Vavuniya. The advice from Rajee and the rest of the guys in Colombo was to just show up here and ask to get in. Not being Tamil, I figured this could backfire on me.

The guard doesn't answer, and he doesn't drop his arm.

I hate border guards. No matter where you go, they all have the same gripe, as if raised in the same family. They are professional bullies, all of them big-bellied army wannabes who never attained the power or education they wanted. So these frustrated *führers* all put their heartbeats to work toward impeding the progress of the masses, of which I am always a part. They all have mustaches, they all wear knee-high boots and fatigues, they all carry little pads of paper in their shirt pockets, and they are all possessors of great wads of inconvenience, which they happily dole out to those who have no need of it. I wait.

"Let me see your passport." Americans aren't particularly hated here, but we're not well liked anywhere these days, so I'm a little leery. I hand over my laminated color copy, leaving the real one buried. I don't like giving people my passport. It's like handing them your head, hands, and feet.

He looks at the photocopy and asks me for proof

of the motorcycle. This is a good sign.

I tell him it's rented.

He tells me he needs photocopies of my passport, international driver's license, and bike registration.

I turn the bike around, head back south, where I came from, and see the rain in front of me.

Back in Vavuniya, at the photocopy shop, my boots are dripping all over the floor. I'm trying to get work done as a good dozen people stand outside and stare through the window. Moving south faster than the rainstorm, I passed through it again, but I'll get a third taste when I return north. As I gradually cover the floor with water draining from inside my boots, I'm running off three copies of everything, just in case.

An aging man in a white shirt and pants pulled up to his ribcage asks me if he can take my picture. Of course, of course. I'm happy for the break, and we shake hands and nod, looking one another in the retina, making sure the other is there. Being a pink this far north in Sri Lanka is a cross between being a rock star and a deformed circus freak. But sometimes I can make people happy simply by standing with them, and that's a kind of honor and it is worth the time, for sure. I expect him to pull out a camera.

He asks me to follow him.

We cross a small ditch and arrive at his house, which is in view of the shop. The man jumps through the door and jogs inside. I am left with two boys, about fourteen or fifteen, and two girls in their early twenties, all just hanging around in front of the house. They smile and nod at me. I wonder how long the man will be inside. I guess he's their father. They ask, in English, where I'm from and what my name is. I answer seriously and slowly, and they tell me their names. We stand there looking at each other with no one knowing what to say next. Somehow I just don't feel myself right now, all sandblasted, bombarded, rain drenched (there are still puddles inside my boots), and a bit wobbly from eight hours of clinging to the motorcycle.

After five minutes of waiting, I start to think about getting my photocopies finished and getting over the border—if it was a border—to find a place to stay for the night and not get shot. And I don't mean by a camera-wielding old man with pants up to his nipples. Here I won't say that I'm Poya from Kandy because I'm in Tamil land, and the joke just won't make sense. They speak a different language here. I'm one hundred kilometers north of Aluvihara. It's another world. Different gods reign here.

The man comes back out with his camera. He groups us all together, and we put hands on shoulders and wear smiles for a second, smiling like we're old friends, he snaps the camera, and then we all pull apart. He tugs his pants up again and thanks me, and pats the camera as if he now has a djinn locked inside.

He has immense front teeth and tiny holes for eyes. The family all have precisely the same forehead and tiny eyes, and two of the boys have his teeth as well. As soon as I notice this, I realize they all move identically. The boys are dressed like their father, with the pants up high. Both boys wear the same shoes, and both boys and their father put all the weight on their left leg, hands in their pockets. They are handsome with big front teeth, the man and the smaller versions of himself. His daughters are pretty, and they have big front teeth, too. I ask them for a trade, and they agree, so I take their picture. We exchange thanks and smiles, and I walk back over to the copy shop to get back to dealing with my photocopies for the damned guards at the LTTE gate.

My passport and bike registration are on the photocopier's flatbed, and the white light is going back and forth across the scanner bed. I close my eyes and feel a hand on my elbow. The man with the buckteeth is there, pulling on my arm. I look at him, and he pulls again, hard. I'm off balance, but he's smiling.

"Come! Come!"

"What is it?"

"I have a personal matter for you."

He lets go of my arm and pulls up his pants.

"But I'm making photocopies."

"It's very important!"

"Then tell me now."

He points toward his house, then hesitates. He looks at me, then looks at his house, then back at me and says, "The woman . . . wants you to marry."

My heart sinks.

She is standing near the door of the building where I took the picture, and her hands hang at her sides. She has huge hands, like a farmer. I notice her for the first time.

She is wearing a pretty blue dress with pants underneath: a salwar kameez, classic Tamil style. She has a thin face and a bindi on her forehead. She has long black hair that is nicely braided and a champagne smile that is demure but still stable. She's looking at me, right in the eye, then at the ground, and I know it took a lot of courage on her part. I can't tell if she's smiling or what the hell is going on. She is soft and has a smart eye and a kind smile. Is it a sincere smile? Did her father tell her to smile? My head gets heavy, and my neck feels like a fulcrum.

Sudden and weird possibilities spring up before me, simply because she's not running and her father is standing there grinning like he's offering me a goat. I could live in Sri Lanka, spend my life making beige, half-Tamil babies, learn the language, and work at the local school teaching English. She probably doesn't have much of a dowry, but hell, I don't either, and, anyway, I haven't gotten laid in a while.

It's so horrible, being human, when you really look at it.

Then, after perhaps a full second of my head being full of this mess, it occurs to me where I am and how absurd all this mating stuff is, despite what any of the three of us might want or not want. I'm smiling at a beautiful woman in blue who is caught between a sad history, an impossible hope, and a lifelong nightmare.

Quick as wings, she nods and disappears into the house.

The more dramatic an event is—someone dying under a truck, meeting your future wife—the faster it occurs. Time moves at speeds we cannot comprehend.

About a month ago, down south, on a little farm near Matara, a man had offered me his fifteen-year-old daughter's hand in marriage for as many dollars, and I told him to quit asking tourists that or he'd sell her to the wrong guy and she'd end up a prostitute in Dubai, or worse. He didn't care and made the offer again, desperate to leverage a better life for her. I told him I was gay.

I tell this man in the white shirt with his hiked-up pants the same thing; and as the response leaves my mouth, I remember why it didn't work last time either.

"What is 'gay'?" he asks.

The column of rain has moved a few miles farther south. I'm legitimately cold and amazed at how it smashes into the highway around me, really driving down from above and grinding me into the bike. I'm driving slowly because it stings if I go too fast, poking my nose and forehead with tiny jackhammers of ice.

The soldiers are still playing cards, the girlie magazine has been moved, the guns are in the same places, but the attitude is a little different: They're not having as much fun now. I hand them my new photocopies, which are only minimally rain-splattered. The same barrel neck from before looks at one paper, then the next, then me, hands the papers back, notes something in Tamil on a dirty little clipboard with a pencil that disappears in his hand, and they go back to playing cards.

After standing there for a few seconds I ask, "Which . . . ?"

"Okay! Go!" one shouts without looking up.

It is a world of documents, not words. I'm back on the bike before I can blink, and go I do.

After over two decades of war and concomitant training, the Tamil population now has tens of thousands of people—mostly men—who have no education or skills other than shifting sheaves of paperwork, playing cards, reading porn, and killing. Not much by way of an education, but they're primed for battle.

A friend who spent a few years in the Israeli army once told me over dinner, "At eighteen you'll do whatever you're told, even if you're told to tear someone's intestines out with your teeth."

The Tamil soldier I'd watched play cards was probably in his mid-twenties, so chances are he'd been recruited by the LTTE some nine or ten years back when things were at their peak. Now he looks bored as a hole so I decide that a bored, uneducated Tamil soldier stationed on the frontier is almost as unpredictable and egoistic, even, as a small-town American cop, for many of the same reasons, and so fast away from them do I drive, with my photocopied documents and newfound hall pass.

Thunder peals and a biblical ocean of water falls on my head. In Sri Lanka there is infinite water in the sky. Fortunately the motor is running fine in this day of Noah. I continue north, checking my compass since I'm not stopping anytime soon, unless I get hit by a truck or decide to sit in the rain and get colder. There aren't usually bars or convenience stores around war-zone checkpoints.

On the map at this point, the funneling of the roads is complete, and I'm passing through that tiny cylinder at the northern end, just before getting spit out into LTTE territory. The ten or twelve kilometers left are more painful than I had thought they would be. The rain is freezing cold on my burned forearms. My eyeballs are getting smashed by water, and my boots are gradually filling up with rain. It occurs to me, first, that I am thirsty and, second, that I could take my boots off and drink out of them. But there is no need: I just lean my head back and open my mouth.

Soaked and decelerating, I boat my motorcycle into the Sri Lankan army checkpoint. It's a Quonset hut with about a hundred people standing next to long benches. The benches are stacked with plastic filing containers, waterproof. The people look sluggish, anemic, forced to stand here for a week without sleep. They don't even search me but send me along the road toward the second LTTE checkpoint. I'm glad I brought extra photocopies.

Back on the bike, into the rain, and up the road another kilometer.

This next camp, more than simply a checkpoint, is a small citadel, and for the first time I get the sense that the LTTE is not an uprising but an established army. There is a vehicle registration area, a personnel registration area, a series of small offices that are nicer than most of the houses I've seen today, and some two hundred people passing through this interrogation station, filing, neat and orderly. A man holding a large gun is watching.

A ray or two of late afternoon sun finds its way through the rain, and then the water stops. I ask the LTTE guy who's dismantling my bag what he's checking for, and he tells me, in one smear of words, "Wearelooking-forweaponsammunitionanddetonationdevices."

He passes me along to the next checkpoint, just over there, within walking distance.

I realize that I am about to be searched by four beautiful women who work at this station. And though I wander in dopey and watery eyed, I think to myself, Wife offer really messed with my head, because now all the women seem gorgeous, and all the men seem threatening. I flirt with the girl who digs through my bags, trading innuendos until her superior officer comes over and looks ready to throw more cold water on me. All five of them give me the comb through, sniff my bag. The woman and I are making eyes at each other while the man looks at my books. I ask if I can take a photo. She's okay with it; he is not. I am briskly shooed up the way to the next building, because, after all, it's a war zone, not a dating service.

A third and final checkpoint inside a small hut. This last fellow likes to bully me around. He's a real bitch, and he's going to make it difficult for me. He looks through my bags and stops when he finds my mechanical pencil. He decides that it merits investigation. Alien technology. He turns it upside down and shakes it and looks at it again. He looks at me but doesn't say a word. I wait. Five minutes later, three of them figure out how to make it work, but during that time they never look at me, never say a word to me, or, heaven forbid, ask me what it is. Satisfied that it's a writing utensil, he stares hard at me and grunts for me to go.

It's sunny again, almost blinding now with all the reflections off puddles. It feels clean to be back on the bike, and I accelerate hard out of there, the wind drying me, the sun opening everything up just for the few hours left in the day.

The red road leads me further into the war zone, and at any moment I'm expecting to see the Tamil homeland I have heard so much about, as if it were a cultural El Dorado or the Elysian Fields. It is worth fighting for, it is worth dying for, it is our land, our home, etc. But the deeper I go, the poorer it gets. Eventually I drive by three boys sleeping on the ground next to the road, one missing a leg, one buck naked, the third with a misshapen head.

In most places, when you enter a new city you are welcomed by signs on the side of the road that say things like WELCOME TO KANSAS CITY, HOME OF THE CHIEFS or maybe BILLINGS, IN THE HEART OF BIG SKY COUNTRY or even just simply, PARIS. You know just where you are with these declarations. It's the same here, in a way.

First are the small red signs. The simplest are square ones with just a white skull and crossbones and two Tamil words across the top. I can't read the Tamil and don't need to. I count ten of these in the first kilometer, at regular intervals. Sure enough, there are no houses out here, no people walking around. Then I come across the blue-and-white UNICEF signs. Trilingual explanations in Sinhalese, Tamil, and English say:

DANGER LANDMINES!
CAN KILL OR PERMANENTLY DISABLE YOU!

Another sign says:

THERE COULD BE LANDMINES!
ANYWHERE OUTSIDE THE ROAD!

A simple illustration shows a sandaled foot about to step on a disk with a big red x through it. Land mines—the gifts that keep on giving. There are other signs, too, such as the handmade sign of a disk and three lines coming off the top, like an exclamation off the happy head of a yellow smiley face. The place is scattered with mines, a great garden of seeds for special flowers that bloom only once, then die.

This is no cultural El Dorado. There is nothing glorious or cultivated about it. It is no homeland. It is a wasteland.

This is no man's land that was trashed, then deserted. When people wanted to come back here to live, they posted signs because the trash was too lethal to clean up. Who was it that said that the first man to claim land as his own was the inventor of civilization? That act was also, perhaps, the invention of orchestrated war.

When an area is really exceptional, it gets an exceptional welcome sign, like HOME OF THE DOUBLE-DECKER WAFFLE or CHEESE STEAK CAPITAL OF THE WORLD! As I pull into a little town—more a corner store with a few soaked boxes than a town—I see the best of all welcome signs. It reads DE-MINED AREA!

I can only assume that these people must be used to a lot of dead cattle, a challenging cricket game, and the occasional three-legged elephant. A big white banner, now dusty, is strung across the road, hanging between two telephone poles. It reads, in Tamil and English, with quaint hand-painted letters across a series of flatly sewn-together bed sheets, MINE AWARENESS WEEK.

It looks for all the world like an Idaho 4-H rally.

Pink Yank Jack Cracker

A family estate, Puttalam, Sri Lanka

The small towns are only a few grass huts clustered together. They have names like Alaikallupoddakulam, Puliyankulam, Mankulam, and Iranamadu, and each of them is a bit sootier, a bit poorer, a little smaller, and all of them are one step closer to the war. I'm getting further and further north, and things are beginning to feel hostile and toxic.

There are no hills. The landscape is as flat as a mirror now. The clouds clear, marching off like silent armies of angels into the south to drop their horrible freezing water on people down there. The sky is big, the road is wide, and the potholes have grown to swimming-pool scale. If I keep the bike moving at more than 140 kilometers per hour (about 90 mph), then the potholes, like a proof of the theory of relativity, shrink in my direction of travel, and I fly over them, not losing altitude before I hit the other side. Fortunately, I have shocks on the bike for when my theory of relativity doesn't work.

The problem with this speeding-bullet approach is that death trucks are solving the pothole problem in the same way I am but in the opposite direction. This is one of those roads that are as much dirt as asphalt. Twice as many vehicles make for half as much road, and my side-view mirror gets tapped more than once. I get run off the road as someone cedes not a breath of space. The calculations between drivers are done in the space of milliseconds and millimeters, and no more.

While I was staying in the south, I stepped into a bank. I was standing there in shorts and flip-flops, envelope in hand, and the twelve folks in line in front of me all turned and stared for a moment. I looked at them and smiled. They all stepped back away from the counter. All at once. An invisible bar had slowly pushed them all to the side. I wasn't sure whether to run out of the bank or bow until I saw the bank teller at the window looking at me, smiling, her eyebrows raised. Since I didn't consider it my role to change the furniture in Prabath's house, I also didn't consider it my role to change the culture in his country, so I walked to the front of the line and tried to thank everyone as I did so.

The Sinhalese culture predominant in the south is known for being racist, but it a form of racism that transcends the casual racism I've seen elsewhere. It is no longer in my realm of "racism." It is more like a national fetish.

In a curious symmetry, here in the north the village people (as Prabath calls them) all treat me the same way. Families stop walking, boys pause in their games of cricket, conversations halt, babies start to cry. Everything stops, everyone stares. Children run up to me screaming "White!" I find out later that I am the first pink who has been north of Vavuniya in over three months, and nobody I speak to knows of another American ever visiting the north of Sri Lanka before. And though I can't believe that is the case, I suppose that, given the absolute lack of cultural or racial range among these folks, their racist bent makes some sense. There are no Chinese, Nigerians, or Spanish. There are no Arabs or Russians. No Brazilians or French. Just yank jack cracker me, roasted as purple as the sun is high, trying to figure out what is going on.

Perhaps I'm riding the aftershocks of imperialism. Sri Lankan caste hierarchies were buttressed by the class-minded English and Portuguese—if you're an imperialist, a country with a built-in caste system will be easier to rule. But the English confused caste with class and overlooked the fact that many Indians and Sri Lankans see no link between your caste and the work that you do. Caste serves many functions, few of them understood by Westerners. As I understand it, caste can make people happier by limiting their choices in life. If you know your caste, then you know your path. Of course, you can move up and down in caste order— just not in this life. Based on how you do in this incarnation, you might come back as a member of a higher (or lower) caste. What stops me from judging this idea of social mobility is the fact that many more people believe in this system than in my own American ideas of social mobility and the role of race. Moreover, this system has been tested since before Plato, Jesus Christ, or George Washington were around.

The issues of race are separate from those of caste, class, and culture and more central to the problems Sri Lanka faces, since one of the key differences that Tamils claim is racial. Sri Lanka takes the prize as the most racist land I've visited. I have never in my life been so discriminated *for*. Despite the mild attitude from the border guards, I have generally been given highest priority as a white Anglophone male. No icon of oppression or modern mask of evil, male white me. No, here I get ushered to the front of lines.

The heat of culture fetish is hot here in Sri Lanka. The island is an ideological bonfire where race, class, caste, ethnicity, history, culture, and politics act as cinders, heating the others they are piled upon. The island's ideological embers emit a heat that has been slowly rising, incinerating the population that walks and works upon the shores and farms.

Gradually, as this internal combustion continues to heat the island, all that will be left will be hatred and ashes.

Boys playing at Madras Kovil, Tamil Nadu, India

Chapter Eight: Kilinochchi

> "What difference does it make to the dead, the orphans, and the homeless, whether the mad destruction is wrought under the name of totalitarianism or the holy name of liberty and democracy?"
> —Mohandas Gandhi

The Man Who Lived in the Horizontal Rain

Highway A9, behind bicyclists, approaching Kilinochchi, Sri Lanka

The bike is humming. The bushes blur. I'm dodging speed bumps and the occasional bird that darts for my face. A truck tries to kill me again, but I'm getting better at off-road driving. It is late afternoon, and the air is cooling. The red earth is below, the blue sky is above, and the windy plain of sand between them is solid and real.

But something in the air sings foul. My heart can hear something wrong in this place; that curious, intuitive feeling you get when you enter a house where someone was murdered, or when the phone rings and you know it won't be good news; that peculiar instinct we humans have evolved that is so important and that we so often discount. There is some ancient problem that has soaked into the dirt here.

Pulling over, I angle my front wheel through a little sand, edging the asphalt (which I assume is safe from mines, since I can see recent tire tracks), and shut off the engine. It's time to have a listen, smell the air, and find my feet.

I get off the bike and stand there in the sand with one heel reassuringly on the asphalt. My legs are wobbly. The soles of my feet buzz. Closing my eyes, I allow the vibration from the motorcycle to wear off, like steam, and let my ears adjust to the silence. I breathe for a minute and wait. The wind hisses in the sand.

When I open my eyes, I see a different world. Next to the road is an old dried-up canal that cuts a line into an otherwise unbroken landscape of orange intestine-colored sand. There is just the sand below and the blue above. A couple of satinwood trees hungrily clutch the ground, crouched under a mighty sky. A few strands of grass sprout up. Red dirt sifts about, running like a tiny transparent army in between the blades of grass. Further out are scrubby bushes, tough as cinder blocks. They also cling to their patch of ground under this weirdly fierce sky. There are no houses, no people, and no signs of civilization other than minefield signs and a crumbling highway.

It is hard to see because it's mostly overgrown, but between the bushes is an old road—perhaps more like vehicle tracks than road. Strange indentations punctuate the ground, perhaps a land mine, or a foundation that was scrubbed out by mortars, or a tree that was bulldozed then burned. As I look more closely and follow the tracks further out, I see several building foundations, now overgrown with colorless grass and unwell bushes. These foundations are chipped and blasted away. There are bones near one of them. I assure myself they're animal bones. I'm tempted to go out to investigate but give up the idea; I don't feel like having my shins blown to splinters. I keep my heel on the asphalt and keep my nose to the wind and keep my eyes on the animal bones.

They're too close to the building.

Decades of war.

The wind smells bitter and moves my shirt.

A jet flies overhead. Singapore to Paris? Jakarta to London? A bird shrieks at me from a low branch near my head, snapping me out of my heavenly reverie. She is not pleased to see a person unattached to his vehicle.

I look down. My boots are sinking into the sand. Red sands shrinking, withdrawing from a shrieking sky, into an earth that is even less safe.

Getting back on the bike, I start the motor and look at the bones. They're the whitest things out here. They're the only white things out here. It's just a red earth and a blue sky, with a few white bones lying around.

I gun the motor and beat the wind at her own game.

Kilinochchi, which means "village of parrots," is

a *real* town, homey, I mean, with the usual assortment of houses, intersections, grocery stores, people talking on the street corner, a motorcycle-repair shop, some blankets for sale, a restaurant where people line up and choose food and sit down to eat together. Everyone is riding bicycles. The men all wear sarongs with nice dress shirts. The women are dressed in saris. They are damn styling for being so poor. The streets are not clean, but the people, individually, are. The notion of hygiene here is focused on personal health and appearance first, on civic health and appearance second. It's mid-afternoon, and the light is so bright that the gray pavement reflects the sky, and the gray road is framed in red with the Tamil dust that peppers everything.

Kilinochchi is vivid and stark. Dilapidated shacks made of some dozen pieces of corrugated steel nailed to trembling frames built with found planks. Tin awnings painted with chipped blue paint. A squiggle of Tamil. An arrow. An occasional bus or tractor, but no cars. Quite a few motorcycles. Forty-two kilometers per hour. I take it easy and move through town. The rpms and temp look fine; gas is getting a little low. The road is broad.

The structures that are not propped up on planks are big buildings with big holes, where a wall sags from a mortar shell that broke it once upon a day. A window has been rather oddly increased in size. More shells. Smaller shell marks, the ones that landed at the base of a wall and threw sand, or the one that just nicked a corner, or hit a tree and left the entire stump split apart, all strange and torn. I slow down to thirty. Here are bullet holes from a machine gun, in a sprayed line up the face of the shaky old wall, across the top, and back down, an upside-down V of bullet scars. I stop the bike.

Not even the moon has been beat up this much. What I thought was textured stucco is really a chalked and shattered dartboard, soaked with a past of heavy fighting. I push the kickstand down with my heel, swing my leg over the bike, and walk up to the wall. There is not a single spot that's untouched. I put my hand, fingers outspread, on the wall. I am touching five bullet holes. I step to the right and do it again. Five. I take another step to the right and do it again. Four. Then I turn around and look at the other buildings nearby, and the veil drops. Every building is the same. It is a village of bullet holes, mortar-shell pockmarks, and burns. A horizontal storm happened here. A rain of heavy lead has decimated this village.

Back on the bike.

About a hundred thousand people live here, but it is hard for me to tell since there are no streetlights or tall buildings. Here, as in other parts of Sri Lanka, sophisticated infrastructure and the population graphs drawn into the skylines of Western cities by skyscrapers have not had the chance to develop. From the looks of it, Kilinochchi could just as well be a town of five thousand people, perhaps somewhere out in Wyoming.

A truck carrying hay and produce swings out of an intersection, cutting me off, so I decelerate and wave to the five guys in the back, who all seem as happy as teenage girls.

I get to the north end of town and flip a U-turn. The turn somehow makes me realize how exhausted and overwhelmed I am. The tank treads; bullet casings; scattered concrete; burned husks; black, molten, smashed cars that were hit from above with something that incinerated the entire vehicle, now black and still inside; the propaganda and documents of psychological warfare that still float in the breeze; the dirty children; the tense jaws; the women holding their babies closer than normal; the men looking malicious — plotting minds, malevolent hearts —

and a world that cannot make itself any better but instead struggles under the weight of violence, poverty, despair, and a sickness that can't be taken to a hospital, because there is neither hospital for such wounds nor money for such luxuries, and if there is, it gets paid to the man who is pointing his gun at your eye. In a kind of confession, an unending and unanswerable admission of pain, despair, weakness, and impossible hope, the village shivers and convulses, and people continue with their lives as if nothing happened. Ultimately, they have no other choice.

I pull over near some buildings that look like houses and turn off the engine again. I'm having problems breathing. I'm riding through a village full of ghosts, and each one is clogging my trachea, mistaking my throat for a door that might let them out of this horrible nightmare named Kilinochchi.

A man comes out of one of the houses. He's about forty, with a beard and glasses. He wears the customary sarong, but he also has a clean white shirt and a thin, tendinous neck, like a math professor. Holding his left hand in his right, he asks, "Iz a prohbellem?"

"No problems, just looking. Thank you."

He raises an index finger, turns, and disappears inside. He comes back with two plastic chairs and sets them down in the shade of the building. I thank him by saying, "*Nandree*" —thank you, in Tamil—and take the load off. I need it. Going back into the building, he disappears for a good five minutes while I sit there and contemplate bullet marks, architectural scars, and what it means to drown a population of very poor people in a civil war. He comes back out with two cups of tea that are steaming hot, but after I drink it I find it has a cooling effect, as does all good tea.

My host has a long slender nose and lower eyelids

that come up higher than they should, all of which makes him look intelligent or angry. He has all of his hair and a straight posture—a Tamil Clark Gable.

His name is Ganesh. His father is a farmer, but Ganesh decided he wanted a more intellectual life. He is indeed a math teacher. He teaches in a high school in Jaffna. He owns a car, and every Friday, after working all week at the school, he drives from Jaffna to Kilinochchi, where he works on his property.

I ask how it's going for him.

"Good, good. But SLA[1] and LTTE keeps damage on thingz."

I'm afraid to ask, wondering if he's referring to his family, his property, his livelihood. We talk about his property. First he had to have the mines cleared from his backyard, he says. That was best done with a tractor.

We get up from our chairs and, with our two cups of tea, walk around his house.

Tractors (these are the John Deere front-end bucket-loader types) cost twenty-one thousand rupees per hour. That's about U.S. $210. If you consider that the average Tamil makes a fraction of that in a year, think of what it would mean to you to put two or three years' savings into clearing mines left in your backyard by the army you are supporting through taxes.

He bends over and hands me the tail end of a mortar shell. It's about as big as my forearm.

I always like to see the "before" and "after:" the starting point, the intent, the execution, those final twists and knots of any such action, which is always the highest accomplishment and the best evidence of thought. On our left is the "before:" the cratered and disheveled dents of automatic weapon spatter across the wall. On our right is the new wall: clean, spackled, painted, and

---

1. The SLA is the Sri Lankan army.

sturdy. It's a skeleton with not only a new skin but new muscle, circulatory system, and clothes to go. On a math teacher's salary, it's hard for him to save the money, but he's making progress each month. I pat the wall and admire the work. It's certainly solid, and I can see the new plaster, and underneath the plaster darker shadows where the holes were. There is a slight texture difference. The building will never be new, of course, but it looks like he's managing to get it back together.

We go into the backyard where, like a bonsai horticulturist, he has been carefully grooming his property. There were mines here, and he couldn't set foot out the back door of his own house. So the tractor came in (here are the tracks, still not wiped out by the rains) and cleaned up the explosives. Then it lifted out the big materiel, twisted metal from some nearby explosion, and a few other large pieces of steel. Then it left. Trusting the yard was safe, he had started to dig—tenuously at first, I imagine—with a shovel and removed all the lumber, bricks, smaller shrapnel, shell casings, a helmet or two, some clothing, plastic sheath assemblies, and other detritus. These things he has stacked into neat piles around the yard, some of which he will put to good use if he ever rebuilds the little greenhouse that he once had back here.

We walk back inside, into the shade. He hands me another cup of tea, then shows me the work he's done on the roof, on the strut between the walls. He explains how it might now be as strong as when it was first built.

I have no idea what it is to clear mines from your yard, clean up after an army, rebuild your house, and all the while keep a job that pays about twenty-five American cents a week in a town some one hundred kilometers away. All I can say is "Good, good" with a little more gusto than I intend to, and hope that he is encouraged to continue his clear, fine work, hard work—something bordering on spiritual. It's all I have to offer.

I leave and walk across the street, where there are more people and a few shops. While the town is withering from the heat and dying from the war, underneath the rot, in the shade, small sprouts are appearing. I meet a family and talk with them for a while. They also commute between Jaffna and Kilinochchi. The woman is beautiful, and she is proud of her child.

A small girl shows me her drawings. Two young men ask me if I play cricket. An old lady begs for some money, and I give her a few candies (and then everyone else gets candies, too, since a candy-handout festival has spontaneously occurred and a good two dozen children materialize with their hands out). A teenage boy wants a ride on the bike, so we take a roll around the block. His mom keeps an eye on us, smiling. He waves at his mom so much I think he'll fall off the bike.

Small sprouts. Just people dragging themselves out of a crater.

"Please welcome, sir. Sit," the man says as he shows me to my table. People are hunched over their plates, jamming fantastic food into their mouths, talking fast like big magic parrots. Little plastic table, little plastic chairs, Kleenex for a napkin. I sit. Looking down the menu, written by hand and a bit orange around the edges from curried fingers, I see many of the usuals. There are a few luxury items—garlic masala, kiwi tea, tea with lime, jasmine. "Please welcome," the man repeats as he stands behind me. I look at him, smile, nod, and keep reading. There are about fifty people in here, but he's still standing behind me. Thank Ganesh for the food here. I look at the waiting man, point to my pick, and say, *"Kari"* (which, by the way, is the Tamil word for "sauce" and the etymological root of the word "curry"). Then I add, in English, "With a pitcher of water," and finally remembering my manners, say, "*Dhayavuseydhu.*" Please.

Just as we did down south, here in the north we eat with our right hands. I sponge out a paddy of rice, then collect a healthy pinch of a gray-and-red sauce, which I spin together on the plate with my fingers. It makes my nose tingle with ancient spices, so I load some more sauce onto it and pinch up a big mouthful, which I shove boldly into my face. Chew, chew. The tangy cumin and cardamom first hit the roof of my mouth, then there's a rebound of tangy tamarind; some sharp cinnamon cuts through with a salty beauty, then a hit of black pepper; finally it is punctured by a deadly chili of some sort that cuts through it all and has me reaching for the bottle of water to wash it down as tears pop out of my eyes. I reach for another, smiling like a drunk lord, not letting go of the water bottle for fear of having my mouth incinerated.

Four guys confidently seat themselves at my table, and for a moment I think they're LTTE, the way they surround me, but they're just happy fellows, tall and skinny, brazen smiles. They are dressed impeccably for war-zone living. After some talking they ask if I'm nervous about visiting. I tell them, "You guys live here and you're okay, so I figure as long as you're here with me, I'm safe." It is both a logical and absurd argument, but it brings us to more important matters such as language, and we laugh as we try to form words that have never taken shape in our mouths. We trade Tamil for English, and the topic of conversation is the items on the table, such real items; and such a gift is a word, and a good thing to trade at that.

We take a break to call over a waiter and order more curries that they've picked this time, another plate that would baffle any high-skipping gourmet restaurant in penthouse Manhattan. Tamils in northern Sri Lanka have access to a surprising list of ingredients, despite the war's weight. This is a simple restaurant, but the guys I am sitting with have ordered a curry that is more a spice party: ginger, garlic, tamarind, coriander, chili, mustard seeds, cinnamon, cloves, cardamom, cumin, and even curry leaves, all together, with lentils and rice.

The waiters move around us, picking up our paper plates, and the bare lightbulbs in the ceiling expose this world in its vivid and brutal reality. We madly scoop the food into our mouths, they work what words they can in English, and I try to remember the dozen or so words they gave me, relying on them to bridge the linguistic span. One of the things I like about speaking with people in a foreign language is that language becomes simple, and smiles and nods become a default.

In 1998 the LTTE set up their administrative offices here, which has brought the town under some fire, but it's worth it, they tell me. Prabhakaran will, they tell me, make this the new Tamil capital. It will be the center of a kingdom. They tell me that Prabhakaran, the head honcho of the LTTE, is a good leader.

"Why?"

They can't say.

They just know it, like Prabath. They tell me that Tamils have lived in northern Sri Lanka for over two thousand years, then left.

"What happened?" I ask. "Why did they leave?"

They don't know. They look at one another.

Then one says "The Sinhalese! They hate us! They hate our culture."

I'm surprised and saddened. These guys are living in LTTE-controlled land, supporting a cause that is not theirs, living on pennies each week, and they have been neatly groomed to spout the party lines, cants, patriot songs, and half-truths that the LTTE has been feeding them for the last thirty years. But perhaps this is how it is everywhere in the world. "They hate our freedoms" is the default response. Perhaps this is, ultimately, the function of government, whenever there is a war, to keep us ignorant, but aligned. After all, I've heard and read and can personally attest to there being massive support for the LTTE in the north of Sri Lanka. Some statistics I've seen indicate a 70 to 80 percent rate of support for Prabhakaran. It's a strange thing to see, really, because it might be that this support was largely created by the racism I've seen among the Sinhalese in the south. It is an impossible balance to measure.

A friend of theirs joins us at our table. He's smiling and excited to see his buddies, and they talk fast with the bubbling sound of Tamil and slap one another on the back and hold hands, and then I am pointed to and some more babbling happens and they are kind enough to shift back to slow English.

They explain that their friend has recently found someone from Colombo—a member of the Sinhalese army—taking notes on the town plan and asking questions at the radio station. There is some discussion about this and he says that he's reported the "spy" to the LTTE office, over near the bank. He is, effectually, an informant, and he is proud of this, so I tell him he'd better go let folks know I am in town, too. This gets a bit of a chuckle but I don't think Mr. Informant finds it too funny.

We smile and nod and eat together. Rice drops on the floor as the stars come out, and more lightbulbs come on in the restaurant, and we laugh more and I am reminded that, ultimately, food and friends are far more important than politics.

After dinner it occurs to me, as I walk toward the only hotel in town, that Kilinochchi is a bit like Woodland

Park, Colorado, a town I lived in for a few years as a boy. The two towns have the same layout, the same population, the same hub-of-transport relation to the major roads, and the people seem to do more or less the same thing: farm, eat, talk, and support and inform the government that, in return, informs and supports them.

What else can they do?

In the end, we all need our literatures.

Mortar (fresh from Ganesh's backyard), Kilinochchi, Sri Lanka

Coughing Morning

Bullet-riddled wall, Kilinochchi, Sri Lanka

Small pain. I wake up. Something behind my knee, above my calf, kind of ... stings. My back stings. Feverish nightmare happening. Forehead sweaty. I'm glad to find I'm still intact because I was dreaming about a truck running over me. My left arm aches.

Lying on my side, I think I can see the ceiling of the hotel room. Someone snores, gulping the cigarette- and Clorox-scented air.

My leg stings.

In Colombo, I could spend about U.S. $20 a night to stay in a nice hotel where three people would watch me eat—one to bring me food, one to clean up, and one to bring drinks. The bed was white with a nice little flower set on the pillow each morning, and there was a bottle of fresh water near the bed and another in the bathroom.

Here I have discovered a very different notion of hotel accommodation. Not only does this room have less than a percent of the amenities of my hotel room in Colombo, it costs four times as much. The architect was clearly a student of minimalism. In the tradition of simplicity and spartan interior design, the bed, set alone in the center of the room, has no sheets. The blue-and-white-striped mattress rests upon a lovely collection of slightly tangled springs quite in keeping with the heady design aesthetic. There is a gray pillow sumptuously decorated in a leopard pattern of drool stains. Sticking with the moderne theme of spare and simple, there is no window. There is no light switch because there is no light. There is no carpet. There is no nightstand.

There is an eight-inch gap where the walls do not quite reach the floor, allowing for the free circulation of air, rats, snakes, cockroaches, and the sounds of your neighbors as they snore.

I blink again at the wall, wishing myself to sleep. The room smells faintly of cigarette smoke, piss, and bleach. The sound of someone choke-snoring next door is suddenly accompanied by the smell of mouth. Yes, it smells like mouths; people around me are sleeping with them open. That gap under the wall kept me attuned last night to the party-happy crowd next door until they finally decided to shut their heads for the evening.

It is the only hotel in town, so it is crowded. I decided that keeping my head attached was worth the cost of this crap hole. This was the only show in town; it was either here with the people or in a minefield with the snakes, so I checked in last night about an hour after sunset. The greasy little man who ran the place was smashingly dressed and incredibly unpleasant and followed me with an open palm until I paid him an uncustomary tip, evidently so he would leave me alone. He then hid himself and offered me no help.

I was not happy to learn that the hotel had no showers, only a shared bathtub. Yes, indeed, there is so little water in the town that there is only a large bath, and if you like you can use it for only about U.S. $10. The communal bathroom is a series of four toilet stalls. To the right of those is a square tile basin large enough for a man to sit in. This is the tub. The basin was already full of gray water. Dead skin and gray hair were sticking to the side, midway up the walls of the thing. The water was partially drained out. After eight hours on a motorcycle in 50°C (122°F) heat, the one thing you really want, more than food, more than sleep, more than rest itself, is fresh water. If I wanted to get the dust and bugs off of me, this was the place to do it, so I paid for my bucket and stood in the filthy little hole, pouring the water over my head, keeping my lips tightly closed, and making the best of it.

The snoring sleeper chokes again, then regains his rhythm.

I'm just lying with my eyes closed, groggy, on my side, my arm under my head. On the back of my leg, in the fold at the back of my knee, I feel something move. There is a small weight on my leg, and it moves. That's when I feel the sting again. I can't see it, but I'm sure some hairy-assed, green-armored, heavy hog of a bug is chewing into a key vein. I spin in the bed. Adrenaline glands spray massive doses of fear into my bloodstream. I swipe at my leg in that one-heartbeat spasm of fear between dead sleep and full battle. Bedsprings screech. My knuckle connects with a very heavy insect, which hits the drywall with a pop. My snoring neighbor chokes again. There's a second of silence as I sit on that striped mattress in the dark, listening. I hear the foul thing skitter along the floor.

I feel something on my lower back. I reach around and grab a wriggling bug about the size of—and, dear God, at least as heavy as—a Zippo lighter. I don't want to touch it any more than I want it touching me, so I fling it against the wall, too. Another whack, another *skitty-skitty-skit* as it scampers to whatever tiny Hades it came from. I'm surprised it survived; I threw it hard.

My feet are numb. My legs have become lunches more than limbs, with mosquitoes, ants, red ants, and red-ant spiders feasting on my ankles. My watch says 2:00 AM.

I sit there breathing the gasoline smell of war. The night scent is full of insects, stifling heat, rusting bullets, and forbidden chemicals, and as I lay there wondering if my two special six-legged Zippo friends will come back, I turn to thinking again.

War is a special trait. Like learning, walking upright, throwing a party, speaking a language, or having sex, humans will engage in war as long as we exist. Someday in the distant future, perhaps on some other planet, when there are only a few humans left, they will engage in battle if they can, because that is ultimately how humans are made. After some hundred thousand years of selection and training, it is one of the things we are best at, both by instinct and intelligence—and in fact, we humans need conflict just like we need language, to help us define who we are.

We use war similarly to the way we use media—as a tool to help ourselves determine our values, our similarities, and our differences. War and media allow us to measure ourselves both against and with our fellows. Also like media, war is driven by popular support, money, and collaboration. Media, after all, is itself a weapon, one that Moggallana, Dhatusena, Rajee, Prabhakaran, Devananda, and Karunaratne all used to strengthen their wars.

War, like media, exists because we are social. War exists because we organize ourselves into groups, and those very groups create a threat to other groups that are neighbors. We are as warlike as we are sociable. It is because we are sociable that we are warlike. These twins require one another, and will always be linked.

Tamils and Sinhalese are about as close, racially and culturally, as two ethnic groups can be, and they have been fraternizing with each other for about as long as any two groups in history. There are some parallels here with the relationship between Palestinians and Israelis, and with the relationship between Iraqis and Kurds. Groups in Africa, such as the Tutsis and Hutus, have been at it for a long time as well—all groups that, from a distance, seem identical to another set of eyes. But these groups hold wars as one might hold a conference. War is a discussion of identity and difference. War defines limits. War creates identity.

Maybe war is just how we compare ourselves with our equals. An equal is needed, and some symmetry in the fight; otherwise we call it genocide, massacre, or holocaust. When all the infrastructure of society, all the water, electricity, roads, advertisements, and laws, are gone, then we see ourselves and our equals clearly. The notion of "asymmetric warfare" was introduced in the 1970s, around the same time that the term "terrorism" began to enter into public dialogue in the United States. The War on Terror (what might be thought of as the fourth world war, if the Cold War was the third) was not, in fact, asymmetric but was, rather, a war waged between two ideological forces that were quite equal: the George W. Bush administration versus Al Qaeda. The efforts of the United States and the primary enemy in the War on Terror seemed not only to be equal in strength, but in outlook as well. Both sides were monotheistic, militant, and media-savvy. Both called themselves conservatives and insisted they had become so because of foreign invasion. Both knew how to foment the formula of God, guns, and government.

Someone snores in the next room and someone else shuffles a bit.

I roll over and stare at the wall. Thinking it might be dawn, I look at my watch. Twenty minutes have passed. Between the probable return of my skittering bed guests, the whine of an orbiting mosquito, my angst over war, and the lingering buzz from the bike, I can't sleep. I roll onto my back and stare at the ceiling. An hour passes like this. I slap my forehead and kill a mosquito that is scaling the cliffs of my temple. I hear a skittering on the floor and lean over the bed to hiss and spit at it. It skitters under the wall. I whisper at it to bite the guys who are keeping me awake.

I come out of my box and step over bodies scattered about in the hall, looking for something that will distract me for a while, keep me from that hateful state of insomnia, something to read, draw, or write, to pass the hours while keeping the bugs from chewing my sunburned meat. Taking a turn down another hallway, I fumble through a closet. I find a sheet I'm probably not supposed to use. I take it and the rest of my drinking water into the bathroom and wet the fabric. Back in my bedroom of death, I tiptoe over the wet tiles to minimize the possibility of stepping on a Zippo bug. The bed seems clear of visitors. I spread out the sheet, crawl under this cool refuge, and lie there in the dark for four hours, willing the sun to rise.

Someone coughs.

War zones—at least the four I have visited—all have some common characteristics. First, there are a few women around and men are generally missing, but

children—kids between five and eleven in particular—
are everywhere. Though young men, those around age
fifteen or so, are usually required to carry arms and fight
with their elders, there is, in most war zones, a huge
surplus of children.

In war zones, life is quiet. Even in an active
bombing raid, the city becomes eerily quiet. The wind
itself is timid. Most of Kilinochchi and Vavuniya—the
two towns in the north with the horrid luck to be located
in no man's land—have electricity only in certain places.
Most Tamils don't have enough money to go from Jaffna
to Kilinochchi and can't travel from one to the other
unless they have a good enough bike and time to pedal
the path. Civic infrastructure has been broken down to
its minimum, its most essential gears, so the war zone
returns to a primitive and preindustrial silence. This
makes a war zone strangely peaceful.

In war zones, a reality of absurdities is built
on what is found. Roadblocks, for example, are made
of burned cars. Or logs, tires, rocks, burned crates of
consumer goods, piles of bottles, rocks from alongside
the road. One time in Gaza I saw a crate of first-aid
packages being used as a roadblock. I once saw a man
use a tampon to dress a wound. I found a car windshield
in Basra that was used as a dining room table, a Coke can
used as a bracelet, copper wiring used as money, and a
curb used as a bed.

In war zones, you can never progress in a straight
line. You constantly come across obstacles that force you
to drive in a Z or a U. These obstacles include potholes,
bag searches, and passport displays, by way of example.
Usually these war obstacles are thrown in the road and
take the shape of a tire, a tree, a transmission, a bag of
sand, or any other thing that will slow a moving vehicle.
These obstacles exist because the world has become

absurd, and the absurdities have forced people to find what they can and build what they're able.

In war zones, and especially here, the sky is terrifyingly large. The roads are wide, and mostly of dirt. There are no resources to raise buildings over one or two stories. There are no planes, no radio towers. There is no reason for these things when all that's accomplished by building is the creation of taller target.

In war zones, people cough. The war zone invades the people, too.

I knew it was getting close to sunrise when I heard a man in the bathroom clearing his throat. At first I thought someone was joking around: *snort, snort, snort, snoooort, hack, hack,* pause, cough. Cough. Spit. Spit. Cough, spit, *hagh.* A minute or two later someone else joined him.

Birds are starting to sing, and a hoarse rooster somewhere outside adds his own voice to the rise of a new day in an old war zone. Men, birds, and rooster, everyone's singing up the sun.

The men leave the bathroom. I take my turn so that I might sooner exit this demonic and expensive excuse for a rest house off the A9 Highway.

I pack my bag and walk out into that sad, bullet-riddled corridor of buildings that was once a city street. The sunrise almost makes things seem fresh. A couple of bicycles whir by, headed toward Jaffna. It is still quiet. The wind is chasing rose-colored streaks of dust into the sucking sky. Everything everyone has built is withered because the LTTE and Sri Lankan army ran out of imagination. They couldn't find a solution.

The motorcycle pulls me out of town.

The Killed Secret Weapon

The secret weapon, Elephant Pass, Sri Lanka

Humans are suicide specialists. Sometimes we kill ourselves to escape our own lives, to dodge our impending deaths, or simply as a solvent for the insoluble problems of the world. Sometimes we have to blow ourselves apart before we can rebuild. Sometimes we have to destroy our bodies so the power of the soul can find its way out of the clogged un-reality of life. I don't know what it is to be a suicide terrorist, but I do know that civil war is a type of large-scale suicide. Sometimes only death can confirm your identity: If you can kill yourself, at least you know you're not under someone else's thumb anymore. Borders appear when a country starts to kill itself in a civil war. Sri Lanka, for example, has been ripped apart by her civil war.

The line north of Vavuniya, called the DMZ, is one of these rips. The rip has become a border between the Sinhalese and the Tamils. It's a suicide that has formed an identity. The Tamil Tigers, however, have taken civil war as a form of suicide one step higher: A bomber will wear explosives strapped around his neck, performing an autodecapitation and leaving his head far from his body in a kind of symbolic representation of a people with no homeland. The suicide bomber sees, in the final seconds of consciousness, a heavenly perspective.

Tyronne Fernando, Sri Lanka's foreign minister from 2001 to 2004, was one of many who credit the Tamil Tigers with the notable distinction of having invented the suicide bomb. Consider the suicide assassination of former Indian prime minister Rajiv Gandhi by the Tamil Tigers in 1991. The Tigers were upset over Indian intervention in the civil war (India had taken back the weapons they'd originally given to the Tamil militants). So the Tamil Tigers sent a suicide bomber to eliminate Gandhi.

The Black Tigers, the LTTE's elite suicide group, had a fairly sophisticated program that, since their targets were usually high profile, required a suicide terrorist to train for a year or more. In addition to training the bomber on methods of walking, dress, facial expressions, and gestures, the Black Tigers also had a research unit that tested the effects of explosives on goats and other animals. Something about the program was successful: The LTTE conducted more suicide operations than any other organization in the world.[1]

Over fifty people were present when Rajiv Gandhi

---

1. "Suicide Terrorism: A Global Threat." Jane's Security News, October 20, 2000, www.janes.com/security/international_security/news/usscole/jir001020_1_n.shtml.

was killed. One of them was an Indian photographer. He was killed in the bombing, but his camera survived. When his film was developed after the bombing, one of the snapshots showed a small, bespectacled woman with braids on both sides of her head, about twenty-five years old.[2] In the picture she is genuflecting. In the next photo, she is closer to Rajiv Gandhi, carrying a sandalwood garland in her hand, again genuflecting. In the third photo we see her stepping up to the stage where Rajiv Gandhi is standing and smiling. She puts the garland around his neck. In the final photo he puts a hand around her arm. At that same moment, at 10:18 AM on May 21, 1991, the officers outside heard an unfamiliar bang.

Of the eighteen people killed in the blast all but one were quickly identified. Most of the body parts were thrown only a few meters. One body, however, was scattered more than sixty meters apart, but the bomb was curiously designed to preserve the head, which was found nearby with a ghastly expression of joy, the mouth open in celebration, the eyes closed, one earring still attached. "The face of the woman was, however, miraculously still identifiable and a bore close resemblance to the one waiting to garland Rajiv Gandhi," wrote Subramanian Swamy.[3]

She was identified as Dhanu (with at least four other sobriquets), a daughter of a Tamil man who, as early as 1966, had begun organizing meetings among potential militants willing to oppose the Sinhalese government. She was the daughter of early militant opposition, and militant opposition was also her inheritance.

The night before the suicide attack, Dhanu had—

2. About 30 percent of the suicide operations in Sri Lanka have been conducted by women.
3. Swamy, Subramanian, *The Assassination of Rajiv Gandhi: Unanswered Questions and Unasked Queries*. Delhi: Konark Publishers, 1994, pages 115–116.

like all suicide bombers do—her last dinner with Prab-hakaran. He gave her—as he did all suicide bombers—a medal.

The sun is rising. I'm driving north, away from my bedbug friends and early-morning nightmares. I keep an eye out, as the general had suggested, for the bulldozer that the Tamil Tigers stole from the cement factory. There's not much to see, really. There is a stretch of salty marshes, and the road goes right up the center. Then I see a grim rhinoceros of a vehicle, settled into a ditch off the side of the road, slowly being devoured by the hungry jungle. I pull over and turn off the bike. I walk around what turns out to be a military tank, slowly circling through the scrub.

This is the tank that Karunaratne told me about, when I was in Colombo, at the Sri Lankan army headquarters.

It's wrapped in chicken wire. I have no clue why. Perhaps to keep people off, but nonetheless I climb up and stare down through the top of the cab, wondering about the last moment of the person who found himself sitting next to a live grenade about to detonate, the man who died here. Morbidity asks if there is a corpse, but there is nothing inside. The vehicle has been rusted and empty for a good decade, and that's okay with me. I sigh a breath of relief, climb down, drop to the safe earth, and start walking around taking photos, kicking through the weeds and thick leaves, picking my way over the rubble of an old building, walking around the front, snapping more photos and wondering about Gamini Kularathna, who threw the fatal bomb into the cab.

The LTTE's efforts to beef up their armory were constant, and when it couldn't buy weapons, it smuggled in the separate parts and assembled them.

In 2007, two Czech-built propeller-driven aircraft known as Zlin 143s were rigged with homemade bombs and used for a series of exploits that included bombing air force barracks, a power station, and several army and air bases. The last attack of 2007 was a run at a military forward-operations base (damaging nothing) at the eastern port of Trincomalee. The following year, in 2008, the Sri Lankan air force intercepted these planes over the northeast of the island; they had been used in an attempted bomb run on an air base in Colombo, and near Vavuniya. The bunked bombing raid was followed by an artillery strike that prompted a series of Sri Lankan army invasions into the north. The militants countered with more air strikes from the north. And so the battle always renewed itself, with each side trading blows, the army growing more embarrassed and frustrated, unable to stop the smaller, weaker planes.

By February of 2009 the LTTE had a new division named the Black Air Tigers. On the night of February 20, at 9:30 PM, two unidentified planes were spotted coming from the north of the island. In less than twenty minutes the power grid had been cut and long streaks of orange could be seen in the skies over Colombo. Several minutes later, one plane crashed into a tax center in the middle of Colombo. The other went down near the airport, crashing into a nearby swamp.

The day of this attack, TamilNet, the LTTE's online soapbox, posted a picture of two men posing with Prabhakaran between them. The website identified them as the pilots. Both of the men are ostensibly smiling, but the expression of the one on the right, slender and in his early twenties, is quite complex. The center of his eyebrows are raised, the lower edges of his mouth are pulled down, and his eyes are squinted, as if he's about to cry.

The image's timestamp says that the photo was taken with a digital camera on the day of the attack, about an hour and a half before they took off for their suicide run: *Camera Model: Canon EOS 350D DIGITAL Date Digitized: 2009:02:20 19:21:16*

This man's face provides a rare glimpse into the atmosphere of the LTTE's honorary meetings. Suicide terrorists, at this point, don't have the freedom to say no; their life has already been assigned a value. Prabhakaran, toadish, glares out from between them. The website refers to these flights as "successful air raids."[4]

Standing next to the old war machine I look back up at it. Like Dhanu's detonation belt, or the Black Air Tigers' airplane, this rusting tank was a vessel for the driver's soul, a sacred object that represented his past, his present, and his future. Now this suicide vehicle is being eaten by the jungle, just oxidizing in the rich air. These Black Tiger suicides left a burn mark on the world. They are remembered for their futility. A deep machinery moved them to this fate, a mechanism that steered them toward their defining end, carried them along its dark conveyor belt, and in the end they could give no more than their deaths. And in the end, the machine does no more than rust, with their futures trapped inside.

Stepping around the tank, avoiding the wires, and ducking under a branch, I move through the low grass and scrub. A small twig snaps.

The image of the sandal with a disk under it comes to mind; the image on a poster I saw back on Highway A9, and only then does it occur to me that I am stupidly, stupidly, standing in a minefield.

But maybe not, though, because surely people

---

4. "Black Air Tiger Attack on Colombo's Air Force HQ, Air Base." TamilNet, February 20, 2009, http://www.tamilnet.com/art.html?catid=13&artid=28478.

walk around this tank. But maybe so, though, because people walk around this tank. I don't have any experience in predicting the likelihood or logic of landmine placement. I look around and take a slow breath.

Fortunately, yes, my legs are still attached, even if common sense clearly isn't. I take a second breath, not really moving, and scan the ground to find the place where I last stepped. My left eye unexpectedly vibrates. The undergrowth seems determined to betray me. I imagine red warning lights flashing under the foliage. Once I find my last footprint, I look carefully to see if there is any metal in sight. I gingerly place my foot, toe to heel, and gradually ease my weight onto it. As if gingerly or gradually would have done any good. There is no explosion. It's normal dirt. I stand, like a stupid bird, on one leg, my camera in my hand. I look for the next footprint. It's impossible to find, and, anyway, I'd been looking at the tank, not the ground, as I walked into this idiotic situation. I figure chances are good enough that the place has been cleared. I am hanging by my fat luck, pants around my ankles. If I die here today, I guess I'll deserve it. I give up logic and just jump wherever feels right.

I hop up onto the chipped foundation of one of the old army buildings and trace a path back. Eventually I get to the bike and, even then, I carefully pick my way through the gravel until I'm back to the safety of paved, sunny asphalt.

The asphalt becomes my trusted friend, my long, black, greasy life preserver that will buoy me up from the bloody oceans of my own stupidity. The road, like tradition itself, will keep me free of deadly mistakes. Or perhaps the road, like tradition itself, will lead me into a repetition of deadly errors.

The Men Who Sold Fish

Fishermen, Elephant Pass, Sri Lanka

Elephant Pass is an oddly slender wedge of sand and sludge whose banks are no further apart than the treads of a tank. A malevolent, surreal place, it does not gladden nor inspire the desire to loiter. I just accelerate out as the land thins, and I trace the final few tendons of dry land up between blue and scabrous lagoons, this salted labyrinth of mines and infested water. The only buildings I see—perhaps four or five in as many kilometers—are bombed and cracked, recoiling from the sky and sagging toward the water. Even the mud, protracted and dried, is in a state of remission before the nuclear gaze of god.

There is no one out here. It's an apocalyptic world of reflection and heat, where the cynical sky bounces off the water. The labyrinth reaches in all directions. The faster I go, the hotter it gets, so hot.

Up the road, a small building becomes visible. I slow a bit, not cooling off at all. It's a small shack with three young men in front. The youngest wears a striped shirt.

"Where are you from?" I ask, beating them to the predictable question.

"Here."

I point to the house. "Is that your home?"

"Yes."

"You swim" —I point to the lagoon—"here?"

"No."

"Why 'no'?"

"Sick."

Ah. "Why?"

"Sick day next. No swim."

"What do you do?"

"We are fishers!" he exclaims like a child, and he waves one hand above his head and shoots the other behind him toward the building. His two friends watch.

It's only 8:00 AM. I look at my forearm and see beads of sweat appearing.

"Let's go see," I tell them.

The counter where they sell their fish is a beach-combed collection that sits in front of the building. It's made of sun-bleached wood slabs from a thousand different sources—houses, boats, warehouses, trees. The boards are different sizes, taped together, wound with coconut twine and coat hangers, and wizened to a mean gray from the salt and sun.

On the countertop are hundreds of dried sardines in organized rows. Each of the tiny silver corpses has its mouth open. I can't remember if sardines die with their mouths open or not. Why are the sardines' mouths open?

A last breath before death, trying to find some final air? If the water is sick, are the sardines sick too? They're lined up on Tamil newspapers that I can't read. They smell good, like a leather jacket. They each have different faces.

Flies are busy with their frenetic duties, grooming the tiny corpses, cleaning, eating, collecting, making deposits.

I've been standing here, I think, staring for longer than I was supposed to. A skinny guy who hasn't said much waves the flies away. The gesture is pointless. A small breeze carries something that smells sulfurous, like a firecracker.

Inside the shack is another table like the one outside. This one has a metal ammunition lockbox on it. It's closed. A wrinkled poster of Mariah Carey is on the wall, from before she had her nervous breakdown. Also on the wall is a calendar, which is a jewelry advertisement. On it is a round-faced Japanese woman dressed in a fancy blue Thai outfit in front of a neon waterfall. The bottom half of the calendar is stained, as if it had been in a puddle for a while. I see no other people, just these men, living here, selling fish, under the watchful eyes of Mariah and the Japanese jewelry woman.

I turn around, squinting at their silhouettes blocking the doorway.

"You like Mariah Carey?" I ask the big one.

"Yes! Mariah has many good things to say! Come," and I think, from the way he says it, that he might introduce me to Mariah as soon as we get back outside.

Three more people are walking up from the beach: a young boy and two men wearing sarongs. One of the men is short, with a beard. They carry plastic sacks. Out of these they take more of the same open-mouthed fish, arrange them on the table in their rows, and stand back to admire their work.

Out on the east coast of the island, in the small town of Vaharai, fishermen were allowed to sell fish only to the LTTE. Even what was taken for their own use had to be accounted for. Around the end of 2002, the LTTE purchased some prawns for two hundred rupees per kilo and sold them off at four hundred rupees. When the fishermen raised this issue with the LTTE's civic administration, they were told that if they didn't like the policy, they could go live somewhere else. Of course they couldn't.

Since the LTTE's civic administration reports to the regional administration, the fishermen got together and decided to take it up a level. Some threats came down the pipeline, and the fishermen, on February 10, 2003, held a demonstration. Some LTTE muscle showed up that afternoon and knocked around some of the demonstrators, a few of whom had to be hospitalized. The fishermen refused to go out and collect fish the next day. The story trailed off into obscurity. The LTTE refused to be interviewed, and the fishermen disappeared.

The LTTE was parroting the Sri Lankan government, which was parroting the British government. But, to be fair, things always get dangerous when someone tells you that you don't have choices. If I push my cat into a corner and don't give her a choice, she'll get angry and eventually scratch me in self-defense, no matter how much she loves me. Government must always give citizens choices, regardless of whether it is an established government state, a de facto terrorist state, or an empire ruling from afar. The choice must at least be offered, or the interaction can't be sustained. Maybe the human heart must have choices because if none remain, then suicide is the final option.

"Fishing!" I holler as he spreads the fish out on the table.

"Yes!" the big one answers, and I suspect there is a pride in what they're doing.

"But no swimming!" I say, looking at the men who have come back with wet fish and dry clothes; even their pant cuffs are dry, and I decide that they must have a boat hidden somewhere. Or are they collecting fish from the beach, maybe dead ones that wash up in the night? I notice that some of the fish aren't that fresh.

The boy starts giggling, and I smile at him.

By this point it's pretty clear I'm not going to be buying any fish, so they show me the local sights. They take me from their shop over to a tank of some sort. It's a junked-out old war vehicle that has been here for many moons—a big, metal, abandoned carapace that had been left on the side of the road. One boy starts climbing on it while the other throws a rock at it. The rock bounces off the side with a clank and rolls down into a little drain-pipe puddle gulley where a couple of fish float, mouths open.

The tank is empty, an old friend with whom they grew up.

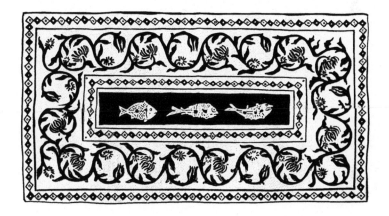

Chapter Nine: Jaffna

"A lot of people are singing about how screwed up the world is, and I don't think that everybody wants to hear about that all the time."
—Mariah Carey

Bicycle City

Bombed house, Elephant Pass, Sri Lanka

In 1284 Marco Polo, his father, his uncle, and fourteen square-masted Chinese ships called junks made their way toward the Arabian Sea.[1] The Polos, accompanied by Kublai Khan's troops, had recently been through Singapore and traveled north to Sumatra and around to Bhutan. They were hugging the Indian coast, sailing down along the western shore, and Polo nearly ran aground on a low-lying red bridge of land. He described how the high winds had pushed up the sea and flattened the land, and how hard it was to see the land, since it lay at the same level as the water. He had arrived in Jaffna, the northernmost point of the island of old Ceylon, where, but for a straight of about a hundred kilometers, it nearly touches India. Marco Polo described the "noble kingdom" he found there, noting the independence of the government as well as the difficulties it was suffering. At that time, a Tamil king by the name of Maaravaramban Kulasekara Pandyan I was in power, and would be for another couple of decades, but his kingdom was threatened not only from the north and south, but also internally.

The Jaffna Peninsula has always been something of an independent state with deep internal conflicts. Then, as now, it had never been clearly Sinhalese or clearly Tamil, or Indian even, but a blend of Sinhalese and Tamils (the Pandyan Tamil kingdom was replaced by the Chola Tamil princes, who then assumed the title of Chola Pandyas about fifty years after Polo's visit; thus even the Tamils cannot be said to have a single heritage). Jaffna has always been more bridge than destination.

Home to more than half Sri Lanka's Tamil population, the Jaffna Peninsula is roughly 1,000 square kilometers (about 386 square miles), about the size of the San

---

1. I am going by Jaffna's history, rather than the Mongolian documentation about his visits with Kublai Khan, which dates the year at 1272. In any case, it was between 1272 and 1292.

Francisco Bay. The land breaks apart into islands that drift toward India. The peninsula gets to be well over 33°C (100°F) during the summer, and the rain that falls during the three-month monsoon season accounts for 90 percent of the rain the area gets all year. Just before the monsoons, when the seasons are still dry, the sky fills with red sandy wind, the water evaporates, and the ground turns to rock, leaving only the wells to provide water for the people and their livestock and red onions and tobacco.

At the extreme end of the peninsula is Valvettithurai, the town where Prabhakaran was born, where heroin is evidently imported, and where the LTTE got its start. This is the heart of Tamil territory, and its red, spotted land and meager vegetation seem more dusty than ancient.

I pull over to wipe off my sunglasses and have a sip of water.

I'm almost out of water. I decide to have a look at the area and leave soon. It doesn't seem dangerous, but if it is anything like Kilinochchi, I don't want to spend the night.

Pulling out my map, I look for the road north to Point Pedro, and from there, through Valvettithurai and then Jaffna. Or, as they're colloquially known, VVT and Jaffna Town.

Marco Polo was caught unawares in Jaffna, but I have no such navigational problems. The A9 forks off into the B68 just ahead, and once I hit the coast at Valvettithurai I can turn a couple of lefts to get back to Jaffna. So I tuck the map away, pull out my sunglasses, and roar on ahead.

There's not much going on. Nicely dressed people on bicycles going about their business make it feel almost like a painting by Georges Seurat or Norman Rockwell:

a dreamy and quiet preindustrial bliss. I'm on the only motorized vehicle I've seen for about an hour now. The bike seems loud, and the noise explains to me why the roads are in such nice shape: The soft tread of bicycles is all they have here.

The highway follows the coast, and I follow the highway in calm celebration as the ocean air wipes my face clean. To my right are sparkling lagoons, clear water, a fisherman, and when the highway starts to turn left, away from the coast, I'm so reluctant to leave it that I stay near the water's edge, skip a couple of small puddles, dodge a few dogs and a boy, miss an ox cart, and land myself in the middle of a fish market. Some hundred people stop their transactions to stare at the pink who just roared into the middle of the market. Bicycles are clustered around the skiffs, and the bicycles as well as the boats have large baskets and reed bags for carrying the fruits of the sea. I don't see, of course, anyone unloading large bags of drugs. All faces are pointed my direction. I shut off the bike, not wanting to cause more of a disruption. But it is too late, and the next hour is spent talking with curious faces at the Valvettithurai fish market.

Talking with people here is like falling back into a preindustrial era when personal contact is of paramount importance. The war has left people here so poor they have no option but to depend on one another, to spend less and use less, and as a result the air is clean, the ocean is clean, and they seem to have a clarity in their eyes that I have only seen in remote places, far away from large cities. They have no money, but they still seem quite rich. It's an odd contradiction for me. I'd expected worse.

This financial poverty changes everything, however. Most people in Valvettithurai or Jaffna don't leave because they can't. The twelve-rupee (U.S. $1.20) bus ride south to Vavuniya, a distance of less than a hundred miles, is prohibitively expensive. Bicycles are the solution for the town. There are a few motorcycles, which are mostly family vehicles, with Dad driving, Mom on the back, and Junior on Mom's lap, facing backward toward Mom.

I don't spend much time in Valvettithurai; it seems peaceful and unconcerned with the war by comparison with Kilinochchi. And by the time I arrive in Jaffna, only about a half hour's drive away, I find that it, too, has more money and less concern than poor old Kilinochchi. When I stop driving long enough to talk to folks, I find that the air is quiet and clean. A city that lacks cars gains a great many other benefits, prime among them being health and human touch. Driving through several main streets, I find hotels, Internet cafés, office buildings, homes with kids playing out front . . . and a severely narrow ethnic range. I am immediately reminded of the south end of the island. In sum, Jaffna is not an unpleasant place to live. The shops are open, the buildings are being repaired, the walls are painted, the streets are swept, people wave to each other, and the temples have attendees.

I'm looking for a port on the south end of town. Though battles were fought everywhere in town, I want to try to understand the details and quirks of the fighting, and some of that happened at the port. I also hope to find out about the fishing industry, which is so important, so traditional, so old, and which accounts for more than just a few points of perspective.

However, the roads are not doing what my now-battered map says they will, and eventually I get lost enough to pull out my compass again. The buildings are mostly gray concrete blocks with doors in front. The street is a yellow dust kicked about by barefoot kids and scattered with fishing nets, people mending the nets, some people washing dishes, and little pools of liquid that smell like the ass end of an elephant.

I have to move slowly through these streets so as not to run over toes. The kids are glomming onto the bike, pulling at my clothes, friendly, curious. Dozens of little voices say in English, "Hello!" and ,"Hello! Where are you going?!" and, "Hello! What is your name?!" But this cluster of kids is more a pile of rags (at least the ones who have clothes, that is; the other half are dusty and snotty). They're smiling and pulling at me like I'm a taffy Santa. Their dark eyes never leave me. There is a mysterious purple light deep in the center of their retinas, like a black light illuminating a velvet painting. They seem to be dreaming and fired up on amphetamines at the same time. They seem to live at an accelerated speed in a remembered time, like ghosts from a past world who have only a split second to live today, to investigate, passively and speedily. This spirit state is my own Hindu mystery and they, too, would watch me for weeks, if I stayed that long, and they would never leave.

Not wanting to hand out money, but knowing that they have real needs, I have candy in my pockets. When I hand them candies they are polite and take them, but not because they are there for treats.

After a couple of rides around the block for one honored boy and one honored girl, I carefully make my way out of the gathering flood of laughing faces, looking for someone who can help me with directions. Down along the gray docks, I meet a sun-scorched bag of a man in his late sixties. He has white hair, thick lips, a big jaw, and boxer's hands. His name is Verrai, and he has lived in Jaffna his whole life, watching the Jaffna constellation spin from Brit to Sinhalese to Tamil. He seals up the caulking on old boats over at the dock and gives me directions to get there, but we end up spending the next two hours sitting on pillars by the water talking about the LTTE. Here is what he tells me:

In 1987 the Indians (specifically the Indian Peace Keeping Force, or IPKF) had been invited in by the Sri Lankan government to clean up the terrorists in Jaffna, specifically the LTTE.

I interrupt Verrai to confirm that this bit about the Sinhalese going to the Tamils to get rid of the Tamils or the Tamils going to the Sinhalese to get rid of the Sinhalese was more or less the same thing that had happened with Moggallana. Verrai agrees, saying that it's just the way things go. Apologizing for the interruption, I sit back again.

The IPKF, after many moons of no movement, decided to get stupid and launch "Operation Wind" on October 10 of that same year. The goal was to land a helicopter at Jaffna University, where Prabhakaran was based, get out of the helicopter, go kill Prabhakaran, take over the LTTE base of operations, then fly home. The commandos did, indeed, fly over in a helicopter, but since the LTTE had gotten wind of Operation Wind (presumably by intercepting radio transmissions), they waited in the bushes with loaded rifles near the university playing field.

The LTTE started firing on the Indian commandos before they could even get everyone out of the helicopter. After the IPKF commandos alighted, the helicopter veered off and didn't return with reinforcements, leaving thirty soldiers at the mercy of the LTTE. By the following morning, out of ammunition, the Indians made a bayonet charge. All but one died, and the survivor was later killed.

The LTTE then carted all the guns and bodies over to a nearby temple and skewered the corpses on big metal meat hooks, doused every one in oil, set them on fire, and hoisted them in front of the temple. They wrote epithets on the concrete in blood and pointed out, in the early morning sun, that the IPKF soldiers hadn't killed Prabhakaran as they had been sent to do.

Verrai tells me that the neighborhood stunk for a week, since some of the bodies didn't burn completely. The LTTE took them off the meat hooks and set fire to some tires, then threw what was left of the corpses on the burning rubber.

In the following fourteen days, the Indian army lost another two hundred men and suffered over five hundred injuries. But India felt it couldn't back down, and so began two years of theatrics, misinformation, and terrorism that boosted the LTTE's international reputation. The IPKF refused to change its strategy and brought in a slew of new troops to patrol Jaffna, claiming that a military presence would be the way to solve the problem. But the LTTE had been trained in guerrilla tactics by some of the best consultants in the worldwide industry of militant terrorism—namely, the PLO. Its members camouflaged themselves in the foliage of the city. They mixed in with crowds and hid under rooftops and trees, taking potshots at the IPKF whenever they had a chance.

The IPKF was taking a drubbing, and many of the army boys didn't even know why they were there in the first place. Who's the enemy? What's the history? What are we supposed to be doing?

The LTTE persisted, taking increasingly drastic measures. Booby-trapping houses around the city became the new rage with the LTTE. The IPKF would find an abandoned house. In searching each building, as instructed, soldiers would flip on the lights, and the entire house would explode. In one instance, the IPKF found over 200 kilograms (440 pounds) of explosives hidden throughout the walls and floors of a house. The IPKF boys were surrounded by devils who cooked people alive.

After nearly a dozen of these traps, the IPKF was so pissed off that it just shut down Jaffna's power supply from mid-October until the end of December of that year. But turning the electricity off in hell doesn't make it any less hot.

The LTTE had other tricks it had been taught: Claymore mines with boxes of rusted nails, remote-detonated plastic explosives, explosive cars, explosive phones, explosive purses and wallets and hats, and even ordinary plastic pipes that could be tossed off rooftops to help paint the town red. The IPKF was under constant attack from all directions. There were no rules to the war. The carnage then continued. IPKF morale was getting twitchy since, it seemed to its troops, the civilians they had been sent to protect were now siding with the LTTE. There were no longer any battle lines. To the IPKF, nothing was clear.

On October 21, 1987 the LTTE holed up in the Jaffna hospital. Despite pleas from doctors, patients, and nurses, the LTTE opened fire on the IPKF from the hospital windows. Of course the IPKF, finding a perfect example of the LTTE hiding behind civilian skirts, saw red and charged. Bullishly, the Indians blew into the building, spraying bullets and throwing grenades in all directions. Doctors and nurses cowered in closets while IPKF soldiers, blind with rage, killed anyone they thought was LTTE. It wasn't until they were firing on hospital staff cowering under tables that they realized their mistake. By then, over forty doctors and staff were shot, and the IPKF was standing in a pool of blood, holding a smoking gun. The LTTE wasn't even in the building anymore.

The LTTE had left the building just as the IPKF had entered. While the IPKF was shooting up the hospital, the LTTE was on the phone with international media, announcing yet another assault on civilians. "International" is the important adjective here. Since 95 percent of Sri Lanka's print-media circulation was owned by three companies—all of them Sinhalese—and reporters were not allowed into the war zone, the LTTE was left to get the word off the island.

It was a media triumph. The LTTE neatly moved the battle from the street to the hospital and the newsrooms. Needless to say, after slaughtering a hospital full of doctors and nurses (and killing not a single LTTE militant), the IPKF did not come out favorably with anyone who heard about what had happened. This marked the beginning of the IPKF's end in Sri Lanka.

The LTTE had needed international attention, and this was its method of getting it. The LTTE walked out of the battle again as the victor, not because of superior firepower or because it lost fewer soldiers, but because it knew how to use the weapon of media.

The Library

The recently reconstructed Jaffna Library, Sri Lanka

On the final night of May 1981, two fires were started in Jaffna. They were both reminiscent of the 1848 burning of the Aluvihara Library.

First, the Jaffna newspaper offices were burned down. Then the Jaffna public library was set ablaze, leaving behind the ashes of nearly ninety-seven thousand publications, some of them thousands of years old.

Francis Whelen, a journalist for the *New Statesman and Nation*, visited the library six weeks later and wrote, "Today its rooms are thickly carpeted with half burnt pages, fluttering in the breeze which comes through broken windows."[1] City officials commissioned local architects to survey the building. It was declared ruined and structurally unsound for renewal. The documents were, of course, completely lost.

---

1. *New Statesman and Nation*, July 17, 1981.

Virginia Leary, an investigator commissioned by the United Nations, in her report to the International Commission of Jurists, advised,

> A primary concern of the government should be the physical security of the minority Tamil population and the avoidance of future communal violence so frequently directed against Tamils in the past . . . In this regard the government should pursue a vigorous policy of investigation and prosecution of police officers responsible for the burning of many areas in Jaffna in May/June 1981.[2]

Two years later Satchi Ponnambalam, investigating the scene, wrote, "The May-June 1981 violence in Jaffna had been state sponsored and carried out by Sinhalese Ministers and high ranking government officials present on the spot."[3]

Most people with whom I've spoken have told me the same thing. They say that the library was ignited by approximately 170 federal police stationed in Jaffna.

Some people, claiming to be eyewitnesses, told me it was by Sri Lankan military operatives. Others said it was the Indian government trying to incense the Tamil army against the Sinhalese army, or the PLOTE against the TULF to incense the LTTE, or the LTTE did it to incite problems with the TULF and the Sri Lankan army, and so on.

As with the 2003 burning of the library in Baghdad, we may never discover who struck the match or who bought the gas. I still can't confirm the data, but in this world, where opinion generally proves to be reality,

---

2. Leary, Virginia A., Ethnic Conflict and Violence in Sri Lanka, Geneva: International Commission of Jurists, 1983.
3. Ponnambalam, Satchi, Sri Lanka: National Conflict and the Tamil Liberation Struggle, Totowa, N.J.: Biblio Distribution Center, 1983.

consensus says it was the Sri Lankan army. After all, the Sri Lankans were taught this lesson by the British during their escapades at Aluvihara.

By 1988, seven years after the fires, people in Jaffna had become accustomed to the charbroiled sight. Meanwhile, in Colombo, funds were collected, a municipal council was put to work, and a lengthy process shifted into gear to restore the old Jaffna town library, install computers, and do what was possible to replace rare Tamil documents that had been lost.

Suddenly, Tamil students (the International Students Union of Gajendran among them) turned up, protesting the project. Prabhakaran and the LTTE, they said, wanted the old library kept as a symbol for posterity to memorialize the crimes committed against the Tamil population. They didn't just want it; they were willing to kill members of the commission to keep it. To quote Ilimparathay, the LTTE's Jaffna political chief, in a meeting with the commissioner head, "If you go ahead with the opening, there will be a bloodbath." The local Tamils and Sinhalese working on the project told the LTTE, in the roundabout way one responds to threats from afar, "Get over it."

The LTTE didn't. These days, the library is finished but unopened, since the entire twenty-three-person commission working on the project resigned en masse one day after the death threats began. Though the LTTE would have liked the library to remain a symbol of "crimes committed against the Tamil people," like Aluvihara, it is now more abortion than monument.

But the LTTE may have had more than one reason not to want a functioning library. After all, libraries in these times, even in places as poor as Jaffna, have more ways than books to provide access to information. The LTTE and Prabhakaran are experts in media manipulation and public opinion. They needed local support. Since education and media freedom are risks that warfare cannot afford, it might not make sense to have people in the north too well informed about life elsewhere.

Dark tales still surround of the town of Jaffna, as they surround Sri Lanka itself. The LTTE, outside the reach of Sri Lanka's government, does as it pleases. I've heard reports of the LTTE bleeding prisoners to death, sometimes after torture, refrigerating the blood and keeping it for battlefront transfusions, a darkly ironic reminder that Tamil and Sinhalese blood has been mixed for millennia.

Still, the problems with blood and books aside, Jaffna seems to me to be moving toward greater well-being. Like Kilinochchi, it's scarred, but it is also showing signs of growth and recovery.

Authority and authorship are always linked, especially in war territories. The lessons offered on Sri Lanka's battlefields and in its libraries have not been lost on the Tamil Tigers. For better and for worse, in sickness and in health, the LTTE has created what political change it could by grabbing hold of the media and using it to portray suffering and victimization. It's hit on a particularly powerful formula in its marriage of media and the military, and the act of authorship becomes more relevant than the veracity of its version of reality, or even the choice of the events it portrays. In other words, it was not that the LTTE was necessarily a good shot, but that it had so much media ammunition that it was guaranteed to hit its target. The LTTE's media military grew far more sophisticated than Karunaratne's army of spin masters.

The LTTE became a marketer of the very highest caliber.

Chaapter Ten:
The Road Back

"While nothing is easier than to denounce the evildoer, nothing is more difficult than to understand him."
—Fyodor Dostoevsky

Recessional

"Demined Area" near Vavuniya, Sri Lanka

Driving back south, down Elephant Pass, I wave at the fishermen as I leave. The highway's been closed to civilian traffic since 1984. Anyone not willing to do U-turns for photocopies or have their mechanical pencils investigated has stayed off of it.[1] The bike hums along well, the knobby tires making strange music on the rhythmic washboard road, through puddles and around potholes, and I travel through the sole point of passage on the thin line of the road. The sand on either side of this narrow place forms it into something of an hourglass, but change here has not been marked by the passing of sand, nor elephants, nor even time itself, but the bullets that have accumulated on each side, in the tidal battles that have surged back and forth over the decades.

By June of 1988, the IPKF had begun causing so many problems—or it had been so neatly crowned with that perception—that it could no longer function as a peacekeeping force and became a common enemy to both the Sri Lankan army and the LTTE. Everyone wanted the IPKF out, but the IPKF refused, claiming it was the sole force that could bring peace.

In one of a number of strange switchbacks, a batch of arms was delivered to the LTTE by the Sri Lankan army's own brigadier Denzil Kobbekaduwa. He offered the LTTE the arms in exchange for an agreement that they stop killing Sinhalese. The arms were to help get the IPKF out of the country. It was really a prompt to the LTTE to cut loose and retreat in among the Sinhalese population, which would only make the IPKF look worse, Kobbekaduwa reasoned. The LTTE, fast as a fly, took the offer and later received not only funding, vehicles, batteries, electronics, and handcuffs, but over ten truckloads

---

1. After demining was completed and mortar damage repaired, the highway was reopened to civilian traffic on March 2, 2009.

of grenades, rifles, mortars, and ammo. It was the final break that prepared them to set up, for a solid decade, a de facto state in the north.

The LTTE was growing accustomed to such patronage; only the year before, India had played the candy man. Let's turn the clock back to 1986 and go a bit north to Tamil Nadu, in southern India, which at that time was a campground for the four main Tamil militant groups. The LTTE, the PLOTE, the EROS, and the EPRLF received training, funding, weaponry, and an early alert to the weak signals of Sri Lanka's political rumblings. The chief minister of Tamil Nadu, M.G. Ramachandran, also served as gunpowder donor to most of the militant Tamils, denying, of course, to public media that these transactions were even conceivable. Nevertheless, the EROS, for example, received courses in "crash training" and finances, and almost a hundred AK-47s were handed out as graduation prizes. The EROS, the PLOTE, and the EPRLF, I learned while speaking with each group, were given hundreds of thousands of rupees on multiple occasions. The LTTE benefited most, as it was the most radical, unwilling to compromise on its aim of creating a separate state. But this wave of success, too, eventually receded.

At last I stop in front of a grocery store where five morose young men stand out in front, waiting for something to happen. Their eyes are hopeless and empty, their arms are crossed, and each have one heel on the wall behind them. They're too poor to afford cigarettes and they've been waiting here for generations. But when I pull up they do not move. I take off my sunglasses, turn off the bike and get off, and put the key in my pocket. They seem to think for a second that I am what they have been waiting for, but as I stretch my back they start talking quietly, discussing, it seems, something up the street.

There is nothing sadder than a small town trapped in a stalled cycle of failed negotiations by faraway people.

The dialogues never went as far as they could have. In 1999, Norway offered to mediate peace negotiations between the Sri Lankan government and the LTTE. The Sri Lankan government accepted the Norwegian offer perhaps to gain a little breathing space, but the real effect was that it gave the Tigers something they'd been fighting for since 1983: international recognition as a legitimate party to peace talks. The talks were booed occasionally, since the LTTE was not asked to shoulder accountability for militant acts. Still, there were enough Tamils who had stepped out of the battlefield and into the senate (Devananda, Rajee, Siddharthan, and many others) that the talks were informed by a balanced collection of opinions.

On the front page of *The Island*, one of Sri Lanka's national newspapers, the headlines on April 24, 2003, read "'LTTE has set up de-facto State' — President Kumaratunga." The Tigers had, by 2003, achieved their goal. The next logical transition for them would have been, again, media based but influenced by politics — not by weaponry. Even up until 2005 they had the choice. For twenty years an important question had been lingering outside the LTTE's very tents: "military strength or political strength?" Tactics could have shifted from war to politics, politics could have been ratcheted up to trust, and a Tamil nation could have been founded. That was how it appeared in 2005, and according to Devananda, that was how it appeared even as far back as 1987.

While the taming of an elephant begins with force, with the use of ropes tied to trees, the relationship quickly shifts to the type found between colleagues. Though the basic fact of coercion is not forgotten, crackers and candies contain more power than blows. The size of the elephant always needs be respected, and physical force is ultimately replaced with conversation and collaboration. By April of 2006, the Tamil militants had forgotten those rules. So indeed had the Sinhalese Sri Lankan government. That month, a suicide bomb was detonated in the same compound where I spoke with Karunaratne, and eight people were killed. The following month, Tamil Tigers attacked a naval convoy that was floating near Jaffna. By August, fighting had really gotten hot in the north again. Suicide bombs, invasions, and accusations mounted until that October the peace talks held in Geneva fell apart with loudmouthed bickering.

For two solid days I drove directly south down the island. The route was clear, the weather was good, and there were no obstacles or guard posts. But because I was alone, even the mundane was charged with meaning. The sky looked larger and more mysterious, the ocean a more saturated aqua, the birds more watchful, the speed of the bike more violent. My emotions were amplified too, as if I had been awake for a week. My highs were elation, my lows seemed closer to despair, hunger was more important, thirst was drier, sleep came faster. All of my reality seemed to have been honed somehow, from only a short visit of a week.

It's beautiful, being human, when you really look at it.

Just south of Chilaw, with trees skittering by on either side, the highway swings by a lake and I think for a moment it is the ocean, but it is too brown and only gives me the desire to see the ocean again, so I hang a right onto the next road I find, a little shallow gravel footpath, really. I follow it west, watching my compass as the trees break apart and yield to the fields farmers are still plowing. The bike feels better on gravel, its natural home;

there is less vibration from the knobs in the tires. A river is ahead and the road goes right into it, so I slow down and watch the waters flow by. Buddha found enlightenment next to a river. And this one's a sweet lullaby, it just keeps on flowing, no worries about where it's going.

I do a tight U-turn, then another, then stop and assess the waters ahead. The river isn't moving too fast and it's got texture to it, so it shouldn't be too deep. I ease forward and drive the bike into the river slowly, steadily pushing forward as the wheel spins the water into the fender's underside. I've got my chin in the air and the water level is now up to the pegs, so I lift my feet a bit and I'm only a third of the way across. There are two boys on the other side, watching me. I think I can push or drag this bike out of the sludge if it gets bogged. The water's now near the motor. The back tire wobbles on a rock and almost causes me to fall, and the movement forces my toes back onto the bike pegs and the water's right at the motor level, up to my knees, and I stand up a bit to keep my ass out of it all, then gas it hard, as I'm halfway, and the water covers the casing and is spraying out either side like some kind of magic water plow but I'm out on the dry bank now and my boots are full of muck so I stop and gun the motor a few times, looking back, exhaust pipes steaming. The bike burps a few times and I rev the engine again. I am not at all clear on how I made it but I feel great. A motorcycle should be required driving for everyone in the world. The two boys come running down and my candies are still in my pocket. The boys are jumping up and down and smiling and I feel like a fucking hero for doing absolutely nothing at all.

Mattakotuwa is a simple little Sinhalese beach town with a fish market, just like they have up in Valvettithurai, in Tamil territory. Like that one there, I manage to disrupt this one, too, but I do not stop, only glance, and glide back to the main road. Like the one I saw in the north, this has dinghies with baskets and people with bikes and everyone is standing around where the boats are drawn up onto the shore to unload their fish. The main difference between the two fish markets is that one is pointed north and the other is pointed west.

I follow the road, wanting to stop, sticking as close to the beach as I can without making more of a ruckus. Coming to a large clearing where I can see south, I decide to stop for a bit, so I slow the bike and pull toward the sand. The motor startles a couple of bright white birds on the beach. There are thousands of them: large white gulls or maybe terns sitting in the sand, facing the wind, which blows from the south. The two I startle jump up and make a low moaning sound, a kind of *ghoo-wer, ghoo-wer*, and hop down the beach away from the bike. "Don't fly, Mister bluebird, I'm just walking down the road," I sing.

One flaps and flies south. Before landing, he scares two more that then leap up and open their wings, and then two more follow, and then fifty, and two hundred are in the air and I already have the motor shut off. So much for not making a ruckus.

After a moment of staring at the waves and stretching my hips, I glance south, then do a double take when I see a swarm of something in the sky. There are thousands and thousands of birds on wing, headed south. The beach has been cleared, utterly emptied. I scared one and now the whole damn species is spooked and headed south, all in terror because of little ole me.

What is it about fear that makes us flock? Or vice versa? Fear is our most basic instinct, our survival key, and our most social emotion. We hear our neighbor coo and hop into the air, and so we do as well, and that is why, as a group, we stay alive. But that is how terrorism functions. Fear transmits quickly.

I swing back onto the A3 in a little town called Marawila. A kid on his bicycle starts chasing me down a little hill and his dog is running behind, ears flapping, and we three zoom past a little grain mill and a corner store and a blue-sky sunny day and all seems quaint as the Carolina countryside.

In May of 2009, with the prime minister's brother firmly grasping the helm of the military machine, the Sri Lankan army headed north and, ignoring calls for restraint from the international community, swept into Kilinochchi and Jaffna and finally cornered the Tamil Tigers on a thin peninsula in the northeast.

In the final month of the war, the international press announced the end of the Tigers, the end of the war, and the end of the dream of Tamil Eelam. But inside the camps, despite the dramatic bombing and 115,000 civilians displaced from the region, the Tigers continued their operations as if it were any other day. After all, they'd lived through decades of war and this was not the first time the Tigers had been cornered. Anyway, cyanide capsule around his neck, Prabhakaran would never accept defeat. Not while alive. In a 1992 interview with *The Los Angeles Times*, he said, "I started the movement with the firm resolve that I will never be caught alive by the enemy." And in that statement about the origin of the movement, he also predicted how it would end.

The typical day for Prabhakaran began with a cup of tea at five AM and a briefing about the battlefront at six thirty. Prabhakaran had high blood pressure and diabetes from nearly thirty years of battle and forty years of being chased by the Sri Lankan army, so he took his tea without milk or sugar. But on the morning of Monday, May 18, 2009, exchanges of fire started before he awoke, and the Sri Lankan army's 53rd Division drove its assault forward into Putumattalan, a small town on Sri Lanka's northeast shore, where the last of the Tamil Tiger chiefs had been corralled. Some said Prabhakaran fled via submarine, others said he slipped out disguised as a Muslim woman. There were reports that he used an ambulance for purposes other than medical and that, just as Rajee had done two decades earlier in Beirut, Prabhakaran had tried to flee the war theater camouflaged in a Red Cross van which was bombed. The news quickly spread that he'd been killed in an ambulance. On Tuesday, May 19, 2009, a report corrected the previous one, saying his corpse was found in the lagoon, but this contradicted another report that said that it had been found on Monday. Yet another report said he had died of burns. Dead Prabhakarans began to appear as quickly as rumors. Some reports claimed he had a single bullet in the back of his head, some say he died of the famous cyanide. Some say he escaped and that his body double was found. The Sri Lankan army, in its official impassioned report, finally stated that it ended in a dramatic gunfight in a mangrove.[2]

---

2. "The End Battle: The Cowardly Death of the LTTE Chief." The Sri Lanka Ministry of Defense,
    http://www.defence.lk/new.asp?fname=20090621LastBattleN.

The Art Form of Terror
(On Imperialism)

School kids, Grandma, and the Tamil Tiger troops, Kilinochchi, Sri Lanka

The week of my return to Colombo, I staggered around in the streets, wallowing in a mud of disequilibrium. I spent a fair amount of time in bars, drinking iced arrack and taking notes on what I'd found. A few days later I went to some outdoor reggae clubs in the south, near Galle, and spent some time swimming in the clear waters to rinse my polluted head. I returned my trusty steed with a pat on the gas tank. I slept about nine hours each night.

Something had been gouged out of me, and something else had been put in its place, and this set me into a head spin as I tried to process what I'd seen up north. Poverty so abject that a buck could change someone's life.

Violence beyond the gates of my worst nightmares. Yet, also, there was the strange kindness that people shared, the closeness and amity that living in such conditions demands. The openness and kindness had crept into the war zone to counterbalance the cruelty. I tried to reconcile this existence with the innocence and reverence for tradition I had found in the south. Both sides seemed to be repeating an ancient history, following what had been played out by their ancestors. Karma had dripped out of the past, saturating the island.

The circumstances in Sri Lanka are so complicated, detailed, and delicate that no one individual can comprehend them. And of course the solution must be equally complicated, detailed, and delicate. But the question now, for Sri Lanka as well as the United States and many other countries involved in counterterrorism, boils down to the same head-scratcher facing the LTTE in the 1980s: Which comes first, military strength or political strength?

The LTTE—and the Sri Lankan government as well—chose military strength first. The LTTE never wavered from its end goal of a separate state for the Tamil population, nor did it waver from its militant approach. It decided to live by the sword. The LTTE generally, and Prabhakaran specifically, refused to be held accountable for their actions and remained unwilling to negotiate. Eventually the PLOTE, the EROS, the EPDP, and even the LTTE's top brass, Colonel Karuna, stopped supporting those self-limiting tactics. Around 2003, the LTTE became politically unanchored and the organization was forced to float on its purely military methods. This worked for a while, but it drifted into increasingly desperate waters and brought the good people of Sri Lanka, and especially the Tamils living in the north, with it. In 2009, the LTTE was sunk—perhaps permanently—because of this decision. If it had maintained some mooring with Sri Lankan ministers, such a defeat could never have happened.

Note, however, that the Sri Lankan government's response was military as well. Ask any terrorist, and you'll hear that, as much as for any other single reason, the purpose of using military methods against a group of people is to incite terror. After a couple of decades of this philosophy, might stops making right and begins to cause blight. A government cannot be run according to militant mentality. Not for long, anyway. It remains to be seen if the Sri Lankan government's military decision will solve the conflict in a permanent way. The EROS, the PLOTE, and the EPDP are all involved in the political process today, and their presence has been instrumental in decapitating the LTTE. Still, that doesn't mean that the war is truly over. This war, assuming it ended in 2009, has been just one in a series of dialogues between the Sinhalese and Tamils over the course of thousands of years. In the last two thousand years of Sri Lankan military history, assaults have not had lasting results, so I have my doubts about whether this peace will last for long. Many Tamils and Sinhalese do as well.

In July of 2008, the RAND Corporation, an American foreign-policy think tank, released a curious and timely report titled "How Terrorist Groups End."[1] RAND researched the final demise of 648 terrorist groups between 1968 and 2006 and found that, more than by any other solution, terrorist groups demilitarized when they were brought into the political process. It is also possible to disband terrorist groups forcibly, but rarely by purely military means. The report points out that if you're interested in ending someone else's terrorist group, this

1. Jones, Seth G. and Libicki, Martin C, "How Terrorist Groups End: Lessons for Countering al Qa'ida." The RAND Corporation, 2008, www.rand.org/pubs/monographs/MG741.

undertaking "requires a range of policy instruments, such as careful police and intelligence work, military force, political negotiations, and economic sanctions." Only in 7 percent of the cases of the 648 groups studied did a military invasion, such as Sri Lanka's 2009 effort, do the trick.[2]

In similar research approached from a different angle, Max Abrahms, then a predoctoral fellow at Stanford's Center for International Security and Cooperation (he's currently a doctoral fellow at UCLA), published a paper in 2006 titled "Why Terrorism Does Not Work."[3] Abrahms had researched twenty-eight groups designated as terrorist organizations by the U.S. State Department. He made a list of forty-two of their objectives. Abrahms found that these groups achieved those objectives about 7 percent of the time, the key variable for success being whether or not they targeted civilians. The groups that attacked civilian targets more often than military targets "systematically failed to achieve their policy objectives."

Guns can stop a negotiation only as far as the bullet will travel. In a world where international networks of sophisticated, wealthy, and highly educated businesspeople are funding operations such as the LTTE, the PLOTE, the EROS, and the EPDP, some negotiation is required to get the battle past the range of the bullet. Nowadays, media and money are more effective than the military. Guns won't do much in the long term but, according to Abrahm's research, negotiation and some form of police-like engagement is evidently a good recipe for a government to follow.

I'm not confident in making these statements. I'm

---

2. The report points out that part of the reason this approach worked against the LTTE was that the LTTE was very large, armed, and well organized. Military means are less effective against smaller and more ideological groups.

3. Abrahms, Max, "Why Terrorism Does Not Work," *International Security*, Vol. 31, No. 2 (Fall 2006), pages 42–78.

looking for truth rather than trying to lay it down, and most of these statements are only questions dressed up to look like conclusions. Questions of long-term government responses aside, there is one thing that I am confident that a public can do, independently from its government, and that is to determine its reaction slowly and discuss it before responding. Panicking prevents you from evaluating the potential danger of a terrorist attack, the effect it has on your daily life, in your home and office, near your bed. A response to terrorism is probably not needed. Certainly not on the part of the public. In the 1980s, the citizens of Colombo did not need to riot. They were not at risk; the Tamils living in Colombo were not the problem. The American public has reacted in the same odd way. The measures taken against terrorism, be they jingoism, patriotism, racism, or the confiscation of my habeas corpus in the airport, have been signs more of panic than consideration. In this respect, the attacks on New York were immensely successful, as Rajee said, because they ended the American way of life that most of us had enjoyed before September 11, 2001. But it was the reaction that caused the damage, not the tumbling of the towers.

You can prick the elephant with something small. You can even get his leg stuck in a noose. But that's about all you can do, regardless of whether the elephant is a government or terrorist group. After that, it's all crackers and sweets.

What I found most interesting, during my tea time with terrorists, wasn't the psychological damage I witnessed or their deep convictions. It wasn't the parallels in their respective stories, or even how unlike my media-built image of terrorists they actually were. What was interesting was the balancing and testing each person had undertaken as he alternated between building up his political and military strength. Each one of them turned to military methods at a relatively young age, but only after trying political methods first. Then, when the military methods failed to work, each returned, at a wiser age, to political tactics. As Siddharthan put it, "The whole struggle is unwarranted and unnecessary. Perhaps it is just because I am growing old that I see this."

The decisions of the terrorists I interviewed seemed to go along with the RAND research. Of the four terrorist groups I followed, three of them went the political route. The fourth, the one that stuck to its guns— the LTTE—was militarily bulldozed. (At least, for now. I maintain that a version of the Tamil Tigers will reappear if the Sri Lankan government does not orchestrate negotiations that more or less appease the seven million Tamils around the world that mostly support the foundation of Eelam.)

What was it they were looking for? What caused each "terrorist" to test the military and political tools of his trade before each decided to follow the political path? Maybe collaboration works better than competition, and maybe it takes time to develop ways of collaborating. On a cultural and national scale, tribes, families, individuals, and nations that live in a region must, it appears, go through a physical and social dialogue to establish a pecking order, goals, resources, limits, cultures, and identities. This type of negotiation can take hundreds of years. Sri Lanka has an even more complicated and obscure problem, since the island has been under imperial rule for five centuries. The country has not had a chance in the last six hundred years to complete this dialogue without a moderator, or at least an external influence.

Terrorism can be defined in many ways. From what I've seen it is a kind of media art that is used for social manipulation. It is the art of using military power, usually against civilians, to gain media control, generally with the goal of achieving political power. It is the destruction and manipulation of symbols, usually linked to human death, for the purpose of controlling public media and gaining attention. The acts against the bo tree, the Temple of the Tooth, and the bombings of Colombo were all symbolic acts performed to gain attention and political power. Even the collapse of the World Trade Center in New York in 2001 was symbolic more than catastrophic. It was the symbol—that of the Twin Towers—that was attacked.

Terrorism is ultimately an art, like writing itself, architecture, or music. The dark art of terrorism is an emotion machine created with, by, and for cultural, ethnic, financial, and religious symbols. Terrorism is the machinery of symbolic destruction. This destruction is framed within a deadly and usually quasimilitary context, so as to manipulate public emotion and, therefore, behavior. Practitioners of terrorism use violence the way a carpenter works with wood: They connect ideas by puncturing both with a spike of deadly violence. It is generally done, perhaps 70 percent of the time, if we are to believe RAND, to gain an opportunity to engage in political dialogue.

Terrorism can be practiced by individuals, groups, or corporations. It can be practiced by governments as well. It has been written that the Sri Lankan government is already using terrorist methods for controlling the island's media. In January of 2009, for a controversial example, Lasantha Wickrematunge, a Sri Lankan journalist, attorney, and politician, was publicly murdered in his car by several unidentified motorcyclists. Wickrematunge's death followed the deaths of other high-profile antigovernment journalists who had also criticized Sri Lanka's president, Mahinda Rajapaksa, and his brother, Defense Secretary Gotabaya Rajapaksa.[4] Prior to Wickrematunge's death, he wrote a lengthy letter in anticipation of his own murder, titled "And Then They Came for Me."[5] In this letter, which was published a few days after his death, he directly accuses the Sri Lankan government, writing, "Murder has become the primary tool whereby the state seeks to control the organs of liberty."

The Sri Lankan government is seeking to control external media as well. In May of 2009, when UN Secretary General Ban Ki-moon visited the island, there was a call for accountability on possible violations of human rights laws, and on the movement of Tamil refugees out of their camps. But the Sri Lankan government rejects the idea of an outside investigation into its rights record, simply saying, "We do not have human rights issues."[6]

But as the city of Colombo learned more than twenty years ago, any response to terrorism, regardless of the source, must be carefully considered. A riot or a "war on terror" was what the LTTE hoped to provoke through terrorism. And while the government of Sri Lanka finally chose a military option, only time will tell if it was the appropriate choice, one that will lead to a peaceful collaboration—or at least a clear definition—between Tamils and Sinhalese, Hindus and Buddhists, majority and minority.

---

4. Other deaths included P. Devakumaran, Sampath de Silva, and Taraki Sivaram.
5. Wickrematunge, Lasantha, "And Then They Came for Me." *The Sunday Leader,* January 11, 2009,
http://www.thesundayleader.lk/20090111/editorial-.htm.
6. "UN Envoy in Sri Lanka for Talks." BBC World, September 16, 2009,
http://news.bbc.co.uk/2/hi/south_asia/8258076.stm.

The coming years will create the karma for the coming decades. Sri Lankan President Mahinda Rajapakse has said he will introduce political reforms that will satisfy Tamil aspirations just as the remnants of the LTTE are warning that their so-called defeat will inspire them to invent yet more innovative forms of guerrilla warfare to be trained, now, on economic targets. If intelligence is exercised, the coming race will not be one of military might or new terrorist tactics, but toward a new era of democracy. Democracy undoubtedly needs reinvention; after all—as Alexis de Tocqueville, the French philosopher who examined emerging democracy in America, said—if the majority rules, it is because they can rule by force. Sri Lanka has the unique opportunity, in redefining its democracy, to exorcise the ghosts of military power and welcome representation for minorities that is not based on physical force.

For now, in 2010, the still-hot embers of the war might best be put to use in warming up some water for a little tea time.

The Message from God

God's own messenger, Colombo, Sri Lanka

It was my last day in Sri Lanka. I was on my way to meet Shankar Rajee, who had read the transcript of his interview and made a few factual corrections. We were supposed to meet at the Hotel Sapphire at 6:15 PM. The city had been washed clean in recent days, and the streets were steaming, smelling of fecund leaves and tossed-out curries. A Hindu convention was taking place. Thousands of Hindus walked in the street, creating a river of humanity. Fruit baskets and carts of vegetables and all of the women draped in Maratha-style saris, the Keralas and Kanchipuram from South India, and of course the Osaria style of sari from Kandy. They floated like lovely flowers through that river, decorated and spiced with earrings and simple perfumes. And everyone had that unblinking third eye, the bindi.

Colombo, despite her history of bombings and riots, was breathing easy. It seemed then that industrialization had nothing to do with civilization, and it was even more clear that these two ancient civilizations of the north and south of the island had more in common than in difference. Those very similarities of culture, mannerism, clothing, and shared history were probably the true reason for the civil war.

An elderly fellow with large glasses and an umbrella stopped me.

"What is your country, sir?" he asked as he stepped neatly between me and my destination. It was clear that English was not his native tongue.

"I was born in the United States, and I live in France. So both?"

"Ah, I lived in San Francisco for some time. Beautiful city!"

I was loath to get into a conversation simply because we had both lived on the same continent (and, in fact, city), but his eyes were so kind, and he was so engaged in properly moving his mouth around the foreign words, that I decided to slow down and talk for a few. Anyway, I was early for the meeting.

"Tell me, sir, are you on vacation here in Sri Lanka?" he asked.

"Not really. I'm researching a book on terrorism and Sri Lanka's civil war. I've been here for a few months, and I leave tomorrow. And you?"

He looked at me for a second and smiled. "God has sent me to speak with you."

I hadn't been expecting a message from God that afternoon. "Oh, really? What does God have to say?"

"Unity is divinity."

That was all he said. He wished me a good day. I

asked if I could take his picture, and he agreed, and I did so. Then he disappeared into the river of saris and fruit baskets.

As I look at the photo now, it seems that I was, indeed, approached by an avatar or an angel. Unfortunately, I was slow to notice this. As often happens, whether it is with our enemies, our relatives, cultures different from ours, or races that are twins, I'd overlooked the common and mistaken his halo for an umbrella.

Addenda

"I am bound to tell what I am told,
but not to always believe it."
—Herodotus

Mahout, Pinnawala, Sri Lanka

SRI LANKAN/EELAM
MILITANT GROUPS

Eelam Revolutionary Organisers (ELO)
Eelam National Democratic Liberation Front (ENDLF)
Eelam National Liberation Front (ENLF)
Eelam People's Revolutionary Liberation Front (EPRLF)
Eelam People's Democratic Party (EPDP)
Eelam Revolutionary Communist Party (ERCP)
Eelam Revolutionary Organisation of Students (EROS)
General Union of Eelam Students (GUES)
Liberation Tigers of Tamil Eelam (LTTE)
People's Liberation Army (PLA)
People's Liberation Front (JVP)
People's Liberation Organisation of Tamil Eelam (PLOTE)
Sri Lanka Freedom Party (SLFP)
Tamil Eelam Army (TEA)
Tamil Eelam Liberation Army (TELA)
Tamil Eelam Liberation Front (TELF)
Tamil Eelam Liberation Organization (TELO)
Tamil Liberation Organisation (TLO)
Tamil New Tigers (TNT)
Tamil Students League (TSL)
Tamil United Liberation Front (TULF)

Militants:
> EPRLF: Eelam People's Revolutionary
> Liberation Front
> TELO: Tamil Eelam Liberation Organization
> PLA: People's Liberation Army

Agitators:
>>ENDLF: Eelam National Democratic
>>>Liberation Front
>>GUES: General Union of Eelam Students
>>TNT: Tamil New Tigers

Freedom Fighters / Terrorists:
>>EROS: Eelam Revolutionary Organisation
>>>of Students
>>LTTE: Liberation Tigers of Tamil Eelam
>>PLOTE (sometimes PLOT): People's Liberation
>>>Organisation of Tamil Eelam
>>TELF: Tamil Eelam Liberation Front

Counterterrorists
>>EPDP: Eelam People's Democratic Party
>>PLA: People's Liberation Army

Anti-Terrorists
>>Black Butterflies
>>Black Cats
>>Yellow Leopards

Suicide Terrorists:
>>LTTE Black Tigers

Foreign Groups:
>>CIA: Central Intelligence Agency (U.S.A.)
>>FBI: Federal Bureau of Investigation (U.S.A.)
>>IPKF: Indian Peace Keeping Force (India)
>>PLO: Palestinian Liberation Organization
>>>(Palestine)
>>PFLP: Popular Front for the Liberation of Palestine
>>>(Palestine)
>>RAW: Research and Analysis Wing (India)

GLOSSARY

arrack: A golden-colored Sri Lankan liquor made from fermented fruit, sugarcane, and the sap of coconut palms.

Bikhu: A fully ordained Buddhist monk.

bindi: The "third eye" decoration, usually a dot, worn on the lower forehead above the nose. It is a traditional Hindu decoration that strengthens concentration and protects one from demons and bad luck.

chapati: An unleavened flatbread, much like a pancake or crepe.

eats: Fried treats served by street vendors in India and Sri Lanka.

hoppers: A griddle cake made from a fermented batter of rice flour, coconut milk and a dash of palm toddy. Sometimes served with eggs, and usually as breakfast.

ola: Dried palm leaves that are used as pages in fan-folded accordion-style books that generally contain sacred content.

Pali Canon: A collection of Buddhist scriptures composed in north India and Sri Lanka, and transcribed into the Tripitaka.

salwar kameez: Traditional wide-cut clothing worn by both men and women in South Asia.

Tamil Eelam: The name given by some Sri Lankan Tamils

to the homeland which they hope to create in the north and east of the island.

tuk-tuk: A three-wheeled taxi and one of the primary modes of urban transport in most of Sri Lanka and India.

The Tripitaka: A Theravada Buddhist canon of scriptures, specifically of the Pali canon.

Holy elephant in shopping mall, Pondicherry, Tamil Nadu, India

TIME LINE

Fifth century BC: Indo-Aryan migrants from northern India immigrate to the island. Prime among them are the Sinhalese.

Third century BC: Tamil migration from India continues.

455–473 AD: Dhatusena's reign as king of Ceylon.

473–495: Kassapa's reign as king of Ceylon.

496–515: Moggallana's reign as king of Ceylon.

1505: The Portuguese arrive in Ceylon.

1517: The Portuguese occupation is consolidated and integrated with local governance.

1658: The Dutch force the Portuguese off the island, establishing control everywhere except for the central kingdom of Kandy.

1659: Robert Knox is shipwrecked in southern Ceylon.

1796: Britain begins to occupy the island.

1815: British takeover of Kandy. Britain employs Tamil laborers from southern India.

1833: The British administration is consolidated.

1931: The British introduce power-sharing with the Sinhalese.

1948: Ceylon gains her independence against a backdrop of widespread antipathy toward Occidental culture.

1949: Indian Tamils are deprived of citizenship.

1955: Land disputes among Tamils and Sinhalese become a political priority.

1956: Solomon Bandaranaike is elected; he makes Sinhalese the island's sole official language. Tamil parliamentarians protest the new laws. Over one hundred Tamils are killed in the subsequent rioting.

1958: Anti-Tamil riots leave over two hundred people dead. Thousands of Tamils flee or are displaced.

1959: Bandaranaike is assassinated by a Buddhist monk.

1965: Opposition party UNP wins elections and attempts to reverse nationalization measures.

1966: Education standardization for university admissions is implemented.

1969: Sivakumaran organizes small meetings in Valvettithurai. Participants include TNT and LTTE founders.

1970: Bandaranaike's widow returns to power, reimplementing nationalization program.

1971: Students and activists lead Sinhalese uprisings.

1972: Ceylon becomes Sri Lanka, and Buddhism (rather

than Hinduism) is given the primary place as the country's religion.

1976: Formation of the LTTE.

1977: The TULF wins all seats in Tamil areas. The TULF demands separate state for Tamils. Anti-Tamil riots in Colombo leave over one hundred Tamils dead.

1981: Sinhalese policemen are accused of burning the Jaffna Library, in Tamil territory, resulting in increased resentment in the Tamil community. At a public meeting in northern Sri Lanka, three Tamil men unexpectedly open fire in a public square, killing two Sinhalese policemen before disappearing into the jungle.

1983: Thirteen soldiers are killed by the LTTE in ambush, sparking anti-Tamil riots and the deaths of several hundred Tamils in Colombo.

1984: The PLOTE robs Kilinochchi's main bank in northern Sri Lanka. The PLOTE robs a magistrate's court in Kilinochchi. The EROS bombs Colombo. Sama the elephant arrives at the Pinnawala Elephant Orphanage.

1985: The first attempt at peace talks between the Sri Lankan government and the LTTE fails.

1985: A large shipment of weaponry arrives for the PLOTE. It is confiscated by the Indian government. The PLOTE raids a police station, steals the weapons, raids a bank, and sets a gas station on fire.

1987: Government forces push the LTTE back into the

northern city of Jaffna. The government signs accords creating new councils for Tamil areas in the north and east and reaches an agreement with India on the deployment of the Indian Peace Keeping Force. Thirteen Buddhist monks on a bus are killed near Kandy by the LTTE.

1988: Sinhalese JVP begins campaign against Indo-Sri Lankan agreement.

1990: Indian troops leave after getting bogged down in fighting in the north. Violence between the Sri Lankan army and separatists escalates. The "Second Eelam War" begins.

1991: The LTTE is implicated in the assassination of former Indian prime minister Rajiv Gandhi in southern India.

1993: Sri Lankan President Premadasa is killed in an LTTE bomb attack.

1994: President Kumaratunga comes to power pledging to end the war. Peace talks are opened with the LTTE.

1995: The "Third Eelam War" begins when rebels sink a naval craft.

1995–2001: War rages across the north and east. Tamil Tigers bomb Sri Lanka's holiest Buddhist site. President Kumaratunga is wounded in a bomb attack. A suicide attack on the international airport destroys half the Sri Lankan Airlines fleet.

2002: The government and Tamil Tiger rebels sign a Norwegian-mediated ceasefire. Decommissioning of weapons begins; the road linking the Jaffna Peninsula with the rest of Sri Lanka reopens after twelve years; passenger flights to Jaffna resume. The government lifts the ban on Tamil Tigers. Rebels drop their demand for a separate state.

2003: The Tigers pull out of talks. The ceasefire holds. The country's worst-ever floods leave more than two hundred people dead and drive some four thousand people from their homes.

2004: The renegade Tamil Tiger commander known as Colonel Karuna leads a split in the rebel movement and goes underground with his supporters. The Tiger offensive regains control of the east. A suicide bomb blasts Colombo—the first such incident since 2001. More than thirty thousand people are killed when massive waves, generated by a powerful undersea earthquake off the coast of Indonesia, devastate coastal communities.

2005: A deal is reached with Tamil Tiger rebels to share nearly $3 billion in tsunami aid among Sinhalese, Tamils, and Muslims. A state of emergency is declared after foreign minister Lakshman Kadirgamar is killed by a suspected Tiger assassin. Mahinda Rajapaksa, prime minister at the time, wins the presidential election. Most Tamils in areas controlled by the Tigers do not vote.

2006: Attacks begin to escalate again. A suicide bomber attacks the main military compound in Colombo, killing at least eight people. The military launches air strikes on Tamil Tiger targets. Tamil Tiger rebels attack a naval convoy near Jaffna. Tamil Tiger rebels and government forces resume fighting in the northeast in the worst clashes since the 2002 ceasefire. The government steadily drives Tamil Tigers out of eastern strongholds over the following year. Peace talks in Geneva fail.

2007: The police force hundreds of Tamils out of the capital, citing security concerns. A court orders an end to the expulsions.

January 2008: The government pulls out of the 2002 ceasefire agreement.

March 2008: An international panel that was invited by the government to monitor investigations into alleged human- rights abuses announces that it is leaving the country. Panel member Sir Nigel Rodley says the authorities were hindering its work. The government rejects the criticism.

July 2008: The Sri Lankan military says it has captured the important Tamil Tiger naval base of Vidattaltivu in the north.

October 2008: A suicide bombing that the government blames on the Tamil Tigers kills twenty-seven people, including a former general, in Anuradhapura.

December 2008: Sri Lankan troops and Tamil rebels claim to have inflicted heavy casualties on each other while fighting in the north.

January 2009: Government troops capture the northern town of Kilinochchi, after ten years as the Tamil Tigers' administrative headquarters. President Mahinda Rajapakse calls it a victory and urges the rebels to surrender.

February 2009: International concern over the humanitarian situation of thousands of civilians trapped in the battle zone enlivens calls for a temporary ceasefire. These calls are rejected by the government, which claims to be on the verge of destroying the Tamil Tigers. The government offers an amnesty to rebels if they surrender. Tamil Tiger planes conduct suicide raids against Colombo.

March 2009: Former rebel leader Colonel Karuna is sworn in as minister of national integration and reconciliation. United Nations high commissioner for human rights Navi Pillay accuses both sides of war crimes. The government rejects conditions attached to an IMF emergency loan worth $1.9 billion and ignores U.S. pressure, causing a delay to an agreement.

May 2009: The government declares the Tamil Tigers defeated after army forces overrun the last rebel-held territory in the northeast. The military says that rebel leader Vellupillai Prabhakaran was killed in the fighting. A Tamil Tiger statement says the group will lay down its arms.

August 2009: The new Tamil Tiger leader, Selvarasa Pathmanathan, is detained by Sri Lankan authorities. The first postwar local elections are held in the north. The governing coalition wins in Jaffna, but voters in Vavuniya choose candidates who supported the Tamil Tigers.

SELECTED BIBLIOGRAPHY

Bhaduri, Shankar and Karim, Afsir, *The Sri Lankan Crisis*. Delhi: Lancer International, 1990.

Geiger, Wilhelm, trans., *The Mahavamsa*. Colombo: Ceylon Government Information Department, 1912.

Gunaratna , Malinga H., *For a Sovereign State*. Ratnamalana, Sri Lanka: Sarvodaya Book Pub. Services, 1988.

Kadian, Rajesh, *India's Sri Lanka Fiasco: Peace Keepers at War*. New Delhi: Vision Books, 1990.

LTTE, Diary of Combat, pamphlet, 1984.

LTTE, Towards Liberation, pamphlet, 1984.

Navaratnam, V., *The Fall and Rise of the Tamil Nation*. Madras: Kaanthalakam, 1991.

Ponnambalam, Satchi, *Sri Lanka, The National Question and the Tamil Liberation Struggle*. London: Zed Books, 1983.

Ponniah, S., *Satyagraha and the Freedom Movement of the Tamils in Ceylon*. Jaffna, Sri Lanka: Kandiah, 1963.

Rasanayagam, Mudaliyar, *Ancient Jaffna*. New Delhi: Asian Educational Services, 1926.

Swamy, M.R. Narayan, *Tigers of Lanka: From Boys to Guerrillas*. Delhi: Konark Publishers, 1994.

Swamy, Subramanian, *The Assassination of Rajiv Gandhi: Unanswered Questions and Unasked Queries*. Delhi: Konark Publishers, 2000.

Ganesh statue, Madurai Kovil, Tamil Nadu, India

Ganesh Statue, Madurai, Tamil Nadu, India

Ganesh statue, Madras Kovil, Tamil Nadu, India

Sama the Elephant, Pinnawala Elephant Orphanage, Sri Lanka